COGNITION IN
LEARNING AND MEMORY

COGNITION
in
LEARNING and MEMORY

LEE W. GREGG
Editor

Contributors for this Volume

GORDON H. BOWER, Stanford University
ROBERT CALFEE, Stanford University
ROBIN CHAPMAN, University of Wisconsin
WILLIAM G. CHASE, Carnegie-Mellon University
HERBERT H. CLARK, Stanford University
ALLAN M. COLLINS, Bolt Beranek & Newman, Inc.,
    Cambridge, Mass.
LEE W. GREGG, Carnegie-Mellon University
JOHN A. MICHON, Institute for Perception,
    Soesterberg, The Netherlands
M. ROSS QUILLIAN, Bolt Beranek & Newman, Inc.,
    Cambridge, Mass.
HERBERT A. SIMON, Carnegie-Mellon University
RICHARD VENEZKY, University of Wisconsin
WAYNE A. WICKELGREN, University of Oregon

*The fifth of an annual series of symposia in the area of cognition
under the sponsorship of Carnegie-Mellon University.*

JOHN WILEY & SONS, INC.
New York, London, Sydney, Toronto

Library of Congress Cataloging in Publication Data:

Symposium on Cognition, 5th, Pittsburgh, 1969.
  Cognition in learning and memory.

Sponsored by Carnegie–Mellon University.
Bibliography: p.

1. Cognition–Congresses. 2. Learning, Psychology of–Congresses.
3. Memory–Congresses.   I. Gregg, Lee W., ed. II. Bowers, Gordon H.
III. Carnegie–Mellon University. IV. Title.

BF311.S83 1969   153.1   72-6107

ISBN 0-471-32658-5

Printed in the United States of America

10 9 8 7 6 5 4 3 2 1

PREFACE

The Fifth Annual Symposium on Cognition was held April 3-4, 1969. Previous volumes in this series dealt with problem solving, concept learning, judgmental processes, and language development. The subject of the present volume—learning and memory—is an appropriate continuation of the fundamental aspects of cognition. The papers by Wickelgren, Bower, Michon, Collins and Quillian, and Calfee, Chapman, and Venezky were presented at the symposium. As in the past, members of the Carnegie-Mellon group contributed to the discussion stimulated by the work reported by the invited speakers. Two papers, one by Simon and the other by Chase and Clark, have been included in this volume. They represent the main themes of interest generated by that discussion—imagery and semantic memory. These topics have become important areas of research over the past few years. Equally important, however, are the sophisticated and mature treatments of memory, cognitive structure, and reading skills discussed in Chapters 2, 4, and 6. The current volume, more than any prior volume of this series, reflects the coming of age of cognitive approaches to the study of complex psychological phenomena.

Publication of this volume was made possible by grants from the National Science Foundation and The Carnegie Corporation. Individual contributors have noted their sources of support. Research on cognitive processes at Carnegie-Mellon University has been supported by Public Health Service Research Grant MH-07722 from the National Institutes of Mental Health.

Lee W. Gregg
Pittsburgh, Pa.

CONTENTS

CHAPTER 1

Lee W. Gregg
Carnegie-Mellon University

SIMULATION MODELS OF LEARNING
AND MEMORY

After more than a decade of research, computer simulation as a technique for integrating and examining the consequences of hypotheses about complex behavioral processes appears still to be in its infancy. Core ideas such as the concept of an information processing system pervade the current psychological literature. Even so, there remains a language problem. It is still the case that only with great difficulty can computer models of complex phenomena be communicated.

A few attempts have made frontal assaults presenting the IPL-V code itself (Reitman, 1965; Laughery and Gregg, 1962). Hunt (1962) and more recently Laughery (1969) used flow charts and diagrams with some success. Simon and Kotovsky (1963) developed a special notational scheme to convey the essential features of their pattern learning model. Then Gregg and Simon (1967) tried an Algol-like language to suggest the processing dynamics of the concept identification models. Nevertheless, there remains a strong feeling that computer simulation is a private science. One critic has remarked that to simulate means to pretend falsely, to feign. But to feign has a second meaning, "to give mental existence to, to imagine, to invent." Surely these are most proper things for the scientist to do—provided he does not invent the data.

Theories are the means by which we give meaning to collections of facts. The remarkable quality that characterizes the use of the computer in theory construction has been the computer's reluctance to let us invent as freely as we might wish. It is difficult to feign (here, the first meaning of the word—"to fashion or shape") radically different explanations that account quantitatively for as many verbal learning phenomena as does EPAM, the theory of human verbal learning developed by Simon and Feigenbaum (1964). One result of this has been the considerable repetition of a few working postulates. These are easy to state. Much more difficult to express are the relationships that give substance and insight into the dynamics of the simulation models and, in turn, a better understanding of information processing mechanisms in man.

Verbal learning, concept formation, and problem solving have been of central interest to those of us who try to model human cognition by computer simulation. Although the cognitive system of an individual human subject brought

1

into the psychology laboratory is such that our subject can walk from room to room participating now in a paired associate learning experiment, and next in a concept identification study, or a serial learning task, we have not yet been able to capture the whole man in a single computer program. To date our efforts have generally produced special purpose programs that are artificially intelligent in limited aspects of the broad range of learning and problem solving functions.

However, in writing simulation models, we are careful to separate data structures, the information on which the postulated mechanisms operate, from the routines defining these processes. An early assumption, at least for the problem solving models, was that a collection of just a few (perhaps 20 or 30) basic information processes could account for much of the complex behavior generated by human problem solvers. Given a suitable representation of a learner's current state of knowledge—the familiarized discrimination tree of EPAM or the current goal—sub-total trees of a chess program—the organized set of learning mechanisms or move generators might well exhibit common features. Thus, we are discovering converging approaches to specifying the cognitive processes of man. Our attempts to generalize the scope and power of our simulation models have pruned and reshaped the tree of unsolved problems.

EPAM—THE THEORY OF VERBAL LEARNING

The association learning mechanism of EPAM is an all-or-none process. The capacity to generate a name, a symbol that stands for an organized set of other symbols, is basic to the theory. In general, forgetting is treated as a failure to retrieve a particular symbol that served as a pointer to the desired information. Information is assumed to be organized in memory as a discrimination net—a tree structure. The explicit outline of this structure provides a set of tests for primitive symbols, for example, for letters of the English alphabet, compound objects, words or syllables, or pairs of these.

The objects on which a discrimination learning process operates are distinguishable either because they are concatenations of more primitive units (compound objects) or because of discernable features (attribute-values) by which the objects can be described. In any event, an assumption is made about the nature of the most elementary units—the primitive symbols—from which compound objects may be constructed.

For EPAM I, the features were visual, binary-valued characteristics of the letters of the English alphabet. Discrimination learning consisted of creating a structure of tests *in some fixed order* so that a letter was recognized by sorting its attribute values with respect to the presence or absence of each feature. Different orderings of the tests were possible, depending on the discrimination learner's experience with the particular letters during acquisition. An object was uniquely defined by associating with a name (internal pointer) either the set of names of its subordinate parts, or the set of features used to describe the object. Order information was important for those compound objects that are defined by the part-whole relationships. Hence, the tests generated by the discrimination learning process were tests of the position of letters in syllables.

In the theory, long term memory is represented by the tree of tests—the discrimination net. Elementary or compound objects can be recognized by the same net sorting process. The net sorter first examines attribute-value characteristics of the object presented to it and then performs whatever tests are appropriate to that type of object, provided the object is of a familiar kind.

Paired Associate Learning

For paired-associates learning, three types of objects are possible. Elementary objects—the letters of the English alphabet—are assumed to be recognizable as integrated units in the current version of the program. Compound objects are the syllables and S-R pairs.

The model assumes that human information processing in learning is serial. The central mechanism is capable of doing just one thing at a time. This means that the cognitive processes to be prescribed by a program must occur sequentially, and that the total time required for executing a complex collection of processes is the sum of the times associated with more elementary components.

The symbols that the information processing system receives as input, and produces as output, are limited by the capacity of the short term memory subsystem. The capacity may be restricted by size (number of storage cells) or by rate (symbols per second). At the present time, there is no empirical way of determining which formulation is correct.

A collection of microprocesses forms the association between any two symbols. For learning to be useful, one of the symbols must be available to serve as the retrieval cue for the other symbol. Presumably the collection of microprocesses accomplishes at least the coding and recognition of two symbols and their transfer from the immediate memory to the long term memory. There are two ways in which these processes are invoked. The first entails associations among pointers to various parts of the long term memory (constructing tests at nodes). The second creates internal representations of objects that have external counterparts, for instance, the verbal materials presented to the learner. In the latter case, we speak of "improving images at terminal nodes."

> Thus, learning in EPAM III involves cycles of the two learning processes. Through familiarization, the stimulus image is elaborated until it contains more information than the minimum required to sort to its terminal. Through discrimination, this information is used

to distinguish between new stimuli and the stimulus that generated
this terminal and grew its image. On the basis of such distinctions,
the net is elaborated. The interaction of these two processes is
fundamental to the whole working of EPAM, and it is not easy
to conjure up alternative schemes that will permit learning. (Simon
and Feigenbaum, 1964.)

Most of the phenomena of paired associates learning can be accounted for
by the EPAM model. Simon and Feigenbaum (1964) ran extensive tests of the
model and showed that it was capable of generating essentially correct predictions
of the effects of similarity and familiarity/meaningfulness. Gregg and Simon
(1967) showed how it was possible to represent learning strategies as modifications of EPAM's short term memory processes and thus explained that under
some conditions learning paired associates appears to be incremental over a
series of learning trials.

In paired-associates learning, the retrievable unit is clearly defined and triggered by the experimenter's presentation of the stimulus member of the pair.
In serial learning, the effective or functional stimulus is less obvious.

Serial Learning

Attempts to determine the functional stimulus in serial verbal learning have
been notably unsuccessful. The results of an experiment by Young (1962)
indicated that neither the preceding item nor the complex of several prior items
uniquely fill the role. Underwood's (1963) analysis suggested that meaningfulness may be a critical variable influencing the extent to which the subject
analyzes a stimulus item and responds selectively to parts of it. However, any
single feature of the nominal stimulus seems unlikely to become *the* effective
stimulus. It is even less likely that a prescription for evoking such a feature
can be had by recourse to a collection of ahistorical variables, like meaningfulness.

A more reasonable assumption is that the nominal stimuli provide a variety
of cueing possibilities, and that these are organized into a complex structure
capable of generating the desired verbal response sequence. In addition to the
stimulus items themselves, there are cue-producing events that occur during
the course of acquisition. Some of these are external to the subject, such as
the experimenter's signaling of repeated trials. Other events are internally
produced by the subject, and grow out of the attentional aspects of his learning
strategy. Precisely which encodings become integrated into the memory
depend on the constraints imposed by the task dynamics, and on the limitations of the subject's information processing strategies.

EXPERIMENTS ON INDUCED CHUNKING

Two experiments that R. S. McLean and I carried out make explicit how structural characteristics of encoding can be derived (McLean & Gregg, 1967). The approach was through an analysis of the temporal properties of ordered recall of serial lists. In examining these properties, it was assumed that groups of items recited quickly form a coherent memory unit or chunk (Miller, 1956). Longer or shorter intervals between chunks indicate different kinds of encoding relationships, not simple differences in the strengths of bonds between pairs of elements in the stimulus list.

There are several possible bases for the chunking that occurs in memory. First, the nominal stimuli may form a unit that was familiar to the subject prior to the experiment. If the subject is learning a list of letters of the alphabet, he may recognize familiar words, parts of words, or initials that stand for a familiar name (e.g., IBM, USA). Second, external punctuation of the stimuli may serve to create groupings of the individual elements. If the stimuli are presented in some external grouping, either temporally, spatially, or logically (e.g., by category), this grouping may serve to delimit substructures that may be used by the subject in managing his learning. Additional cues for retrieval of the sublists may be provided by this organizational scheme. Closely related is a third possibility: internal structuring as a result of the subject's own monitoring of the acquisition process. That is, given a serial list that exceeds the immediate memory capacity, the subject may choose to disregard all items except the first few items following an already learned item. In this way he acquires n_1 items on the first trial, and then adds n_i items on each succeeding trial until the list is learned.

The second of these techniques—specifically, spatial grouping of letters of the English alphabet—was used to impose external structure upon the serial list. It was hypothesized that the temporal structure in ordered recall—and hence the inferred structure of the subject's internal representation—would reflect both the number and size of the letter groups.

In the first experiment, letters of the English alphabet, excluding *e* and *i*, were randomly permuted to form five different 24-letter lists. The letters were typed on 3 x 5 file cards to form groups of 1, 3, 4, 6, or 8 letters on a card. The design of the experiment was a 5 x 5 factorial with three subjects per cell. Seventy-five undergraduate college students served individually in the first experiment to fulfill a course requirement. Each subject received one list in one grouping condition. A follow-up experiment used a total of 200 subjects, 40 per group. The experiment was self-paced. In the instructions, the subject was asked to turn over the cards, one at a time, reciting aloud the letters that appeared on that card. After each pass through the deck, the subject attempted to recall the list in the correct order. The study-recall trials were continued to a criterion of one perfect recitation. When this criterion was reached, the subject was requested to say the entire list in reverse order—but he was not instructed about the backwards trial until criterion had been reached.

For each subject the time of occurrence of each response for the criterion trial and backward recall trial was obtained. This was accomplished by a fairly elaborate procedure involving a voice-key triggered by the tape-recorded recitation and a computer-generated time base and display for the letter sequences.

The extent to which grouping of responses in recall paralleled the grouping of stimuli was tested by comparing the interletter response times of the subject with hypothetical perfect grouping strategies. The 23 interletter times were designated interchunk or intrachunk times depending upon their serial location within the list and according to the grouping strategy being tested. For example, if a three's grouping strategy was being tested, the first and second interletter times would be considered to be intrachunk times and the third interletter time would be considered an interchunk time. For each strategy to be tested each subject's interletter times were summed in their appropriate categories. A grouping strategy score was then computed by forming a weighted ratio of interchunk to intrachunk times. If the effect of some stimulus grouping was present in the responses, the score of the grouping strategy that corresponds to it should have been greater than the other grouping strategy scores.

An independent measure of grouping was obtained by dividing the letters into groups separated according to decreasing interletter times. Interletter times within the group were smaller than those between the groups. The smallest groupings were obtained which did not isolate a single letter. This measure provided information about the regularity of the subjects' verbalizations. A test of the grouping uniformity within the criterion recall responses was made by computing the standard deviation (of grouping size) for each subject. The effect of stimulus grouping on memory structure was also seen in backwards recall, applying the same grouping strategy measure.

The results of the several analyses provide evidence that stimulus grouping leads to stable chunks of the size induced by the grouping. Stability was shown by the good correspondence between the temporal aspects of the criterion trial and the backward recall. Subjects who received the items one at a time also produced stable chunks, but chunk size varied. There was a tendency for these subjects to group by three's. However, in the one-at-a-time condition, no two subjects produced the same chunking patterns for the entire list.

The evidence suggests that no single feature intrinsic to any of the serial lists produced unique encodings of the 24-letter strings. The chunking patterns of the subjects were easily manipulated by the stimulus grouping imposed experimentally. That operation, independent of the particular letter sequences, far overshadows any other perceptual or associational relationships; and there were many such relationships within these randomly selected lists. No effort was made to eliminate them. There were, for example, embedded words—*sky* and *ox* in List 1, *at* in List 3, *dog* in List 4, and two words, *up* and *now* in List 5.

It would appear, then, that information both from features of the lists themselves and from the manipulation of stimulus grouping induces chunking in the organization of a serial list. It seems likely that this organization takes on an hierarchical form. At the top level of the hierarchy are those cueing features that allow the subject to get from one chunk to another. At a lower level, within chunks, additional cues enable the subject to produce the integrated strings that become his overt verbal responses.

While the distinction between paired associates learning and serial learning is a useful one for describing experimental procedures, behavior in any learning task rests upon internalized sets of relationships that are neither purely paired-associate nor serial-motor in form. Particularly in grouping conditions of size six or eight, where there were only three or four separate 3 x 5 cards, the obvious pairing of serial position name and card label occurred. During acquisition and during the backward recitation, many subjects referred to the "first card" and "last card," for example, and were able, then, to state a specific fact about the content of the card, the first or last letter, or an idiosyncratic feature of the letter sequence on that card. Having once located a desired card in memory, the subject might then produce a completely integrated response, or he might have to search further for the subunits representing the serial-motor level of the hierarchy (e.g., "first half," "last half").

One issue posed by the fact that subjects must learn both the index and the order of elements within subunits is how to determine the proportion of learning time devoted to each of these components of the learning task. Serial position data from the induced chunking experiment provide an approach to this issue.

Attention in Serial Learning

Feigenbaum and Simon (1962) accounted for serial position error curves in serial anticipation learning by assuming a "relatively orderly and systematic method for organizing the learning task, using items with features of uniqueness as anchor points." Their explanation simply states that subjects pay attention to items of a serial list in a particular, ordered way—not the same order as presented. They computed the relative proportion of errors at each serial position, and showed that the typical bowed serial curve follows from the particular order of attention to list items. Their analysis also incorporated an attentional mechanism that could handle one or more isolated items occurring within the serial list. An isolated item serves as an anchor similar to the first or last item and changes the noticing or attentional order.

The study-recall method used in the induced chunking experiment imposes a set of conditions that constrain learning strategies. In the recall phase, guessing or repeating segments out of order is discouraged by the instructions. In any event, the payoff occurs only when the subject can recite items from the first to last in their proper order. Even so, many subjects will remark "I don't know what comes next, but there's an 'OX' toward the end of the list." Ordered recall tends to force subjects to eliminate this kind of forward looking behavior, and to focus attention on early items until they are mastered.

In contrast to the anticipation method, there is a sharp break between phases of study and recall. The initial item anchor is emphasized by changes in the format of the experiment. Repetition of the initial segment, anchored strongly by the first item in the serial list, tends to produce overlearning of that segment.

In the study-recall method, subjects may generate anchor points successively throughout the list. Generally, we suppose these will extend from the first item toward the last. Hence, for averaged data, we would expect the serial position error curve to be a monotonic, increasing function. The broken curve of Figure 1.1a is a plot for the subjects who learned the items one at a time, averaged for comparison with the three-at-a-time condition over adjacent segments of length three. The solid line for the three-at-a-time condition differs systematically at the extremes, beginning items and last items. Similar graphs for stimulus grouping of 4, 6, and 8 items show an increasing and systematic departure from the one-at-a-time values. The systematic departures are such that the segments take on the appearance of bowed curves—the classical serial position curves obtained in serial learning experiments.

In Figure 1.2 (page 13), within-chunk serial position curves are shown. Once again, the pairs of curves contrast the averaged one-at-a-time data with each of the other experimental conditions. In general, the pairs of curves are linear and parallel, and have about the same slope. The inference that one can draw from the differences between the shapes of the intrachunk and interchunk serial position data is that separate processes govern their generation.

We take these results as evidence that the processes of EPAM are, in fact, sufficient to describe these phenomena. The net-growing discrimination process builds a structure of tests that serve as retrieval cues for the chunks. The familiarization process elaborates images of the segments to which the retrieval cues point. Image elaboration proceeds from the well anchored initial item and is linear. The discrimination process, on the other hand,

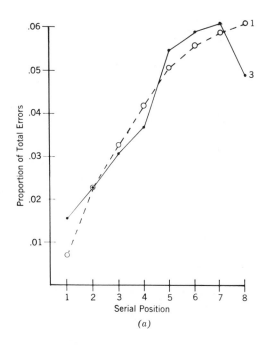

(a)

Figure 1.1   Serial position curves for comparing single letter presentation (broken line) with stimulus grouping conditions of 3, 4, 6, and 8 letters, the solid lines of (a), (b), (c), and (d), respectively.

depends on attentional factors of a different sort. The bow-shaped curves reflect distributions of the learners' attention to later segments of the lists.

Association Time, t_c

For many years we have attempted to ascertain the time charges for the learning process in the EPAM theory. Analyses of earlier data in the psychological literature suggested a range of 5 to 10 seconds for the execution of the collection of microprocesses specified by EPAM's net building subroutines. A few direct attacks on the problem were made by our own group and by other psychologists. Bugelski (1962), for example, found that total learning time was approximately constant for lists of 8 paired associates presented at different rates. Subjects took more trials to learn the S-R pairs at the faster rates, but overall learning times were about the same at 25 seconds per pair. We can assume that some feature of the stimulus

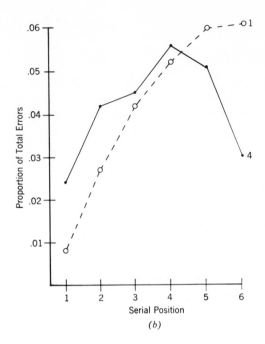

Serial Position

(b)

Figure 1.1(b)

syllable had to be fixated in order to retrieve the first letter of the response syllable. To complete the response, two more letters of the consonant-vowel-consonant response syllable had to be added—a total of three executions of the discrimination learning process. Hence, for such familiar units as letters of the English alphabet, a total time charge of about 8 seconds per execution seems appropriate.

The difficulty with this analysis is that once the retrieval cue is established (i.e., once a pointer to the terminal image is created), image elaboration should proceed without restructuring the test nodes of the discrimination tree. It should, therefore, take much less time to elaborate an image at a terminal than to construct new test nodes.

I believe the resolution of the question lies in the manner in which order information is preserved in the serial integration of responses. In the McLean and Gregg experiments, it is possible to see how total learning time is affected by segments of varying lengths. We observed that induced chunking provides stable retrieval units for subjects who received the 3- , 4- , 6- , and 8-item

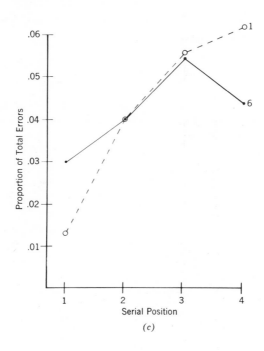

Figure 1.1(c)

displays. Serial integration *within chunks* occurs, I believe, from the first letter to the last. Thus, there are two distinct ways in which the order information in the serial lists becomes internally represented. The first involves the construction of retrieval cues for whole segments; the second, the creation of sequentially ordered images at the terminal node. Figure 1.3 (page 14) shows the total learning time for groups of 40 subjects in each of the experimental conditions. It is clear that the external organization imposed by the induced chunking reduced the total time required to learn the lists of 24 letters by a factor of about two. We can approximate the number of hypothetical executions of the discrimination learning and familiarization processes by the following expression:

$$N \simeq m\,(m+1)\,{}_{/2} + \tfrac{1}{2}\,[\,n\,(n+1)\,{}_{/2}\,]$$

where: N is the total number of operations
m is the number of chunks
n is the number of letters within each chunk

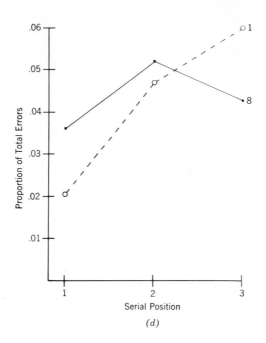

Figure 1.1(d)

The first part of the expression represents the strictly hierarchical tree of tests that discriminates among retrieval cues while the second part describes the linear ordering of pairs of letters within each chunk. Hence, total learning time is given by

$$T \simeq t_c \, \text{N}$$

The parameter t_c is the time required for a single operation of an association learning process.

The open circles of Figure 1.3 are computed values of total learning times using an estimated t_c of 8.8 seconds per operation. Since the subjects who received the letters one at a time exhibited varying chunking patterns, it is not possible to apply the approximation to that group. The value of about 950 seconds is an extrapolation of the values for 2 and 3 letter groups.

It is unfortunate that we do not know more precisely just what organizing strategies and attention-directing mechanisms are used by these subjects. Nor can we be certain of the particular retrieval cues used by the individual subjects in the induced chunking groups. However, these observations suggest

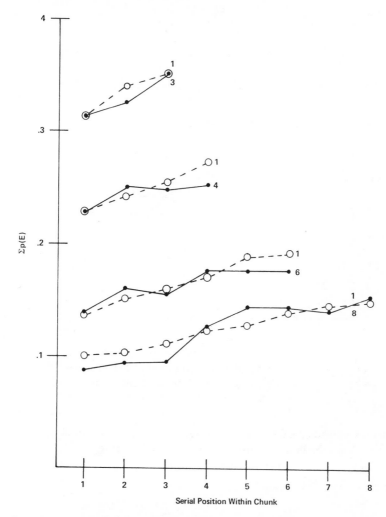

Figure 1.2   Within chunk serial position curves comparing single letter
presentation with stimulus grouping conditions of 3, 4, 6, and 8
letters, the solid lines.

that the EPAM model and its fundamental parameter t_c are essentially correct.
Further, we can make a heuristic comment on the issue raised earlier concerning the distribution of learning time in the serial learning task. If learning
were a simple matter of response integration, so that each of the 24 letters
were added to the terminal image of the list by a single associative act, we
would predict a total learning time of 111 seconds, the product of t_c and
the number of familiar items. In fact, observed learning times are about four
times that value when appropriate external structure is imposed. Left to

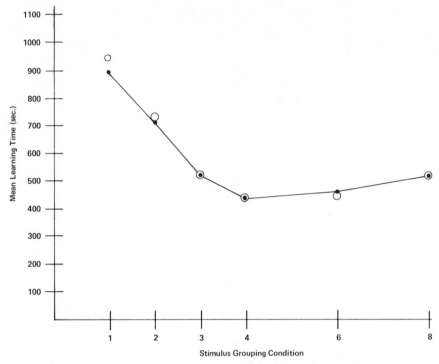

Figure 1.3   Observed and predicted values of total learning time in the
induced chunking experiment. The solid line connects the data
points and open circles are the predicted values.

their own organizing devices, subjects required even greater total amounts of
time to learn the lists. Therefore, we can conclude that the bulk of our learning effort, perhaps 75 percent of it, must be and should be directed toward
building the index.

SOME IMPLICATIONS FOR COMPLEX TASKS

In describing learning effects in complex tasks, there are three very global
possibilities. First, the learner through practice enlarges the data base available
for problem solving while keeping the program constant. An example might be
the child's acquisition of the multiplication tables. He does much the same
thing in the same way—but he knows more answers as his learning progresses.
And when we retrieve the answer to 25 x 25 = 625 or $\log_{10} 2 = .30103$, our
program for doing whatever numerical computations we are engaged in
remains relatively unchanged. A second possibility is to change the program

while keeping the data base reasonably constant. Here, we suppose that learning certain short-cut procedures $(a + b)(a - b) = a^2 - b^2$ or special methods, like the one reported in Dansereau's dissertation (1968), represent real changes in the performance program, but 5 x 5 is still 25. In the sense that a new program must be learned and remembered, the data base has become larger, and so it may not be necessary to treat the third possibility—learning which involves changes in both program and data—as a separate case at all.

On the other hand, there is a great deal of evidence for the notion that restructuring, recoding, and renaming information in memory occurs as a concommitant of changes in information processing sequences that I have called the program. We learn formal taxonomies that then change the "relatedness" of objects. Jonah and the whale was a fish story before the concept "mammals" was introduced. We learn a procedure for calculating moments, and the shapes of distributions take on new meaning. In learning to read, several changes occur. From an early attentional strategy that weights each letter in a word equally and in serial order from left to right, a more sophisticated strategy evolves. The information content for word recognition was beginning, end, and then middle letter groups. I still believe it is fair to say that the visual cues—word features—used by adults in reading are largely unknown. But it must be the case that they are different from the elementary symmetries that lead children to reverse letters. There are many more examples of perceptual changes when processing strategies are learned. Maps, logic diagrams or schematic drawings make sense to the expert who knows where to look for related information.

With conceptual cognitive behavior, the act of learning new executable sequences is often one of discovery, a consequence of problem solving processes. But having labelled subroutines and fixated the order in which they are called and organized them with due regard to decision-making branches, learning effects may be detected during automatization and serial integration of the program.

Some experiments seem relevant to the second kind of learning effect where changes in the program can be equated with rule learning, procedural task performance, and certain motor skills learning. Usually the limited duration of the observations, the fact that subjects are given unlimited time to perform, or, in the motor skills case, lack of interest in cognitive behavior provide little information about the data base. Where very different behaviors crop up, the subject is thrown out of the experiment because he did not follow instructions. In general, there is a gap in our knowledge of the range of strategies subjects evolve for different tasks and also a great deal of uncertainty about the heuristics they use to program themselves.

Most psychological learning experiments, especially in verbal learning, focus on effects of the first kind—changing the data base. And I would conclude that *the* theory of verbal learning (EPAM) accounts for most of what needs to be accounted for in those experiments.

If an item is attended to for at least t_c seconds (in the range 5 to 10 seconds for familiar items from a large set), the necessary condition for learning is fulfilled. The item (1) can be retrieved by means of an appropriate retrieval cue (Tulving, 1968), or (2) it can be recognized as "old" on subsequent presentation of the items provided that no interpolated learning interferes with the structural properties of the memory system. The collection of microprocesses involving transfers among components of the memory system consume, in the aggregate, the interval defined by the time constant. Hence this view of an all-or-none learning process can explain incremental learning phenomena provided new items are presented faster than one every t_c seconds. The time constant may be an average value (and hence probabilistic) with a potentially large range. I believe that as the size of the set of items is restricted, say from familiar words, to familiar letters, to familiar digits—all chunks, there is a corresponding increase in t_c as additional chunks are added. This may occur because (1) the difficulty in generating distinctive retrieval cues increases primarily as a result of conceptual or perceptual set or (2) items from smaller sets are necessarily repeated in long learning sequences with the result that only temporal estimates, time tags, serve as distinctive features for retrieval.

AN OVERVIEW

This does not mean that there are no unsolved questions. There are many. Some have been central to the development of simulation models such as the issues of internal representations and the detailed analysis of problem solving strategies. Other problems have their origin in the general progression of psychological research where information processing concepts have guided a large share of the efforts of investigators during the past decade.

In the chapters that follow, several of the more crucial problems are treated. Wicklegren, in Chapter 2, presents an integrated picture of the relationships between short term, intermediate term, and long term memory systems. He describes from his view the dynamics of what we have come to call the immediate processor. In Chapter 3, Bower reports research directed toward understanding the role of visual imagery, a particular form of representation, in learning. His chapter is followed by Michon's, where a more general approach and methodology is suggested for determining precisely what form internal representations take on during the course of learning. Collins and Quillian, Chapter 5, report their research on the comprehension of language based on the kind of representation proposed earlier by Quillian for a semantic memory network. How such a network grows and is elaborated through experience, particularly through reading, is the concern of Calfee, Chapman, and Venezky. Their approach is presented in Chapter 6 in which basic reading skills, information processes necessary for acquisition of reading, are identified. The last two chapters, Chapter 7 by Simon and Chapter 8 by Chase and Clark, take as their theme the explanation of how visual and linguistic information is represented and processed.

CHAPTER 2

Wayne A. Wickelgren
University of Oregon

CODING, RETRIEVAL, AND DYNAMICS OF
MULTITRACE ASSOCIATIVE MEMORY

Perhaps the most useful theoretical distinction in the field of memory has been the distinction between three phases of the memory process: acquisition, storage, and retrieval. I propose that a substitute trichotomy will prove more useful in the analysis of the memory process, namely: coding, retrieval, and dynamics.

Coding refers to the internal representation in memory of events and the relations between events, including such topics as: the modalities of memory, the similarity functions defined over pairs of events, the dimensions of similarity spaces and the loci of events in these spaces, the associative or nonassociative nature of any memory modality (content addressability, uniqueness of representation, contiguity conditioning), the coding of events and associations of events making use of previously learned cognitive structures (learned concept representatives and associations between concept representatives), and, finally, the number of traces within any one modality, each mediating memory for a different period of time or with other differences in their trace properties. Coding refers to the structure of memory, what its components are and how they are organized into a system. In short, coding is concerned with the question, "What is learned?"

Retrieval refers to how such memory traces are used in a variety of situations. Having specified what the different traces are in the coding assumptions of a theory of memory, it is necessary to say which of these traces are used in various situations, that is, "What is judged in retrieval?" Also, we must specify the decision rules which translate the values of the traces that are judged into responses in different types of judgment tasks.

Dynamics refers to the time course of the strengths of different traces through the various phases of the memory process. However, it seems worthwhile to distinguish four phases: acquisition, consolidation, decay, and retrieval, in place of the more conventional three phases: acquisition, storage, and retrieval. Acquisition refers to the period during which a potential trace is formed, often as a result of the input of new information. However, potential traces are assumed not to be retrievable until after they have been converted into retrievable traces by the consolidation process. In the case of long-term memory, LTM (days to years), the period of consolidation could be hours or days. In intermediate-term memory, ITM (minutes to hours), the period of consolidation could be tens of seconds. If this is so, then in either case, it would be quite important to explicitly characterize consolidation as a phase of the memory trace, distinct from both acquisition and decay. Undoubtedly, short-term memory, STM (1-20 seconds) or very-short-term memory, VSTM (generally less than 1 or 2 seconds) consolidates so quickly that the distinction between acquisition and consolidation is a mere formality. Decay refers to the period during which the retrievable trace is subject to degradation from a variety of possible sources. Retrieval, as a phase in trace dynamics, focuses on how retrieval of a trace affects its strength. For example, is retrieval destructive, nondestructive, or constructive? To characterize the dynamics of any memory trace, there must be laws specifying the form of the time function for each phase and how the parameters of these functions depend on the type of trace, the modality, and the conditions. Finally, there must be a law specifying how to combine the phases.

OVERVIEW OF MULTITRACE THEORY

Multitrace theory is a modification and extension of the theory described in Wickelgren (1969e). The basic assumptions of multitrace theory fall into three categories: coding, retrieval, and dynamics of memory traces.

Coding

There appear to be two basic types of memory structures, associative and nonassociative. In associative memories, each event or concept has a unique internal representative, and the internal representatives have different degrees of association to each other depending upon how frequently they have been contiguously activated. In nonassociative memories, there is an ordered set of locations (cells, registers, boxes, etc.) into which the internal representative of any event or concept can be coded, and sequences of events or concepts are stored in order in this ordered set of locations. A tape recorder is a good example of a nonassociative memory. From a hardware viewpoint, virtually all computer memories are also nonassociative, though with suitable programming, an associative memory can be simulated. Multitrace theory assumes that human memory is largely associative, with the exception of very short-term sensory memory (e.g., visual and auditory "afterimages" of one kind or another), which is probably nonassociative.

In specifying more precisely the nature of the internal representative of any event, it seems to be necessary to distinguish between the representation of the *attributes* of the event in whatever sensory or motor modality or modalities are relevant and the representation of some more general *concept* which is cued by the event under some particular interpretation of the event. Many events have more than one conceptual interpretation, with the frequency of each interpretation being manipulable to some extent by the conditions surrounding presentation of the event. This can complicate matters to whatever extent one wishes, but there are many situations under which particular conceptual interpretations of each of a set of events can be made overwhelmingly predominant.

For example, in visual presentation of a list of letters, there must be a visual attribute representation of these letters at one stage of the representation process. In a very young child, this may be all the representation these letters have. In an adult, the visual attribute representation of the letters is strongly associated to a conceptual representation of each letter. If the list of letters forms a word, the visual attribute representation and/or the conceptual representation of the letters is associated to the conceptual representation of the word. The conceptual representation of a letter can also be activated by auditory and tactile stimulation, and the variety of different visual, auditory, and tactile patterns that can activate the same concept representative for most concepts is astounding. Certainly, no one conjunction of attributes is common to all events which activate the representative of most concepts. Thus, we cannot identify the conceptual (semantic) modality with any sensory modality. Nor can we identify the conceptual modality with any motor modality, as there are generally representatives in at least two motor modalities (speech and writing) associated with each concept and frequently several different representatives in each of these two modalities associated with the concept (e.g., different ways of speaking or writing the same word).

The simplest, adequate way to describe the relation between attribute representatives and concept representatives is to say that concept representatives are disjunctions of conjunctions of attributes. Elsewhere, I have argued that single neurons could be concept representatives, if it is assumed that there are free neurons which are unspecified genetically and come to be specified by learning (Wickelgren, 1969d). The plausibility arguments for this position will not be repeated here, but the present version of multitrace theory does assume a process of learned representation of concepts which is consistent with this position.

Thus, multitrace theory assumes that there is a cognitive (concept) modality in addition to a variety of sensory and motor attribute modalities. Since associations apply to ordered pairs of internal representatives, the number of possibly different modalities of memory is the number of different ordered pairs of sensory, motor, and cognitive modalities.

Multitrace theory distinguishes four types of associations within or between modalities: (a) interevent associations (direct forward and backward associations between the representatives of successively presented events), (b) intraevent associations (associations between the representatives of the simultaneously presented components of an event), (c) concept associations (associations between the representatives of the simultaneously presented components of an event and a concept representative for the event), and (d) structured associations (associations between the representative of an event and cognitive structure representatives such as the familiarity representative, serial position concepts like beginning, middle, and end, subgroup labels, syntactic structures, visual images, mediators, mnemonics, rules, etc.).

Simultaneous or immediately-successive contiguity of activation of internal representatives is assumed to produce learning of the associations between these representatives in all but the initial learned specification of each concept representative. Within the present framework, concept learning requires the contiguously activated representatives to become associated to an input site of a previously unspecified representative.

Associations involving cognitive structure representatives undoubtedly play an increasingly important role in learning as the child develops, and structured associations probably play a dominant role in adult learning. Even when the task is to associate two events (A and B) in paired associate (PA) learning, it has become increasing clear that the A-B association is very frequently mediated by some cognitive-structure representative, which may be represented abstractly as A-M-B. In many cases it may be necessary to consider performance in PA learning to result from a combination of a direct A-B association and a "mediated" A-M-B association.

In addition to the different modalities of memory and the different types of associations within and between modalities, multitrace theory assumes that there are different traces mediating each type of association in each modality, namely, short-term memory (STM), intermediate-term memory (ITM), and long-term memory (LTM). STM is assumed to have a time constant in the range from 1 to 10 seconds, ITM a time constant from 2 minutes to several hours, and LTM from days to years.

Finally, mention must be made of sensory very short-term memory (VSTM), which clearly exists at least in vision (Sperling, 1960; Averbach and Coriell, 1961; Averbach and Sperling, 1961; and perceptual work on after images). It is not yet clear how many different types of visual VSTM there may be, nor are the properties of any one kind of visual VSTM completely specified. However, it does seem likely that visual VSTM is a nonassociative memory, where any pattern can be imposed on any location of an overlapping set of locations in a two (or three?) dimensional visual space. Associations are probably not formed between adjacent patterns (i.e., letters in array) in visual VSTM. Exactly such results were obtained for visual VSTM by Wickelgren and Whitman (1970).

Retrieval

There are two principal aspects to the analysis of retrieval: (a) What memory traces are judged in retrieval? and (b) What judgment rule is used? Multitrace theory designates two basic types of elementary retrieval processes, recall and recognition. Recall is a comparative judgment on a set of strengths corresponding to the alternative responses. The simplest judgment rule for recall seems to be the maximum rule (choose the alternative with maximum strength), which is the same as Thurstone's (1927) Law of Comparative Judgment. Recognition can be either a comparative judgment (as in multiple-choice tests), or an absolute judgment (as in "yes-no" recognition) on the total strength (across modalities and traces) of some association. The simplest judgment rule for absolute-judgment recognition seems to be the criterion rule (choose the one of a set of ordered responses whose criteria bracket the total strength) of Thurstonian successive intervals scaling and signal detection theory (Tanner and Swets, 1954.)

Nonassociative VSTM only permits recall of the representative in a location, with the recalled representative being the one with the greatest VSTM strength of activation. It seems likely that any attempt to superimpose a test item on the location of the previously presented item would simply destroy the VSTM trace for the previously presented item. Presenting the test item in a location sufficiently removed to avoid this problem might well result in above-chance recognition performance, but, according to multitrace theory, subjects would be recalling the test item and answering "yes or no" depending on whether what they recalled matched the test item. This is not elementary recognition, but a more complex retrieval process based on the elementary recall process.

Associative memory permits both recall and recognition. What is judged in recall are the comparative strengths of associations from the representatives of the cue event to the representatives of the alternative responses, either direct associations or indirect associations via structure representatives.

What is judged in recognition varies greatly with the nature of the recognition task. In event recognition or recency memory, the strength of association between the event and the familiarity representative is assumed to be judged. In associative (or serial order) recognition memory, the sum of the direct and indirect associations between the representatives of the two test events is assumed to be judged.

Many retrieval processes are quite complex, such as trying to remember someone's name when it is not immediately recalled. However, according to multitrace theory, all such complex retrieval processes are, in principle, analyzable as a sequence of elementary retrieval processes.

Dynamics

The most fundamental assumption of multitrace theory regarding trace dynamics is the analysis into four phases: acquisition of potential strength, consolidation of retrievable strength, decay of strength, and retrieval of strength. With appropriate (non-)rehearsal instructions and other conditions of presentation, it is reasonable to assume that acquisition can be confined to the period of occurrence of each event prior to the presentation of the next event. Consolidation takes place perhaps partly during the occurrence of the event, but, for ITM and LTM, largely or entirely after the event and during the acquisition or other processing of subsequent events. It is reasonable to suppose that the lag from event onset or offset to the beginning or end of consolidation is greater for LTM than for ITM or STM, if indeed there is any consolidation lag at all for STM. Decay begins as soon as the trace is fully consolidated. In retrieval, the strength of the trace at the moment of retrieval is the input to the judgment processes. This terminates a complete cycle of the four memory phases, though retrieval may initiate further acquisition followed by consolidation and decay.

Each phase has its own dynamic function (strength as a function of time). The retrievable strength at any time in the acquisition period prior to consolidation is zero. During consolidation it is the product of the acquisition function and the consolidation function. During the decay period, retrievable strength is the product of all three functions. This multiplicative combination of phases is obviously valid if the phases are strictly successive and nonoverlapping. If the phases overlap, such as would occur if decay of already consolidated strength occurred during the consolidation of new strength, then multiplicative combination of phases is less obviously valid. However, one can interpret the acquisition and consolidation phases to include the effects of the decay process for already consolidated strength in addition to the effects of the true acquisition and consolidation processes on the increment in trace strength due to the last presentation of an event. Now the phases in multitrace theory are successive and strictly nonoverlapping, despite some overlap in the true phases. The advantages of a simple multiplicative combination of dynamic functions are so great that some added complexity in the acquisition and consolidation functions is a small price to pay. Also, it is not clear that there is any added complexity in the acquisition and consolidation functions, since these functions are likely to be approximations without an elegant derivation from an underlying more molecular theory.

It seems necessary to have three different acquisition functions, one for associative acquisition, one for nonassociative acquisition, and one for concept acquisition. Since there is nothing known regarding the dynamics of concept acquisition, in the present sense of the term, there is little point in stating anything but that activating a set of representatives in simultaneous contiguity increases the strength of association of each to an input site of the concept representative for which this set is a cue. Note that in order for a concept representative to be a disjunction of conjunctions of attribute representatives, the strengths of associations from attribute representatives should sum only within each conjunction. That is the purpose of specifying that a concept representative has many input sites.

The associative acquisition function is assumed to be the product of two exponentials which approach a limit as a function of the durations of the two events presented in simultaneous or immediately successive contiguity. The limit is formulated with sufficient generality to include the effects of contiguous activation of two internal representatives i and j on the association from each to the other (forward and backward associations in successive contiguity) and also the generalized increment in strength of association between any two representatives k and l resulting from contiguous activation of i and j. The accounting for generalized strength depends upon the estimation of similarity functions for any unordered pair of internal representatives in the modality involved. There is no provision for remote associations between successively activated event representatives, except indirectly via serial position representatives. This may or may not be the correct formulation, but it turns out to be simpler to handle it this way. I know of no evidence that distinguishes between the relative contributions of remote event-to-event associations and indirect effects due to generalization of associations with serial position concepts.

It should be noted that event familiarity or recency judgments can be handled by the associative acquisition function, by interpreting event familiarity and recency as determined by the strength of association between the event representative and the familiarity representative. If one assumes that the familiarity representative is always activated simultaneously with the activation of each event representative, this is a special case of simultaneous conditioning.

Provision is made in the associative acquisition function for acquisition to begin only after a lag which is assumed to be a function of the memory modality. The principal purpose of this is to account for the apparent finding that moderately rapid presentation of verbal events (0.2 to 1 second per auditory event, 0.5 to 1 second per visual event) leads primarily, though perhaps not entirely, to acquisition of associations in the phonetic attribute modality, not in the concept modality. The evidence for this is that errors and interference similarity effects tend to be primarily determined by phonetic attribute similarity, rather than by conceptual (semantic) similarity (Baddeley, 1966a, 1968; Cole, Haber, and Sales, 1968; Conrad, 1963, 1964; Conrad and Hull, 1964; Conrad, Freeman, and Hull, 1965; Hintzman, 1967; Laughery and Pinkus, 1966; Posner and Konick, 1966; Wickelgren, 1965a, b, c, d, 1966a, b). There is also some auditory and visual nonverbal attribute memory (Murray, 1968; Sperling, 1960; Wickelgren, 1969a).

However, given sufficient time to study each event, conceptual coding can be demonstrated (Anisfeld and Knapp, 1968; Baddeley and Dale, 1966; Kimble, 1968; McGeoch and McDonald, 1931; Underwood, 1965; Underwood and Freund, 1968; Underwood and Goad, 1951). The time required for conceptual coding of an event probably varies somewhat with the event and the precise determination of average lag and rate parameters requires careful control of what the subject is thinking of at each moment. However, under steady-state conditions where the subject must conceptually code each of a long series of events, the lag before any conceptual coding takes place is probably on the order of 1 second, and the time constant of the subsequent exponential approach to a limit in conceptual coding is probably also on the order of 1 second.

The nonassociative acquisition function is simply a degenerate version of the associative acquisition function where the duration of only one event needs to be considered. It should be noted that the nonassociative acquisition function has the same form as the associative acquisition function for single-event familiarity or recency judgments, making the reasonable assumption that the similarity of the familiarity representative and any event representative is zero.

The form of the consolidation function for all traces in all modalities is assumed to be some power-function approach to a limit that starts only after a lag, which is assumed to be close to zero for VSTM and STM, on the order of seconds or tens of seconds for ITM, and on the order of hours for LTM. Complete consolidation of VSTM and STM is assumed to occur essentially immediately. Complete consolidation of ITM is assumed to require seconds or tens of seconds, and complete consolidation of LTM is assumed to require hours or days.

Decay of all traces in all modalities is assumed to be exponential, though the rate of trace decay may vary with the modality and the conditions. The range for visual VSTM time constants appears to be 0 to several seconds. The range for STM time constants appears to be 1 to 10 seconds. The range for ITM time constants appears to be 2 minutes to several hours. The range for LTM time constants appears to be days to years. One point must be made clear. I use the word decay to refer to the degradation of a memory trace in storage for whatever reason. Thus, decay, as I use the term, does not exclude storage interference effects (such as unlearning), though it does exclude all retrieval interference (competition) effects. One of the primary reasons for the variability in the decay rate for any given type of trace is undoubtedly that the storage interference effects vary with the modality of the trace and the nature of the experimental conditions. However, recognition of the variability of the decay rate with the storage modality and the conditions should not overshadow the importance of the simple assumption that under constant conditions the rate of decay of a trace does not vary with its age. This is a contradiction of Jost's (1897) Second Law that the rate of decay of a trace decreases with its age. The crux of the decision between Jost's Second Law and the assumption that trace decay rate is invariant with trace age is whether trace decay curves look more like single trace decay with a continuously decelerating rate or the sum of several exponentially decaying traces.

AXIOMS OF MULTITRACE THEORY

Coding

A1   (Attribute Coding) Every event has an innate internal representation such that every pair of events i and j has similarity η_{ij} determined by their sensory and motor attributes, where $0 \leqslant \eta_{ij} \leqslant 1$.

A2 (Concept Coding) For some events, the attribute representation of event i is associated to a learned conceptual representation with strength s_i, under a given interpretation of the event. Events may have several learned conceptual interpretations. The conceptual representation is such that every pair of events i and j under particular interpretations has semantic similarity δ_{ij}, where $0 \leqslant \delta_{ij} \leqslant 1$.

A3 (Types of Associations) The principal types of associations within or between modalities are: (a) interevent associations (direct forward and backward associations between the representatives of successively presented events), (b) intraevent associations (associations among the representatives of the simultaneously presented components of an event), (c) concept associations (associations between the representatives of the simultaneously presented components of an event and a concept representative for the event), and (d) structured associations (associations between the representative of an event and cognitive-structure representatives such as the familiarity representative, serial position concepts like beginning, middle, and end, subgroup labels, syntactic structures, visual images, mediators, mnemonics, rules, etc).

A4 (Modalities of Associative Memory) Every ordered pair of sensory, motor, or cognitive modalities is a memory modality. The traces involving representatives in different memory modalities may have different dynamics.

A5. (Traces in a Modality) An association in a memory modality is the sum of as many as three component traces with different dynamics: short-term memory (STM) with a time constant varying from 1 to 10 seconds, intermediate-term memory (ITM) with a time constant varying from 2 minutes to several hours, and long-term memory (LTM) with a time constant varying from days to years.

A6 (Non-Associative Very-Short-Term Memory, VSTM) Presentation of an event activates the internal representative of the event and the VSTM strength (of activation) persists for a very brief time (generally less than 1 or 2 seconds) after presentation.

Retrieval

A7 (Elementary Retrieval Processes) The principal types of elementary retrieval processes are: (a) Recall, which is a comparative judgment (1) on the STM, ITM, and LTM strengths of the associations from the representative of the cue event to the representatives of the alternative events or (2) on the VSTM activation strength of the events, and (b) Recognition, which can be either a comparative or an absolute judgment of (1) direct forward and backward event associations, (2) intraevent associations, (3) associations from event representatives to the familiarity representative,

(4) indirect event associations via a mediating structure such as serial position, or (5) any weighted additive combination of the above.

A8   (Complex Retrieval Processes) Complex retrieval processes are composed of sequences of elementary retrieval processes with final decisions being based on logical combinations of the elementary absolute and comparate judgments.

A9   (Criterion Rule for Absolute Judgment) One-dimensional n-alternative absolute judgments are based on a 1 to 1, order-preserving, mapping of an n-way, interval partitioning of the judged dimension onto the n responses. The criteria c_i ($i = 1, \ldots, n - 1$) for the interval partitioning are normally distributed random variables, $c_i \sim N[\bar{c}_i, \sigma_c]$.

A10   (Maximum Rule for Comparative Judgment) One-dimensional, n-alternative comparative judgment is an n to 1 mapping from the n values on the judged dimension and their uniquely associated responses to the response associated with the maximum of these n values.

Dynamics

A11   (Phases) Memory traces have four phases: acquisition, consolidation, decay, and retrieval, in that temporal order. Activation initiates acquisition in VSTM. Contiguous activation initiates acquisition in associative STM, ITM, and LTM. Acquisition is the addition of an increment A to potential strength. Acquisition of potential strength for the same association on each trial of a sequence of n trials is A_q, $q = 1, \ldots, n$. In the consolidation phase, this potential increment in strength is converted into retrievable strength according to the function $C(t_q)$, where t_q is the delay since onset or offset of the acquisition period. In the decay phase, the activation strength decays according to the function $D(t)$, where t is the delay since the last acquisition trial (n). Retrieval is nondestructive and also can serve to produce further acquisition.

A12   (Multiplicative Combination of Phases) The memory trace available for retrieval is $M = \left[\sum_{q=1}^{n} A_q C(t_q)\right] D(t) + X$, where X is a normally distributed random variable, representing all the noise in the memory process, $X \sim N [0, \sigma]$.

A13   (Associative Acquisition) Activating two internal representatives i and j in simultaneous or immediately successive contiguity strengthens the association between the internal representatives k and l by the increment $A_q = (1 - e^{-\psi [T_i - \mu]})(1 - e^{-\psi [T_j - \mu]})(\sigma_{ik} \sigma_{jl} \alpha_f + \sigma_{il} \sigma_{jk} \alpha_b)$, where T_i is the presentation time for event i and where ψ (the rate of acquisition), μ (the lag after onset of an event before acquisition begins), σ_{xy} (the similarity of x and y in some modality), α_f (the forward association parameter), and

α_b (the backward association parameter) depend on the modality, the trace, and the state of the trace prior to presentation of events i and j on trial q. In particular, μ for the concept modality exceeds μ for any attribute modality. $\alpha_f > \alpha_b$ in successive contiguity, $\alpha_f = \alpha_b$ in simultaneous contiguity, $\alpha_{xx} = 1, \sigma_{xx} \geq \sigma_{xy} > 0$, and $[z] = \max(z, 0)$.

A14 (Nonassociative Acquisition) Activating an internal representative i increments the VSTM trace for item k by

$$A_k = (1 - e^{-\psi[T_i - \mu]}) \sigma_{ik} \alpha$$

A15 (Concept Acquisition) Activating a set of internal representatives $\{i\}$ in simultaneous contiguity increments the strength, s_i, of association of each to an input site of the concept representative for which this set is a cue.

A16 (Delayed Consolidation)

$$C(t_q) = \begin{cases} 0 & \text{for } t_q < \tau \\ [(t_q - \tau)/(\epsilon - \tau)]^{\varphi} & \text{for } \tau \leq t_q \leq \epsilon \\ 1 & \text{for } t_q > \epsilon, \end{cases}$$

where τ, ϵ, and φ depend on the trace and the conditions. For present purposes, we can assume $\varphi = 1$ so that $C(t_q)$ is a ramp function from $t_q = \tau$ to $t_q = \epsilon$.

A17 (Exponential Decay)

$$D(t) = \begin{cases} 1 & \text{for } t < \epsilon \\ e^{-\beta(t - \tau)} & \text{for } t \geq \epsilon, \end{cases}$$

where β depends on the trace and the conditions.

CODING

Associative Versus Nonassociative Memory

Verbal ITM and LTM. Since the same types of arguments on this question apply to both ITM and LTM and existing data gives no reason to doubt that both ITM and LTM are associative, the two types of traces will be lumped together in the present discussion. The arguments favoring an associative theory of verbal ITM and LTM are as follows.

First, there are at least hundreds of thousands of event pairs stored with reasonable strength in LTM, and at least a thousand event pairs can be stored with reasonable strength in ITM (Wallace, Turner, and Perkins, 1957). A memory which was nonassociative in both storage and retrieval would, on the average, have to search half of all the locations in the storage system looking for the cue word in order to come up with the correct response word, stored in the adjacent location. A reasonable neurophysiological estimate of the time required to "search" a location might be on the order of 10 to 100 milliseconds, since a single synaptic delay is on the order of 1 millisecond. This yields response times for LTM that are completely absurd, and to get reasonable response times even for ITM would require some rather remarkable new discoveries in neurophysiology. Of course, the present argument only requires an associative (content addressable) retrieval scheme. Storage could still be nonassociative. However, if a system has the capacity for content-addressability in retrieval, it seems silly not to use it in storage and instead to faithfully record each occurrence of an event in a separate location. Such nonassociative storage puts great strain on the retrieval system to achieve integration of temporally distributed information concerning identical or similar events or concepts, which is achieved automatically by an associative storage system.

Second, the principal advantage of a nonassociative memory is that it could realize extremely precise temporal resolution of events. However, this appears to be an ability humans do not have, except for very brief delays on the order of seconds (Brelsford, Freund, and Rundus, 1967; Henrichs and Buschke, 1968; Peterson, 1967; Yntema and Trask, 1963). Recency judgments for delays of seconds appear to be best explained by STM associations to a familiarity representative. Recency judgments for delays of minutes or hours may make some use of ITM associations to a familiarity representative. But even for delays of minutes or hours and certainly for delays of days, weeks, and years, recency judgments are mediated by ITM and LTM associations directly to certain timing events (like the time of day or the month or season of the year) or indirectly by way of association to certain larger events (such as one's stay in a certain location) which are associated to timing events. Handling recency judgments of events by means of associations which can be quite separate from other associations involving these events accounts for the fact that recency judgments can be quite poor when other associations to the events are extremely strong. With a nonassociative memory, it is difficult to see how one could be virtually incapable of remembering when an event occurred, but could recall an event associated with the cue event. It could be explained by the retrieval system, but it is difficult to see why one would have a nonassociative storage system and then throw away by an inadequate retrieval system the precise timing information that such a system can give you. It is particularly odd when you consider that the retrieval system for associative information has to be so complex because it must operate on a nonassociative storage system.

Third, retroactive (Bugelski and Cadwallader, 1956; Gibson, 1941; McGeoch and McDonald, 1931; Osgood, 1949, 1953) and proactive (Blankenship and Whitely, 1941; Melton and Von Lackum, 1941) interference in recall is a function of the similarity of the two lists. At a minimum, this requires an associative retrieval system. However, recently, there is a growing body of evidence to indicate that similarity-dependent retroactive interference is not solely a retrieval phenomenon in verbal ITM and LTM. Numerous studies have demonstrated that interpolated A-C learning causes greater storage interference (unlearning or inhibition of consolidation) for previously learned A-B association than does interpolated C-D learning (Houston, 1967; McGovern, 1964; Postman, 1965). Similarity-dependent storage interference is inconceivable with a nonassociative storage system. In a nonassociative memory, there is just no reason why storing A-C in one pair of adjacent locations should cause greater decay of A-B in another pair of locations than should the storage of C-D in the prior pair of locations. In an associative memory, it is perfectly reasonable to suppose that the connection capacity of any single internal representative is limited, so that increasing an A-C association will tend to weaken an A-B association.

Fourth, some position must be taken in the nonassociative theory as to whether repetition of a sequence of events can strengthen the traces for the events in the same sequence of locations or whether new occurrences of events are always stored in new locations. If it were possible to increase the probability of correct recall as much by strengthening the trace in a particular sequence of locations as by replication and if the subject were deliberately practicing a particular sequence, one would assume that strengthening would be the storage method of choice. Improving memory by replication causes problems in retrieval, particularly in the time required to come up with the correct response and particularly in learning by the part method. If one is learning the sequence ABCDEF in two parts, ABC and DEF, replication leads to a memory structure like the following ABCABCABCABCDEFDEFDEFDEF, whereas strengthening leads to a memory structure that parallels the sequence structure, namely, ABCDEF. Nevertheless, the results of experiments on learning by the part method make it clear that, if humans had a nonassociative memory, they would have to be assumed to be using replication not strengthening learning. This is because substantial practice is required to connect the parts after each part has been learned separately and subjects make CA type errors in attempting to connect the parts, as if the end of a part had been associated to the beginning of the part in learning the part (see McGeoch and Irion, 1952, for a review of whole vs. part learning). However, the nonassociative theory with replication has its own problems. How does the subject ever learn to connect the parts? How could he ever stop making CA errors, if the previous part learning is to be of benefit to him, as it clearly is? The simple linear structure of nonassociative memory is inadequate to account for the more complex topological (connection) structure of human memory.

An associative memory is completely consistent with all the facts of whole vs. part learning. It explains why the whole method is often superior to the part method in efficiency of learning, despite the fact that subjects strongly prefer the part method and receive more immediate reward in the form of correct performance with the part method. The advantage of the whole method is that it secures the greatest efficiency ratio of direct event-to-event associations rehearsed to events rehearsed, namely $n-1/n$, where n is the length of the list. The part method, particularly in the combination of the parts, has a very much lower efficiency ratio. Furthermore, an associative memory predicts that combining the parts should be particularly inefficient, and also predicts that there should be frequent errors involving the end of a part being associated to its beginning, if rehearsal of a part involved close temporal contiguity of the end and the beginning of the part.

Verbal STM. Since the capacity of verbal STM is small in comparison to ITM and LTM and since work on STM began in earnest about the time that computers were being developed, many people interested in STM assumed explicitly or implicitly that STM was nonassociative (buffer storage). The earliest focus of my research on STM was to show that this was false and that STM was associative, just as is ITM and LTM.

First, RI and PI in short-term recall are similarity dependent, when the phonetic similarity of the interfering list to the list to be remembered are manipulated (Wickelgren, 1965a, 1966b).

Second, in at least one case intralist phonemic similarity facilitated item memory while severely depressing order memory, exactly as predicted by an associative theory of STM (Wickelgren, 1965e). Taking as an example the phonemically similar list of consonant-vowel digrams, *na fa ta*, versus the phonemically different list, *na fo ti*, with only the consonants having to be recalled, the argument is essentially as follows: in an associative memory, all of the consonant representatives will be associated to the single vowel representative, *a*, in the similar list. Since *a* is very frequently activated, it will be certain to be recalled producing a very good item-recall for all of the consonants, but it will give no information about the order of the consonants. Considering only the direct forward associations between the components of adjacent CV digrams, order information is carried only by the single association between the adjacent consonants in the similar lists, but is carried by all four associations from and to adjacent consonants and vowels in the different lists. Thus, an associative theory of STM predicts that order memory might well be better for different lists, while item memory is better for similar lists. This was what was found, and it is difficult to see how a nonassociative theory could account for such a dissociation between item and order memory.

Third, an associative theory of STM predicts that the topological structure of the associations between item representatives will be different for lists with repeated items than for lists with no repeated items. A nonassociative theory of STM predicts no such differences, though of course one can construct *ad hoc* hypotheses to graft onto the nonassociative memory structure to account for some of the same repeated item phenomena predicted by an associative memory structure. A rather large number of differences in STM for lists with and without repeated items have been found (Wickelgren, 1965f, 1966c), perhaps the simplest of which to describe is the associative intrusion phenomenon. Lists which have the form...*AB*...*AC*...show frequencies of substituting *B* for *C* and *C* for *B* that significantly exceed the frequencies of substituting items in these positions when they are not preceded by a repeated item. The reason for such associative intrusions is obvious with an associative theory of memory, the representative of *A* is associated to both *B* and *C* and the differentiating serial position cues do not completely swamp the effect of the ambiguous prior item cue. In a nonassociative theory, there is no logical reason to expect such associative intrusions, at least not in STM for relatively short lists.

Fourth, in STM experiments on the effects of rehearsal grouping, subjects give evidence of the ability to cross-classify items by beginning, middle, or end group and by beginning, middle, and end position within the group (Wickelgren, 1964, 1967a). Several phenomena in rehearsal grouping experiments support this interpretation, the most definitive of which is that errors tend to be within the group or in the same position of a different group. In an associative memory, an item can have associations to a group label and a position within a group label, but it is very difficult to see how this could be accomplished by a one-dimensional nonassociative memory.

Visual VSTM. Wickelgren and Whitman (1970) have obtained experimental evidence which indicates that visual VSTM (e.g., Sperling, 1960) is nonassociative. Similar experiments to those used to show that verbal STM is associative can probably be done to show that visual VSTM is nonassociative, namely, storage of a visual pattern in each of some array of locations on the retina, with no associations between the item representatives in each location.

Attribute Versus Concept Representation

Verbal ITM and LTM. Since the same phonetic and visual attributes characterize an enormous number of different verbal events, it is not likely that interevent associations in ITM and LTM would be primarily based on ITM and LTM associations between the phonetic or visual attribute representatives of the events. The retrieval and storage interference effects of subsequent events and the retrieval, and possibly storage, interference effects of prior events would simply be too great at the phonetic attribute level of coding. Thus, it is not surprising that errors and interference effects in verbal ITM (and presumably also LTM) for words are primarily based on conceptual similarity as shown by studies in serial learning (McGeoch and McDonald, 1931; Underwood and Goad, 1951), paired associate learning (Baddeley, 1966b; Baddeley and Dale, 1966), and recognition learning (Anisfeld and Knapp, 1968; Kimble, 1968; Underwood, 1965; Underwood and Freund, 1968) with delays on the order of minutes or tens of minutes.

The learning of verbal lists (nonsense syllables or words) generally does show interference effects due to phonemic or graphemic (letter) attribute similarity, often called "formal" similarity, (e.g., Baddeley, 1966b; Cohen and Musgrave, 1966; Dallett, 1966; Feldman and Underwood, 1957; Horowitz, 1962; Runquist, 1966; Underwood, 1953). However, the influence of attribute similarity may be largely due to a substantial STM component in precriterion performance on standard verbal learning tasks. When 16 second delays are introduced between learning trials and a rehearsal-preventing task is used to fill these delays, the effect of attribute similarity on verbal learning disappears (Baddeley, 1966b).

This does not imply that there is no ITM or LTM involving attribute representatives. There must be LTM for the associations from attribute representatives that specify concept representatives. Furthermore, in the present theory, the distinction between attribute representation and concept representation of an event must be considered to be relative to the event, with the attributes of an event being its immediate constituents. Thus, the immediate constituents of a word or other multiphonemic item might be an ordered set of its syllables, phonemes, or graphemes (letters). Alternatively, the immediate constituent of a word might be an unordered set of its context-sensitive allophones (Wickelgren, 1969c). According to the context-sensitive allophonic theory of the coding of speech at the phonetic level, there is an internal representative for every ordered triple of phonemes that appears in any word in one's language. Thus, *stop* is coded as the unordered set, $/_{\#}s_t, s_{t_0}, t_{o_p}, {_o}p_{\#}/$. It is a remarkable feature of context-sensitive allophonic coding of words that the ordered set can always (to my knowledge) be recovered from the unordered set. This recovery of the ordered set from the unordered set is accomplished largely by the use of long-term associations between the allophone representatives. The context-sensitive coding theory solves the problem of serial order in the articulation of speech at the word level and also solves the two most celebrated problems in the recognition of speech at the word level, namely, segmentation (partitioning the acoustic signal for a word into segments) and the immediate left and right context-conditioned variation in the acoustic features of a phoneme. Thus, there is considerable support for a theory which requires the assumption of LTM associations between the immediate constituents (attributes) of a word.

It is probably the case that the ITM and LTM traces involving attribute representatives play a small role in most adult memory tasks because of the interference factors. Nevertheless, according to multitrace theory, it ought to be possible to find situations in which they play a large enough role to demonstrate their existence.

Verbal STM. Errors and interference effects in verbal STM for rapidly presented multiphonemic items such as words, nonsense syllables, letters,

and digits in many studies appear to be primarily dependent upon phonemic
similarity (Conrad, 1963, 1964; Conrad, Freeman, and Hull, 1965; Conrad
and Hull, 1964; Posner and Konick, 1966; Wickelgren, 1965a, b, c, e, 1966b).
Errors in verbal STM for rapidly presented single vowel or consonant phonemes
in many studies appear to be primarily dependent upon distinctive feature
similarity (Cole, Haber, and Sales, 1968; Hintzman, 1967; Wickelgren, 1965d,
1966a).

This does not mean that there is no STM in the concept system. Generally
small, but statistically significant, effects of conceptual similarity have been
found in several types of situations usually thought to be primarily measuring
STM (Corman and Wickens, 1968; Dale and Gregory, 1966; Henley, Noyes,
and Deese, 1968; Turvey, 1967; Wickens and Eckler, 1968; Wickens and
Simpson, 1968). Even those STM studies which failed to find statistically
significant effects of conceptual similarity have found effects in the same
direction (Baddeley and Dale, 1966; Dale, 1967). All of these demonstrations
of small effects of conceptual similarity are open to the charge that they are
assessing the conceptual coding, not of STM, but of a small ITM component
which may be present in the situations studied. The study by Turvey (1967)
supports the interpretation of the conceptual similarity effects as being due
to ITM, since Turvey found effects of conceptual similarity with delays of
24 seconds but not with delays of 12 seconds. Henley, Noyes, and Deese
(1968) also found greater effects of conceptual similarity with delays of 16
seconds than with delays of 0, 4, and 8 seconds. However, until one has
the ability to assess conceptual similarity effects in memory situations which
are known, by some independent criterion, to be mediated entirely by STM,
or until we have a well established quantitative analysis of trace components in
some situation, it will not be possible to definitely conclude whether there is
STM facilitation of associations in the concept system.

Nonverbal Auditory STM. Errors in STM for the pitch of pure tones
follow a generalization gradient which has one maximum at the pitch of the
tone to be remembered (standard tone), at least within a single octave
(Wickelgren, 1969a). Although this has not been established quantitatively
to my knowledge, the accuracy of the ability to recognize a difference between the standard and comparison tones with short delays between them
is probably vastly greater than the accuracy of one's ability to sing a tone of
a given pitch. Furthermore, the ability to recognize pitch differences extends
beyond the range of the human voice. Therefore, it is likely that the memory
is in the auditory system, rather than being in a vocal motor system. A
variety of unpublished attempts to attribute part or all of this pitch memory
to verbal memory for absolute or comparative judgments of pitch have all
failed to provide any support for the presence of verbal memory components
when the number of alternative standard tones is 10 or more. Thus, I think

it is quite certain that there is nonverbal attribute STM for pitch and undoubtedly for many other psychophysical attributes in sensory, and probably
also motor, modalities.

Visual VSTM. Visual VSTM presumably is coded in some visual attribute
system, and indeed it is very susceptible to visual interference, but not very
susceptible to verbal or nonverbal auditory interference (Sperling, 1963).
An unsystematic error analysis in one situation which probably is mediated
in part by visual VSTM and in part by verbal STM suggested the presence of
both visual and phonetic coding (Sperling, 1960). Presumably the visually
similar errors were due to the visual VSTM component and the phonetically
similar errors were due to the verbal STM component, but it would be nice
to have this shown in a precise quantitative manner.

Rote Versus Structured Learning

Rote learning refers to the strengthening of a direct association between
the internal representatives of two actually occurring events or components
of a single event, without use of any associations to or from other (cognitive
structure) representatives which are not representatives of the occurring
events or event components. Structured learning refers to every type of learning
that involves the strengthening of associations to, or from, internal representatives which are not the representatives of currently occurring events or
event components. Such representatives are called *cognitive structure*
representatives. As such, structured learning includes the direct association
of an event representative to a cognitive structure representative and the
indirect association between two event representatives (*A* and *B*) mediated
by a chain of associations involving cognitive structure representatives.
Such a chain presumably starts with associating event *A* to one or more
cognitive structure representatives which may be associated to other cognitive structure representatives and so on until some terminal set of cognitive structure representatives is elicited which is associated to event *B*.

If we summarize the sequence of sets of cognitive structure representatives
by M (mediator), getting A-M-B, we have the conventional diagram for
mediated association. In those cases where M is a single internal representative
unadorned by the presence of cognitive operations (logical, syntactically
structured, etc., thought processes, whatever they are), there seems to be little
reason to complain with this formulation. Where M hides a multiplicity of
cognitive operations, the formulation is open to the charge that it does just
that, namely, hides a multiplicity of cognitive operations without any attempt
to understand them. However, that is just the point, to study learning and
memory, it would be extremely desirable to be able to give cognition its due
in relation to learning and memory, without having to explain everything
in cognition as well.

The current formulation of multitrace theory adopts the mediated-association approach to the influence of cognition upon memory. Following Jarrett and Scheibe (1962), multitrace theory takes the further step in the quantitative formulation of mediation theory of assuming that one can represent a mediational chain of associations, A-M-B, by a single strength. This mediated strength of association is just like the strength of a direct association, A-B, and can be added to any direct association to determine the total strength of association between A and B. Whether this simple approach to the effect of cognition on memory will be successful remains to be seen, but the determination of its success depends upon how adequately it accounts for learning and memory phenomena, not upon how adequately it accounts for thinking and language phenomena.

Although I am not, at present, in a position to make a quantitative evaluation of the mediational approach to structured learning, the need for some incorporation of structured learning is clear and will be described in the following sections. From an introspective viewpoint, most of adult learning involves association of the representatives of occurring events to a cognitive structure, and very little is rote. Multitrace theory says that all of the basic principles of rote learning apply to structured learning. Nevertheless, it seems to me to be important for an adequate theory of learning and memory to make the distinction between rote and structured learning and to describe the important classes of structured learning, because this is important in and of itself, not because it interacts with any other part of the multitrace theory of memory.

Verbal Paired Associates Learning. Subjects very frequently report the use of verbal mediators in paired associate (PA) learning, and there is now rather substantial evidence that PA learning is facilitated by good verbal mediators whether supplied by the subject or the experimenter (Dallett, 1964; Davidson, 1964; Jarrett and Scheibe, 1962; Jensen and Rohwer, 1963a,b; Kiess and Montague, 1965; Wood and Bolt, 1968). Good mediators also facilitate retention (Adams and McIntyre, 1967; Montague, Adams, and Kiess, 1966; Runquist and Farley, 1964; Reed, 1918) and reduce retroactive interference of A-B pairs due to subsequent A-C learning (Adams and Montague, 1967).

Good mediators can be defined theoretically as those mediating concepts which have strong previously established associations from the stimulus event and to the response event, such as the example given by Dallett (1964) of *bacon* as a good mediator between the stimulus trigram *bac* and the word response *eggs*. Poor mediators have low levels of previously established associations from the stimulus event and to the response event. Empirical measures of the goodness of mediators can be derived from free association data, subjects' or experimenters' ratings, or even from whether the mediator is or is not recalled on some later trial or retention test. Poor mediators can

inhibit PA learning (Dallett, 1964), and generally fail to facilitate retention
or possibly inhibit it (Adams and McIntyre, 1967; Montague, Adams, and
Kiess, 1966). However, as one might expect, most mediators chosen by
subjects are good mediators and so the net effect of natural language
mediation by subjects is facilitatory in both learning and retention.

In addition to verbal mediation, it appears that combining the stimulus
and response events into a single visual image facilitates PA learning and
memory (Bugelski, 1968; Epstein, Rock, and Zuckerman, 1960; Paivio,
1969). The mediator in this case is a visual image that includes both the
stimulus and response events in some sense, and this seems somewhat different
from a natural language mediator, which does not necessarily include the
stimulus and response event in any sense. However, multitrace theory
treats both verbal and visual mediation in the same manner, namely, by means
of a mediated strength of association between the stimulus and response
events.

Serial Learning. To the extent that serial learning (SL) in STM, ITM,
or LTM is achieved by facilitation of associations between adjacent item-
representatives (Postman and Stark, 1967; Shuell and Keppel, 1967; Wickelgren, 1965f, 1966c), verbal or visual mediation of the type just described
ought to be facilitatory in SL, and indeed there is some evidence for this
(Houston, 1964). However, the interesting new type of structured learning
that appears with SL is mediation by the use of serial position concepts.

There is evidence for the use of serial position concepts in STM studies
of serial learning. Melton and Von Lackum (1941), Conrad (1959, 1960)
found that there was a significant tendency for intrusion errors in immediate
recall of a list to come from the same position in the previous list. Wickelgren
(1964, 1967a) in a study of rehearsal grouping in groups of different sizes
found a significant tendency for intrusion errors to be other items in the
same group or to be items in the same relative position in other groups.
It is difficult to see how the latter within-position errors could have occurred
above chance, except if subjects were using a two level cross-classification
of serial position concepts for groups and for positions within a group.
Furthermore, the error patterns and the optimum rehearsal group size at
around 3 or 4 suggested that subjects in this situation can use on the order of
3 distinct serial position concepts, beginning, middle, and end. However, the
ordering power of these 3 serial position concepts can be greatly extended by
the human capacity for two-level use of these concepts through grouping.

Intermediate term memory studies of SL also indicate the importance of
serial-position-to-item associations. Evidence for this comes from a variety
of sources. First, positive transfer between a serial list and a PA list derived
from adjacent pairs of items in the serial list is far from 100 percent (Jensen
and Rohwer, 1965; Postman and Stark, 1967; Shuell and Keppel, 1967; Young,

1959, 1961, 1962; Young and Casey, 1964; Young and Clark, 1964), though it can sometimes be substantial on early transfer trials. This indicates that some other cues besides the direct forward item-to-item associations play a role in SL, and while this does not prove that the other cues are serial position cues, they are the most likely candidates. Second, when the serial list is learned by varying the starting position on each learning trial, the transfer from SL to a compatible PA list is significantly enhanced (Shuell and Keppel, 1967). Since varying the starting position in SL must primarily reduce the reliance upon serial position cues, this effect indicates that serial position cues are important in ordinary SL. Third, SL with variable starting position is more difficult than ordinary SL (Bowman and Thurlow, 1963; Ebenholtz, 1963a; Keppel, 1964; Saufley, 1967; Shuell and Keppel, 1967; Winnick and Dornbush, 1963). Fourth, there is positive transfer from SL to a PA list which pairs the items from the serial list with numbers referring to their previous serial positions (Jensen and Rohwer, 1963). Fifth, there is positive transfer from one SL task to another SL task for items that are common to the two lists and maintain the same serial position (Ebenholtz, 1963a). Sixth, presenting a list of items in a spatial order without temporal ordering can be just as efficient for learning a serial list as presenting the list in temporal order (Slamecka, 1967), though under other conditions, conventional SL has been found to be somewhat faster (Ebenholtz, 1963b). Seventh, in the Ebenholtz (1963b) study there was heavy positive transfer between conventional SL and the spatial position learning.

RETRIEVAL

Event

Recognition Memory. Event recognition memory is measured by presenting a test event, such as a verbal item (letter, digit, nonsense syllable, word, etc.), and asking the subject to say whether or not that event has occurred in some period of time. The only reason for using the term *event* rather than *item* is to include motor and nonverbal sensory events which are not so naturally referred to as *items*.

Most studies of event recognition memory have been concerned with judgments of the occurrence or nonoccurrence of the test event in a period of time that could be considered to end with the presentation of the test event. Under such circumstances it is easy to think of event recognition memory judgments as being based on the familiarity of the test event, where familiarity is based on the strength of the STM, ITM, and/or LTM association from the representative of the test event to the familiarity representative. Recently presented events have STM and/or ITM facilitation of these associations on the hypothesis that the familiarity representative is always activated in contiguity with the representative of any occurring event.

However, when a subject is asked to recognize whether a test word was presented previously in a 1-hour session that occurred a week ago, the ITM or LTM strength of the association from the test word to the familiarity representative is not likely to be the primary basis for making the judgment. Such associative strengths would not distinguish between words presented in the critical period and words presented before or after in the subject's daily life. Thus, it is undoubtedly necessary to assume that, if it is familiarity that is being judged in this type of event recognition, it is the familiarity of the compound event consisting of the test event and the situation in which it occurred. This might be called associative recognition memory because it seems reasonable to assume that the strength of association of the representative of a compound event to the familiarity representative must be determined largely or completely by the strength of the associations between the representatives of the components of the compound event.

In either case, multitrace theory can treat the recognition of an event as being based on a single strength characterizing the familiarity of that event. Judgments in event recognition memory are assumed to be made by the criterion rule, namely, respond yes, if and only if the strength (familiarity) of the test event exceeds a criterion, and no otherwise. Further partitioning of the strength scale can be achieved by having the subject give confidence ratings in addition to the yes-no response. A yes-no decision combined with n levels of confidence yields $2n$ possible responses, which are assumed to be determined by the placement of $2n-1$ criteria that partition the strength scale into $2n$ not necessarily equal intervals. This makes event recognition memory an absolute judgment on trace strength.

Under constant experimental conditions, this strength may vary due to uncontrolled noise in the memory process, acquisition, consolidation, decay, and retrieval. In multitrace theory, the presence of such noise is handled by the addition of a random variable to the retrieved strength with zero mean and a variance that is often constant over the different conditions in an experiment, but could be assumed to vary with the conditions, if that were necessary.

In addition to noise in the memory process, there is undoubtedly a very large source of noise in a subject's criterion placements. Under the assumption that memory noise and criterion noise are normally distributed, the two can be combined into a single normally distributed noise. The combined noise can then be considered to add to a real-valued memory strength, converting it into a random variable whose mean is the same as the real-valued strength, and whose variance is the variance of the noise distribution. This is exactly the same trick used by Hull (1943) known by the name of *behavioral oscillation*. The advantage of this way of handling noise is that it permits one to have a real-variable memory theory almost everywhere, converting real variables to random variables only at the end of all computation regarding the passage of memory traces through different phases. To the extent that retrieval and criterion noise are large in relation to the noise in acquisition, consolidation, and decay, there can be no better way of handling the uncontrolled stochastic aspects of memory. With appropriate experimental control of coding and rehearsal, it seems reasonably likely that criterion noise overshadows all other noise, so this is a particularly attractive way of handling noise. However, even if the noise in acquisition, consolidation, or decay were substantial, the present approach could still be the simplest way of handling the stochastic aspect of memory, though, of course, it is somewhat *ad hoc*.

Like any strength theory, multitrace theory has the desirable property of allowing one to use the judgment rule of the theory, in combination with the noise assumptions, to convert response probabilities in event recognition memory into interval scale measures of the total memory strength of the event. The fact that measurement is on an interval scale means that one only measures the difference in the strength of two types of test events, for example, an event presented i seconds ago and an event that was not presented at all in the period in question. Furthermore, the unit of measurement is the standard deviation of the noise in the strength of one of these events. If the noise affecting the measured strength of each event is the same for all types of events in an experiment, then this is no problem. If there is some reason to suspect that the noise may vary for different events, then it may be necessary to take special care to measure all strength differences with the same unit of measurement. The latter problem is discussed at length in Wickelgren (1968a).

Operating Characteristics. In most cases, it suffices to estimate strength differences and the ratios of the standard deviations of the noise in two different strength distributions by means of a special plot called an operating characteristic (OC). The present section explains how to plot and interpret OCs for an event recognition memory experiment using confidence ratings.

Imagine that you have presented a list of items followed by a test item which is sometimes an item from the previous list (correct item) with i intervening items and sometimes an item not from the previous list (incorrect item). Call these conditions i and *, respectively. On each trial a subject answers yes or no and states his confidence on a scale from 1 (least) to 4 (most). We consider the subject's yes-no and rating responses to be a choice of one of 8 responses ordered on a single dimension of sureness that the test item was in the list: $Y4, Y3, Y2, Y1, N1, N2, N3, N4$.

Ideally, we have enough data for single subjects to do all analyses separately for each subject. This avoids any possibility of being misled as to the form of various functions due to averaging subjects with very different values of various parameters. More important, it gives us some idea of the

range of individual variation and whether this variation can be accounted for
by different values of parameters.

From our experiment we obtain the frequency of each of the 8 responses
in each condition. OCs are generated from the data for two conditions, say
for i and $*$. The first step in generating an OC is to convert the frequency of
each response in each condition into an empirical cumulative probability of
a response with a certain degree of sureness or greater sureness (that the test
item was in the list). This means that for condition i you divide the frequency
of $Y4$ responses by the N_i for condition i, then you divide the frequency of
$Y3 + Y4$ responses by N_i, then you divide the frequency of $Y2 + Y3 + Y4$
responses by N_i, ..., then you divide the frequency of $N3 + N2 + N1 + Y1$
$+ Y2 + Y3 + Y4$ responses by N_i. Thus, you obtain 7 empirical probabilities
(which must be monotonic nondecreasing) for condition i; call them p_{1i},
p_{2i}, ..., p_{7i}. In an identical manner, you obtain the 7 probabilities for
condition $*$, $p_1*, p_2*, ..., p_7*$.

The second step is to plot on normal-normal probability paper, the 7 pairs
of points: (p_j*, p_{ji}) for $j = 1, ..., 7$, where p_j* is the horizontal coordinate
and p_{ji} is the vertical coordinate.

The third step is to fit a straight line to the points, assuming that the
points do not deviate systematically from a straight line in this and other OCs
for the same subject in similar conditions (say the OCs for each of the various
i conditions against the $*$ condition). The best fitting straight line is our
empirical estimate of the true OC. The absence of any systematic deviation
of the empirical points of the various OCs from straight lines is evidence that the
noise in both i and $*$ conditions is approximately normally distributed.

The fourth step is to determine the slope and horizontal intercept of the
best-fitting straight line. The slope provides an estimate of the ratio of the
noise in the $*$ condition to the noise in the i condition, $\sigma*/\sigma_i$. The horizontal
intercept provides an estimate of the difference between the trace strengths
of i and $*$ test items in units of $\sigma*$, namely, $D(i. *) = (M_i - M*)/\sigma*$.

Empirical Adequacy. The only direct test of the retrieval assumptions
for event recognition that is currently available is the fit of the OCs to
straight lines on normal-normal plots. In almost all cases, there is no systematic
deviation, but there can be a lot of unsystematic variation. Appropriate
goodness of fit tests are now being developed (Dorfman and Alf, 1968),
so this test can be made more powerful in the future. However, this is
mainly a test of the normal distribution assumption. As long as the strength
distributions are unimodal, slight deviations from normality, no matter how
significant statistically, are of little significance theoretically. Hence, I think
that the results of such tests of the fit of OCs to straight lines on normal-
normal plots are of very limited value in determining the accuracy of the retrieval assumptions of multitrace theory.

The principal evidence for the validity of the retrieval assumptions for event
recognition appears to be largely indirect, namely, how elegant are the laws

for the dynamics of memory traces that result when these retrieval assumptions are made. So far the laws of trace dynamics for event recognition memory appear to be rather elegant, but it is far too early to be sure of this.

Associative Recognition Memory

Although, as mentioned in the previous section, event recognition memory may sometimes or always be merely a special case of associative recognition memory, it is clearer, and perhaps safer, to distinguish them at the present time than to lump them together. Associative recognition memory refers to the subject's memory for the temporal contiguity or temporal order of events, namely, his ability to discriminate correctly and incorrectly paired events in PA recognition memory and his ability to discriminate direct forward associations from backward or remote associations in SL using a recognition test of serial order memory. In each case, multitrace theory assumes that it is the strength of association between the two test events that is judged in a recognition test, with the forward association between the test events being weighted more heavily than the backward association in the serial order case at least.

In the case of associative recognition memory, it is possible to devise a very strong test of the central property of the retrieval assumptions for recognition memory. This central property is called *independence from irrelevant associations* because it asserts that only the strength of the test association is judged in recognition memory. For example, if the test pair is A-B and subjects are to decide whether B followed A in the previous list, only the strength of the A-B association is assumed to enter into the judgment. The strengths of presented or nonpresented A-C pairs are assumed to have no effect on the A-B recognition judgment. Another way to refer to this is to say that recognition tests are free of retrieval interference.

Independence from irrelevant associations has been tested in STM studies of SL and PA by comparing recognition memory judgments for A-B pairs in cases where the lists that were presented contained both A-B and A-C pairs, and in cases where the lists that were presented contained only A-B pairs with X-C pairs used in place of the A-C pairs. No differences in recognition memory performance were obtained (Bower and Bostrom, 1968; Wickelgren, 1967b and unpublished data), confirming the central property of the multi-trace retrieval assumptions for recognition memory.

Multiple-Choice Recognition

In multiple-choice recognition, subjects must choose which of n events occurred in some previous list. The events are frequently compound events, $A-X_i, i=1, \ldots, n$, where the subject's task is to choose the X_i which was paired with A in some previous list. Multitrace theory assumes that only the strengths of the test associations are judged in multiple-choice (independence from irrelevant associations) and that the maximum decision rule is employed, namely, choose the event with the greatest strength of association to the cue event. If these retrieval assumptions are correct, it should be possible in many cases to predict performance on a multiple-choice test with m alternatives from performance on a multiple-choice test with n alternatives. Such predictions have been reasonably successful (Kintsch, 1967; Norman and Wickelgren, 1969).

Recall

Although the mechanism of recall with even a small known set of n alternatives may be different from n-alternative multiple-choice, they may both be describable by the maximum decision rule applied to the strengths of the associations from the cue event to the n alternatives. Evidence for different mechanisms was obtained by Norman and Wickelgren (1969) who found recall with 4 alternatives to be substantially faster than 4-alternative multiple-choice recognition. No systematic differences were found in the probabilities of correct choice in 4-alternative recall and multiple-choice, but large unsystematic differences were found. No definite conclusion regarding recall from small specified populations can be drawn at the present time. Recall from large populations of events is largely an unexplored frontier in the testing of multitrace theory.

However, some plausible speculations can be made regarding recall. First, it may be a simultaneous search through the alternatives, while multiple-choice is a sequential search. This is suggested by my introspection and by the latency differences obtained by Norman and Wickelgren (1969). Of course, I am referring to an elementary recall process, not a complicated recall task where a subject is allowed a lot of time to consider and reject alternatives. The latter task may have lots of elementary recall processes arranged in a series interspersed with elementary recognition processes. Of course, both a simultaneous and a successive search through the alternatives could be described by the maximum rule, but there might be some minor or major differences, for example, greater noise in the retrieval of associative strengths with the simultaneous search, or greater opportunity for decay of associative strengths during retrieval with the successive search.

Second, the total strengths of the alternatives judged in recall and multiple-choice may have somewhat different components. For example, subjects can be guaranteed that both items in a pair were in the previous list and they are only to decide whether the second item immediately followed the first in the previous list. Formally, this makes item strengths irrelevant to the judgment, and it may make them psychologically irrelevant. In recall, the item strengths of the different alternative response items may be important in addition to the strengths of association from the cue to the response items. Furthermore, in multiple-choice recognition, the backward association may help to discriminate correct and incorrect pairs, whereas in recall it is less likely that the backward association plays any role.

Predicting Recall and Multiple-Choice from Recognition

Another way of testing all of the retrieval assumptions of multitrace theory is to attempt to predict recall and multiple-choice with different numbers of alternatives from recognition memory data. The prediction is sensitive to hordes of minor assumptions (see Norman and Wickelgren, 1969 and Wickelgren, 1968a for a discussion), but, surprisingly enough, the prediction has been reasonably successful in at least two cases (Green and Moses, 1966; Kintsch, 1968). In a third case (Norman and Wickelgren, 1969), there appeared to be some minor complications in the prediction, but there was no reason to fault the basic retrieval assumptions of multitrace theory.

DYNAMICS

Two-Phase Studies of Verbal STM

Two-phase studies of verbal STM involve presenting a list of items followed immediately by a probe item or pair of items, with the subject required to say whether the probe was in the previous list or not. When the probe is a single item, this is an example of event recognition memory. When the probe is a pair of items and the subject is guaranteed that both items were in the list, though not necessarily as a pair in the presented order, this is an example of associative recognition memory. The two independently manipulatable experimental phases are the acquisition-consolidation-decay phase on the one hand and the retrieval (decision) phase on the other hand. This does place some limitations on the power of the two-phase design in testing theories of memory, by comparison to designs with more independently manipulatable phases. The principal example of the latter is the three-phase design of Brown (1958) and Peterson and Peterson (1959) where a third type of activity is interpolated between the presentation of the list to be remembered and the test.

However, the two-phase design does have an important advantage, which is that it appears to produce the least amount of active STM trace maintenance (rehearsal) of earlier items and the least amount of ITM difference between items presented and not presented on a trial. The evidence for the absence of ITM is that the two-phase STM strength decay curves are virtually always simple exponentials, whereas, three-phase STM strength decay curves always require the assumption of two traces (STM and ITM) decaying at very different rates (Wickelgren, 1970a). Furthermore, the STM component of three-phase strength decay curves is decaying somewhat more slowly than the STM trace in two-phase studies (Wickelgren, 1969b, 1970b).

Simple exponential decay of trace strength in STM has been obtained with two-phase studies on: (a) event recognition memory for three-digit numbers (Wickelgren and Norman, 1966) and single letters (Wickelgren 1970b), (b) associative recognition memory for the serial order of digits in SL (Wickelgren, 1967e) and of letter-digit pairs in PA (Wickelgren, unpublished), and recall of single digits (Norman, 1966). All of these studies carefully instructed subjects to think of the current items only and not try to rehearse previous items. This may be of critical importance in obtaining simple exponential decay in two-phase studies of STM.

One possible explanation of the absence of ITM in the above two-phase studies is that the presentation rate was too fast and the number of items to be learned was too great to permit the consolidation of appreciable amounts of ITM. This seems unlikely to account for the apparently complete absence of ITM in the strength decay curves. More likely, the explanation is, at least in part, as follows. The ITM traces are decaying at a rate which is slower than the decay rate of the STM traces by a factor of about 10^2 (Wickelgren, 1970a). With short lists constructed from a small population of items and with a short intertrial interval, the ITM traces for all items, whether correct or incorrect for that trial would be relatively constant. Thus, they would contribute nothing to the strength discriminability of correct and incorrect test items and would leave the strength decay curve reflecting only the STM strength discriminability.

This interpretation is confirmed by an unpublished two-phase study with words from a rather large population of 1000 words where a modest ITM component appears in the strength decay curve. One might well ask why about the same amount of ITM did not appear in the Wickelgren and Norman (1966) study which used a population of a little under 700 three-digit numbers. The reason is undoubtedly that three-digit numbers are much more similar to each other in their internal representation than are words, leading to a much greater amount of ITM strength generalization for three-digit numbers than for words.

Obtaining simple exponential decay of strength in STM is a very important simplifying result for multitrace theory. It would be very messy to have trace decay rate depend on trace age. However, one further simplification does not hold, namely, STM decay rate is not invariant over the conditions in the delay interval. At present, the primary variable that is known to affect the temporal decay rate of STM is the density of items to be learned in the delay interval. The evidence for this is a study by Wickelgren (1970b) in which rate of decay for letters (with time measured in seconds) was a linear function of rate of presentation of the list, with a positive intercept. The positive intercept, obtained for all subjects in all conditions, disproves the hypothesis that decay rate is invariant over rate of presentation if time is measured by the number of intervening items. Furthermore, the extrapolated rate of decay of STM at a hypothetical rate of 0 items to be learned per second is of the same order of magnitude as the rate of decay of the STM component in three-phase studies where the material that fills the delay interval does not have to be learned (Wickelgren, 1970b). The interpretation placed on the dependence of decay rate on the rate of presentation of new items to be learned is as follows. There is an active STM trace maintenance process which is partially counteracting a passive temporal decay process. However, the STM trace maintenance process requires some of the same neural apparatus as the STM trace acquisition and consolidation processes and thus cannot maintain previous STM traces as well during a period of around .25 seconds/letter in which the STM trace for each new letter is established. During any blank time between letters, the STM trace maintenance process operates much more effectively in counteracting decay. According to this hypothesis, rehearsal is the conscious top of the unconscious trace-maintenance iceberg. The simple assumptions formulated by Wickelgren (1970b) to account for this STM trace maintenance process may very well be approximately valid only for cases where the frequency of conscious rehearsal is kept minimal by nonrehearsal instructions.

Three-Phase Studies of Verbal STM and ITM

Three-phase studies involve presenting a short list of events to be remembered, followed by a delay which is filled with a task involving material that usually does not have to be remembered, followed by a test of the first list. The test may be event or associative recognition or recall and may be either a complete recall or recognition of the list or a probe recall or recognition of an individual event in the list. Strength decay curves for such three-phase studies (e.g., Peterson and Peterson, 1959; Murdock, 1961; Helleyer, 1962; Melton, 1963) deviate from a simple exponential decay in a manner which suggests the presence of a significant amount of ITM (Wickelgren, 1970d). This presumably results from the relatively greater temporal separation between repetitions of an item in these studies. However, studies with longer delays are needed to determine whether the decay curve is well fit by the sum of two exponentially decaying traces with very different time constants. Furthermore, according to multitrace theory, it ought to be possible to achieve a simple exponentially decaying trace with the three-phase design by modifications that decrease the temporal separation between repetitions of an item, for instance, reducing the population of items, increasing the number of items in a list, requiring learning of the interpolated material and using interpolated material from the same population as the list.

Continuous Studies of Verbal ITM

Continuous recognition studies (e.g., Donaldson and Murdock, 1968; Melton, Sameroff, and Schubot, 1963; Shepard and Teghtsoonian, 1961) involve presenting a long list of events, each of which is a new event to learn, a delay filling event, and a test event. In the multiple-choice version of continuous recognition memory (e.g., Shepard and Chang, 1963), the subject sees two (or more) events on each trial, must learn both, and must choose the one that has been presented before. In continuous recall studies (e.g., Atkinson, Brelsford, and Shiffrin, 1967; Brelsford, Shiffrin, and Atkinson, 1968), a trial has two parts: a test phase followed by a study phase. In the study phase, one pair of events is presented to be learned. In the test phase, a cue event is presented for which the subject is to recall the correct response event.

Continuous recognition studies are one-phase designs and continuous recall studies are two-phase designs. However, the continuous design has an enormous advantage over other designs, namely, the efficiency with which really long delays can be studied. In addition, it is easy to have short delays also, so one can easily study the memory trace over a very wide range of delays. Finally, the number of events to be remembered is often (but not always) so large that one can be sure that conscious rehearsal is of negligible significance, except perhaps at very short delays in the absence of non-rehearsal instructions.

When probabilities of correct recall are transformed to strengths in the continuous recall studies of Atkinson, Brelsford, and Shiffrin (1967) and Brelsford, Shiffrin, and Atkinson (1968), very nice fits to simple exponential decay of ITM are found over a range from 10 seconds to 3 minutes. Strength decay curves for continuous recognition memory over roughly the same period of time are also well fit by a simple exponential decay (Melton, Sameroff, and Schubot, 1963; Shepard and Teghtsoonian, 1961; unpublished data of mine). The decay rates for these different studies are all within the same order of magnitude (time constant of around 3 minutes), but they are not invariant over the different conditions. Thus, just as for STM, the functional decay rate for ITM must be assumed to vary over a range. What conditions affect the functional decay rates for ITM are not yet clear, but a strength analysis of the Melton, Sameroff, and Schubot (1963) study suggested that the number of intervening items to be learned is irrelevant, provided the total delay time is constant. This must be replicated in future studies with longer delays, but, if it is true, it is an important difference between ITM and STM. Within the same theoretical framework used to explain the dependence of STM decay rate on the rate of presentation of items to be learned, one would conclude that ITM has no active trace maintenance process or at least not one which interacts with the trace acquisition process.

All this would make a fairly neat story if it were not for the presence in some unpublished data of mine on continuous recognition memory (one example of which is shown in Wickelgren, 1970a) of yet another, more slowly decaying ITM trace, which appears when delays of 3 to 12 (or presumably more) minutes are used. One ITM is bad enough without two of them. However, at present, the continuous recognition decay curves from 10 seconds to 12 minutes do look somewhat more like the sum of two exponential decays than like a monotonic deceleration of decay rate (Jost's Second Law). Obviously, much more data are needed before the number of ITM traces and the relations between them are clear.

Verbal LTM

Unpublished studies of mine of recognition memory for Russian-English word pairs over a 2-year retention interval yielded decay curves which were not well fit by a single exponentially decaying trace. However, the experiment was not well suited to the determination of the shape of the decay function, being intended only to determine the order of magnitude of the decay rate in verbal LTM for overlearned verbal materials. Thus, further experiments will be needed to determine whether the decay function for LTM is a single exponential, the sum of two exponentials, or some version of Jost's Second Law.

The time constant of the LTM decay curve for overlearned Russian-English word pairs was on the order of 2 years. This means that there is a factor of around 10^7 or 10^8 between the decay rates of the fastest decaying verbal STM and a very slowly decaying verbal LTM. This is truly a staggering range of decay rates for human memory. This enormous range suggests both that several different types of traces may be required and that each trace may have a range of possible decay rates over a factor of 10 or 100.

Successive Comparison of Pitch

All psychophysical successive comparison studies involve memory for the standard (S) stimulus which is judged in relation to the comparison (C) stimulus. Successive comparison studies are recognition memory studies, and decay curves can be determined by plotting the decline in the discriminability of the trace strength for C stimuli identical to or different from the S stimulus as a function of the delay between the two stimuli. In the case of a one-dimensional judgment, such as pitch over intervals less than one octave, there are a large variety of possible C stimuli that could be chosen differing from the S stimulus by different amounts on the relevant dimension.

In the case of pitch judgments for S tones, Wickelgren (1969a) has investigated the discriminability of C tones identical to the S tone versus C tones that are 10, 20, 30, 40, or 50 Hz. different from the S tone. The decay curves from 0 to 3 minutes are well fit by the sum of two exponentially decaying traces, with the STM and ITM components having about the same decay rates as the STM and ITM components over the same delays in verbal memory experiments. Acquisition of the STM trace approaches a limit (approximately exponentially) as a function of S tone duration, and the rate of decay of STM is invariant over the degree of acquisition manipulated in this way. The rate of decay of STM for pitch is also invariant with the distance of the C tone from the S tone over the range from 10 to 50 Hz. Although I have felt it was necessary to fill the delay interval between the S and C tones with another tone to control rehearsal of the S tone, the intensity of this interpolated tone and its similarity to the S and C tones (beyond 50 Hz.) are irrelevant to the decay of STM trace for pitch.

CONCLUSION

Multitrace theory requires much more extensive testing before any definite conclusion can be reached regarding its suitability as a general theory of memory. Very likely, future testing will indicate that modification or extension of the theory is required, especially to specify the nature of the dependence of the parameters of trace dynamics upon various conditions. However, the theory already has considerable generality, and there is every reason to hope that future modifications and extensions can be made within the same basic theoretical framework.

CHAPTER 3   *Gordon H. Bower*
                                            Stanford University

MENTAL IMAGERY AND ASSOCIATIVE LEARNING*

I wish to discuss some of our research on mental imagery in associative learning. I think there are some fascinating but difficult intellectual and scientific puzzles connected with imagery, problems whose solution would significantly advance our understanding of mental life.

My discussion will be divided into two parts—the first predominantly philosophical and phenomenological in tone, and the second within the proper confines of experimental psychology. Although I am an amateur at it, I still think that some philosophical discussion of imagery is necessary, and mainly for therapeutic reasons, because many experimental psychologists cannot entertain thoughts about imagery without some deep sense of guilt associated with forbidden taboos. Our fraternal indoctrination that imagery is the forbidden fruit has been handed down to us, of course, from the heydays of radical behaviorism, which consigned it to the flames along with other cognitive concepts. Because speaking and writing were observable behaviors of a person, words or utterances were let pass as mere motor responses. Today, the domain of studies of human memory is almost coextensive with verbal learning and motor-skills learning.

Now, whether or not psychologists wish to admit it, the radical behaviorism of John Watson was a philosophical doctrine. More specifically, it contained an implicit epistemology about how we acquire reliable knowledge of the world—in particular, knowledge about other persons. So I think the defense of imagery also has to be partly philosophical, with a healthy sprinkling of subjective experience. In much of this discussion, I am drawing from arguments in a book by Brian Smith (1966).

THE NATURE OF MEMORY IMAGERY

The primary distinction I wish to draw between types of cognitive memories is remembering in imagery versus remembering in propositions. *Remembering* is

This research was supported by a grant, MH-13950, to the author from the National Institutes of Mental Health. Thanks are due several students who helped conduct these experiments. They include Michal Clark, Samuel Bobrow, David Tieman, David Winzenz, Alan Lesgold, Laura Bolton, and Michael Fehling. Their assistance was indispensable in the preparation of this chapter.

51

a performance term, and many performances involve one or another of our
motor skills (e.g., speaking, writing). When we are reporting or acting upon what
we are remembering some of our learned motor-output skills are likely to be engaged. But we just as frequently remember something without reporting it, so
the overt motor-output skills need not be engaged. So with this nod to motor-
skills, let us turn to remembering in imagery and how it differs from remembering in propositions.

How Versus What

The function of memory imagery is to put us in direct contact with *how*
things looked, or sounded, or felt, or tasted, as distinct from *what* they resem-
bled, what they sounded like, looked like, felt or tasted like. This "how something looks" is called by philosophers its *appearance*. And the claim is that
imagery is our only way of remembering appearances. Said differently,
memory imagery is our means of re-presenting to ourselves the appearances
of past events we have witnessed.

This distinction between how something looked and what it looked like runs
parallel to the distinction between images and propositional memory. That is,
we remember appearances in imagery, and we also remember propositions,
propositions sometimes containing higher-order perceptual inferences about
events witnessed.

The difference between how something looked and what it looked like is
the same as the difference between a sighted and a blind person's knowledge
of the visual world. In the auditory domain, it is the difference between
how an orchestral symphony sounds and how one might try to describe it to
a deaf person. William James (1890) put it as follows: "The best taught
blind pupil...yet lacks a knowledge which the least instructed seeing baby has.
They can never show him what light is in its 'first intention'; and the loss of
that sensible knowledge no book learning can replace." This "first intention"
is what is meant by *how* something looked or sounded.

The unfortunate difficulty with this distinction is that our descriptive
terms are adequate only for describing what something looks like, not for how
it appears. One resorts to citing cases which exemplify the difference between
how something looks or sounds and a catalogue of descriptive propositions
concerning what it looks or sounds like. For example, most of us know how
an oboe or a clarinet sounds—that is, we can recognize their sounds, we can
have auditory imagery in remembering them, and we can compare them in
memory—but our verbal descriptions of such sounds are woefully meager,
impoverished, and metaphorical. A second example is that one's chances
of apprehending a wanted criminal are very much better given a few photographs of him compared to a book-length, verbal description of him. Part of

the problem here is simply an absence of appropriate verbal terms to label or describe the vast array of stimulus variables which we can differentiate (e.g., Gibson, 1966). But even when we have verbal labels, they are usually very broad categories, so that much stimulus information is lost when some unique perceptual event is replaced by a class label. A descriptive category is a many-one mapping or compression of the information available in the stimulus. For instance, *The Science of Color* (Optical Society, 1953) estimates that the color solid is divisible into about 7,500,000 just-noticeable differences, yet English speakers commonly use only about eight color names. But the many-one coding imposed by our color naming does not force us to judge, when remembering, that green peas are the same color as green Christmas trees. There need be no claim that our discriminations from memory images are as sharp as those from present appearances. All that needs to be claimed is that memory images contain some information, and that it is structured in ways resembling the structure of our present perceptions.

Roger Shepard at Stanford has done some work on this question. In one completed experiment, similarity ratings were obtained for the shapes of pairs of U.S. states either when the person is shown outlined pictures of the states, or when he merely remembers what they look like. In another study being planned, musically-knowledged subjects will give similarity ratings for pairs of instruments (e.g., oboe, bassoon, clarinet, etc.) either when the person actually hears the two instruments alternately playing a short passage, or when he remembers how they sounded when playing the same passage. Given a matrix of similarity measures for a set of stimuli, analytic techniques exist for extracting their underlying pattern, representing stimuli as points in Euclidean space (Shepard, 1962). The question is whether one gets approximately the same spatial configuration of the stimuli under the sensing and imaging conditions. Rapaport and Fillenbaum (1968) have shown that the configural representations are about the same for sensed versus imaged colors. Shepard showed that the configurations are about the same for sensed versus imaged shapes of states. It is a reasonable presumption that the representations will also be about the same for sensed versus imaged sounds of instruments. If so, then one could assert that a set of memory images has a similarity structure isomorphic to the structure of the set of original perceptual events. The alternate interpretation is that the subject is not really comparing auditory images but is remembering the verbal judgment he made during his past perceptions. But this requires the implausible assumption that the subject has perceived all $n(n-1)/2$ instrument-pair comparisons in the past, pronounced similarity judgments at that time, and now remembers those judgments and transforms them to the appropriate scale for the experimental report.

Now strictly speaking, we do not remember events in the world; rather we remember our autobiography—the appearances presented to us by events, our perceptual inferences, and propositions we formulated about past events as they happened or as we later revive them and rethink them. As a result, our memory for some event ordinarily includes both some imagery of it and some propositions about it. This makes operational separation of the two modes of remembering difficult, but I think there are sufficient instances where we remember predominantly in one way without the other. For example, much of my memory of my preschool childhood is propositional, remembering either my own judgments or propositions my parents told me about my early childhood. I remember that my father's elderly aunt had a small wrinkled moonface, and that she once told a terribly ribald joke in my presence, but I have no remembrance or imagery of her. I am only recalling a proposition I formulated about her when I was very young. My knowledge in this case is about on a par with my knowledge that Brutus stabbed Caesar, even though I was a witness to the former but not the latter event. I could easily be argued out of either proposition by contrary evidence, because the memory is not supported in either case by remembered appearances.

Contrariwise, we can remember in imagery without propositions. Examples would be our memories of paintings, or ballet choreography, or photographs (Shepard, 1967); or the memory imagery of a person after a good trip on LSD, which he finds to be such an ineffable and noncommunicable experience. Certainly, our memory for musical melodies can hardly be called propositional.

Problems With a Purely Verbal Approach

In the visual cases above, it should be clear that I am distinguishing between the imagery in which a person is remembering, and the propositions or descriptive statements he might be presently formulating about what he is remembering. Radical behaviorism would not allow that distinction, insisting in fact that my present verbal utterances are my remembering, that one does not remember images but only earlier utterances or other responses made at the time a particular stimulus event happened.

I think this view is indefensible for several reasons. First, there is sometimes a strong introspective feel to the difference between remembering an appearance and remembering propositions about an appearance. Second, even though we might remember the appearance of some event and some propositions we formulated about that event, we occasionally do reinterpret that experience and alter our propositional memory about it in the light of new evidence or a new frame of reference. What we took to be a motorcycle policeman by the side of the road we later agree must have been a painted, wooden dummy set up to frighten speeding motorists. The banging night-time noises I take to be a prowler turn out to be a cat rummaging in the garbage cans. Such reinterpretations, double-takes on our perceptual inferences, would be pointless if all we remembered were propositions that we formulated at the time of the event. The validity of such reinterpretations presupposes that we remember something else which constitutes the evidence to be reinterpreted. This "something else" is what I call the appearance of the event.

Third, against the verbal descriptive doctrine, one is seldom aware of formulating propositions when perceiving, for example, a painting, but this nevertheless does not prevent at least some recall of these appearances. Or a subject in the laboratory can learn a serial list of pictures even though his vocal apparatus is continuously engaged, say, in counting backwards by 3's. A standard defense of the verbal theorist to such counterexamples is to postulate that implicit verbalization, categorization, and naming go on in all such instances. That is, the same central mechanisms of linguistic description are activated but the motor outflow is inhibited. At this point the verbal approach loses whatever operational advantage it might have had over an imagery approach. Unconscious, inhibited verbalizations are operationally no better than images. A final move by the verbal theorist is to say that whether or not verbalizing is necessary for remembering some scene, verbal description surely improves one's memory for it (cf. Kurtz & Hovland, 1953). As a matter of fact, I doubt whether this is generally true; but even those cases where it is correct raise no problems for my position, since two alternate codings of an event may make it more memorable than one coding does (see Wallach & Averbach, 1955).

A final criticism of the strictly verbal approach is that our memory of a proposition can only rarely be described as a memory of a verbal utterance or a sentence. Although laboratory tasks often demand verbatim reproduction, a salient feature of our day-to-day discourse is our competence at paraphrasing, our ability to generate and recognize roughly synonymous expressions. Such casual evidence suggests that we remember propositions that are reasonably indifferent to the sentences by which they are expressed. For bilinguals, the propositions are indifferent even to the language in which they are expressed. One of Smith's (1966) examples is of a German scientist who immigrates to America, learns English and forgets most of his German. He would not thereby be expected to forget all the scientific propositions he had learned in German. Most of them would still be available, only now they would be in English. The behaviorist doctrine that we primarily remember verbal utterances has not faced up to the most elementary facts about linguistic competence.

The Imagist Theory of Cognition

A good deal of philosophical analysis has gone into the view that all our conceptualizing, cognition and thinking is in mental imagery. For example, one tenet is that words are derivative tokens whose "cash values" are a capacity for arousing associated imagery. There are a number of difficulties with this imagist view of cognition. One problem is that many concepts (e.g., animals, flowers) are names for heterogeneous instances, so that an image of any particular instance could not possibly represent the concept in all its applications. Another problem is that there are no criteria for deciding which of several superordinate classes an image of an instance may be representing. Does an image of a dachshund represent the class of dachshunds, dogs, mammals, animals, or living things? A third problem is raised by abstract concepts like *infinity, interpretation*, and so on, where imagery is either absent, or is at best metaphorical and nonreferential.

One avoids all such problems by admitting that we have concepts which have nothing to do with images. We infer that a person possesses a concept, for example, of dogs, when he can recognize instances. But we cannot have an image of a generalized DOG, only of numerous individual dogs. Similarly, I have no image of a generalized Lee Gregg, but only several images of his appearances in several contacts we have had.

The old imagist view that a concept is an image bears a strong resemblance to the template-matching view of pattern recognition, which we know to be weak for several reasons. I would say that images can exemplify but not substitute for concepts. For example, I can have no imagery *of* relational concepts like above or between; but I can image a spatial organization of objects exemplifying such relations.

I am proposing that we can assign an important role to imagery in cognition and memory, without subscribing to the entire imagist view of such matters. Let us now consider some of the functions of imagery in our thinking.

Imagination Imagery

One of the primary uses of memory images is in productive imagination. Such imagery may be characterized as a new assemblage of memory images; that is, the recombining of memory images together into scenes which the person has not witnessed. For example, I can remember Al Newell in imagery and I can remember an elephant in imagery, so I can also image a scene in which Al Newell is riding on the back of an elephant, even though I know that this does not correspond to any actual scene I have witnessed. We construct these novel assemblages by using our memory images as the basic components.

This imagination game resembles a picture-blocks game my children have, in which one independently selects a picture-block with a mouth, another for the nose, another for the eyes, ears, hair, neck and so on, all put together to make a composite but very bizarre face. Our imaginative images differ from the blocks in being less determinate but more manipulable in shape, size, color and perspective. The wings we imagine on a flea are a different subjective size than those we imagine on an elephant. In some people's visual imagery, geometric forms (e.g., a parabolid or a box) can be made to undergo deformations and perspective transformations like rotation, reflection, and shearing, as though the observer were walking around and/or changing his distance from a three-dimensional object.

In such instances, imaging is being used like the flexible, on-line CRT displays connected to a computer program such as Sutherland's (1963) "Sketch Pad" or Green's (1961) or Roberts' (1965) programs for rigid 3-D rotation of figures. The manipulability of imagery is one of its chief advantages in thinking. We often use tangible replicas or models as an aid to our thinking. We draw diagrams, graph structures, benzene rings, build solid models of DNA molecules, etc., and we manipulate these tangible tokens in thinking. The principal limitation of imagery in this respect arises from the limited capacity of our short-term memory. Our imaginal sketch pad can be focalized on just a few symbols or manipulations at any one time.

To mention one further role of imagery in thinking: it can sometimes serve as a supplementary aid in understanding novel sentences. One way to comprehend a statement is to imagine some situation or state of affairs which would make it true. This view is the picture-theory of Wittgenstein's (1922) *Tractatus*, that a proposition corresponds to a picture (true or false) of reality. Pictoriability or imaginability of a sentence may be a sufficient but is clearly not a necessary condition for comprehension, since we use millions of meaningful sentences that require no imaging to understand them (e.g., this sentence). Furthermore, although imaging may ensure comprehension, it would be indeterminate whether the click of semantic comprehension came before, after, or was noncausally coincident with the imaginal construction. That is, the ability to generate appropriate imagery may sometimes be just one of many behavioral dispositions that issue from comprehension of a linguistic proposition.

Characteristics of Imagery

Our memory imagery, like any picture or verbal description of an object or event, can be more or less precise. Faint memory images are sketchy, lacking in detail, and elusive. Moreover, faint memories cannot readily be expanded into an associated context; that is, it is difficult to fill in other objects and happenings. This expansion of a memory image into its associated context is the principal way by which we build up subjective confidence in the validity of a given memory. Old cronies who meet at class reunions may pride themselves on reproducing details associated with some football game. It is notorious that some of these reconstructions are imagined.

Introspectively, the memory image of a visual scene is usually fairly faithful in its perspective, in the relative sizes and locations of parts of the scene, and it may be colored. Frequently only part of the scene is figure, the rest being indeterminate ground until we generate another part of the scene.

To say that a person is remembering an event in imagery is to say that some central mechanisms are generating a (probably sequential) pattern of information which corresponds more or less to the structural information in the original perception. Imaging is a generative process and a performance. There is a very strong tendency in our everyday language to "substantify" our activities, to talk about a performance as though it resulted in a tangible entity. Performance verbs tend to become nouns. We run a long run, breathe a deep breath, perceive a clear percept, and think a bright thought. Imaging is likewise a performance verb: one "has" images. This use is quite innocent and no one need be seriously misled into believing that there is a palpable entity located in some definite place, that it can be weighed, and so on. To say that we are remembering in imagery is to say that there is some structural isomorphism between the information presently available to us and the information picked up from the stimulus event we are remembering. Needless to say, this structure need not be apparent in the person's overt response, which may simply consist of his answering "yes" to the question "Are you remembering x now?"

Problematical Issues With Imagery

The common man says that imaging is very much like constructing mental pictures. His critics are fond of pointing out how unlike photographs or tape recording images are. Images surely do have a large degree of indeterminateness to them, much like impressionist paintings. People can visualize a zebra but not be able to count its stripes; or rehear the twangy, nasal voice quality of an orator without recalling any particular part of his oration; or visualize the front of a building but not know how many stories it has. This is all quite true; but to disparage imagery in this way is unfair because most of our perceptions are similarly vague, indeterminate, and lacking in detail. A tachistoscopic flash of a building or zebra would produce similar inaccuracies. When the object is continuously before us, we move our eyes successively over it and count. But this we cannot do with our memory imagery.

Another issue concerns individual differences. The classic questionnaire study of Sir Francis Galton (1883) turned up some people who reported having no imagery. A more recent and adequate survey by McKellar (1965) of 500 British adults from a variety of occupations turned up none who reported no imagery; 97% reported availability of visual imagery, 92% had auditory imagery, and over half had a variety of sensory imagery available, including movement, touch, taste, smell, pain, and temperature. We may still wonder what to make of those occasional respondents who report no imagery whatsoever.

Smith (1966) lists three alternatives: they are liars, they have only propositional memory, or they have misunderstood the reference of the question. The first may be discounted; of the last two, I prefer the "misunderstanding" account. Psychologists are familiar with respondents' misunderstandings of self-descriptive terms. Respectable society matrons will deny giving vent to erotic impulses although their behavior and their husbands speak otherwise.

To indict misunderstanding is to say that the problem is one of semantics. Having imagery is a private affair, and Skinner (1953) has told us why it is difficult to teach people to have the same referent for names of private events. Since, by definition, I am not aware of my son's private mental event, I have to infer it either from an instigating stimulus or from his behavior. Either of these provides me, as the trainer, with an S^D for applying the label or saying "You're experiencing X now". Thus, I can teach him to label pain by saying "Ouch, that's painful, isn't it?" when I see him crack his shin, double up, and howl. Remembering in imagery has neither unique instigating stimuli nor unique behavioral signs. Learning to use imagery terms would therefore derive mainly from induction or stimulus generalization. Verbal labels acquired with respect to public events (where the reinforcing community can train us to sharp discriminations) are then transferred to private events on the basis of common properties. Thus, children learn the referent of words like *picture* and learn how to copy, or make up and draw pictures, and games are played with them where they close their eyes and try to see an imaginary picture. I presume this is how most of us came to learn imagery terms and it may account for the prevalence of "mental picture" descriptions. Most of our subjective terms are probably learned by induction from public terms, which may be why our subjective descriptions (e.g., of emotions) are predominantly metaphorical. In our metaphor talk, passion is a consuming fire, anger is a raging storm, and intellect or wit is a sparkling instrument that is piercing or dull.

Indicators of Imagery

Because imaging is customarily a private event, the scientist's first inclination is to try to achieve some sort of public measurement of it. Whatever nervous mechanisms generate imagery, they conceivably might also send efferent messages to the periphery where they can be recorded. The analytic leverage provided by such a reliable, public indicant should not be underestimated. For example, the tremendous surge of recent research on dreaming must in part be attributable to Dement and Kleitman's (1957) discovery that rapid-eye-movement sleep is temporally correlated with subjective reports of dreaming. For such reasons, one searches for indicants of imagery.

The obvious first candidate is spontaneous eye movement during visual imagery. This has been studied in detail by Singer (1966), and Singer and Antrobus (1965). Their results are most curious: generally, visual imaging was associated with *minimal* eye movements except when the person's task was to follow moving objects in imagery (e.g., an imaginary tennis game). Instructions to engage in "hard thinking" (e.g., adding three-digit numbers) increased eye movements. Although there were minimal eye movements during passive day-dreaming or fantasying, numerous eye movements occurred when subjects were instructed to break off and stop their daydreaming. A possible interpretation is that one breaks off a given daydream by deliberately replacing that theme by a rapid succession of unrelated images, with corresponding eye movements. Although the technique requires further exploration, these preliminary results do not suggest that eye movements are a perfect indicant of imaging. Corresponding eye movements seem to be neither a necessary nor a sufficient condition for visual imaging.

A learning experiment of ours may be added here. College students learned pairs of concrete nouns, operating under instructions to generate visual images linking the objects denoted by the concrete nouns of each pair. Some subjects were told to close their eyes and scan the mental picture as they constructed it. Other imagery-instructed subjects were required to maintain a steady gaze fixated upon a small spot on the wall opposite them. The items were spoken to the subject, and eye-condition during study and immediate paired-associate recall were varied. This experiment found no recall differences whatsoever due to eye-condition either at study or recall test. Fixation subjects reported no difficulty in having images. This is not implausible; a notorious characteristic of the daydreamer is the far-away look in his eyes and the glassy stare.

Another possible indicator of imaging is eye-pupil size, which may index cognitive events. Pupils during imaging have been measured by Paivio and Simpson (1966) and Simpson and Paivio (1968). The pupil dilates when the person is told to image the object denoted by a concrete noun. The pupil dilates even more when the person is asked to get an image for an abstract noun. In fact, the pupil dilates whenever the person is given any sort of mental task (e.g., adding numbers), and the dilation seems correlated with the amount of mental effort involved. The results also depend on how the subject has been instructed to report accomplishing the cognitive task. Such results imply that pupil dilation may not discriminate imaging from other types of cognitive processing.

Further attempts to track down imagery have involved the electroencephalogram (EEG). This literature (Oswald, 1962; Simpson, Paivio and Rogers, 1967) is distinctly unencouraging. No one has yet turned up a distinctive EEG pattern that correlates with subjective reports of imaging. Kamiya (1969) taught people to discriminate and then to control alpha rhythm in EEG recorded from scalp electrodes. Blocking of alpha activity can be induced by imaging a familiar object. Alpha activity can be induced by letting go of deliberate conscious engagement, and maintaining a placid, receptive state of suspended cognition. However a variety of cognitive activities other than imaging will also block alpha rhythms.

In contrast to the unpromising outlook for physiological measures of imagery, research on behavioral indicants of imagery (particularly visual imagery) has been more successful.

Behavioral Evidence of Imagery

If we have a person describe from memory a picture or some spatial arrangement of information, he will usually have the subjective feeling of generating an internal spatial representation (an image) and deriving his verbal description from that. If, on the other hand, he is asked to give verbatim recall of a sentence he has just heard, his performance seems to involve predominantly the speech mode with little or no internal spatial representations. Lee Brooks (1968) has performed some highly ingenious experiments to support this idea that visual (or spatial) and verbal information are dealt with in distinct, modality-specific manners.

Brooks' method hinges on the conflicting processing that may occur if the modality of the remembered material is the same as the modality in which the subject has to report his judgments. In one condition, the subject learned a short sentence, and then at a signal reported some particular categorization of the successive words in the sentence. For example, the sentence "a bird in the hand is not in the bush" might have to be categorized into noun versus nonnoun words, with the subject reporting "no, yes, no, no, yes, no, no, no, no, yes". Since different categorizations were requested, the subject could not anticipate the judgments to be required. There were two methods of report: either saying "yes" or "no", or pointing to a "y" or "n" printed in a column of y-n pairs before the subject. When the remembered material was a sentence, the visually-guided pointing responses were much faster than the speech reports. In the other condition, the subject studied and learned a simple visual diagram, such as the block letter F. He was later asked for a particular categorization of each corner of the diagram. For example, the categorization might be whether each point is on the periphery or is an interior point. In this case, the speech reports were very much faster than the visually-guided pointing responses.

In several experiments, Brooks has found a similar interaction between modality of the memory and modality of the reports. His interpretation is that spoken sentences and spatial diagrams are processed in memory by separate systems (speech versus visual imagery). Requiring judgments in the same modality produces conflict or strains the capacity of that system. In another work, Brooks (1967) showed that visual reading conflicted with a task for which visual imaging was used, but not with a task for which visualizing was not used.

A recent experiment of ours followed Brooks' ideas. The basic task was paired associate learning of 30 concrete noun pairs read to the subject. Half of the subjects learned these by overt rote rehearsal of each pair, while the remaining subjects were instructed to connect the words of each pair by visualizing a scene of some vivid interaction linking the two objects denoted by the words. During study and recall testing of all pairs, the subject was continuously engaged in a subsidiary tracking task, which either did or did not engage the visual analyzing system. The tracking task involved an irregular wavy line which moved rapidly and continuously past the 1-inch window of a memory drum. The subject was required to track the horizontal location of the weaving line by keeping it between the extended index and middle fingers of his right hand. In the *visual* tracking task, a clear plastic shield covered the window and only visual cues were available for locating and tracking the target. In the *tactile* tracking task, the wavy line was composed of string glued to the paper in the same pattern. The subject was instructed to close his eyes and to keep the raised string touching the sides of his extended index and middle fingers. Each subject had one study and one recall test trial on four different lists of 30 noun pairs. Two lists were learned during the visual task, and two during the tactile tracking task. (Task order was counterbalanced.) Subjects learning with visual imaging were expected to learn and/or recall more poorly with the visual than with the tactile tracking task. Subjects learning by rote rehearsal were expected to recall equally well under the two tracking tasks. The paired associate recall scores were in perfect agreement with these expectations. For visual imagery subjects, recall percentages were 66% under tactile tracking and 55% under visual tracking, a difference significant at the 2% level. For rote rehearsal subjects, recall percentages were 23% under both visual and tactile tracking. Although the effect here is not as large as one would like it to be, it was quite consistent over subjects and does agree with expectations.

Interference between imaging and perceiving in the same modality has been demonstrated by Segal and Fusella (1969). In a signal detection and identification task, their subjects were presented with a near-threshold visual or auditory signal (or neither signal) and had to report which event occurred. In different series of detection trials, the subjects were instructed to generate either a visual image (e.g., of a tree) or an auditory image (e.g., a ringing telephone) with the detection trial presented only after the subject had the image clearly. A control detection series was also run without subsidiary imaging. Measuring sensitivity in terms of the d' parameter of signal detection theory (which takes into account possible criterion shifts), Segal and Fusella found that although either type of imaging reduced d', the reduction was about twice as large when the signal was in the modality of the person's imagery. Averaging together their visual and auditory d' values, the control d' was 2.70. It dropped to 2.18 with imaging in the opposite modality from the signal, and dropped to 1.74 with imaging in the same modality as the signal. They also found a significant effect of image familiarity. Imaging of relatively unfamiliar events produced greater reductions in sensitivity. It is not yet clear whether the effect is central or peripheral in origin. For example, we know that visual imaging produced pupil dilation and possibly misfocussing on the visual target, which might reduce visual sensitivity.

Posner, Boies, Eichelman, and Taylor (1969) have some recent evidence on visual images and long-term memory. In initial experiments, they found that subjects more quickly judged whether two successive alphabetic letters had the same name if the two letters were physically identical (for example, *B* and *B* as opposed to *B* and *b*). But the faster physical-identity match disappeared if there was a delay of about 2 seconds between the two flashed letters. The effect is presumably due to a rapidly fading visual icon. The first letter becomes less available for effecting a physical-identity match to the second flash (much as in template-matching at lower afferent stations). In subsequent experiments, however, they obtained a similar effect with verbal (auditory) prewarnings. If the auditory prewarning occurs .5-1.0 seconds or more before the test flash, the person can respond "same name" as quickly as in the two-flash, physical-identity condition at those interstimulus intervals. This .5-1.0 seconds is presumably the time the subject requires to generate from long-term memory implicit icons of the pre-warned letter, in readiness for matching against the test flash. A fast name-identity match of a first *B* to a second *B* can apparently be achieved either by flashing the first shortly before the second, or by letting the subject generate a first B from his long-term visual memory.

A more definitive experiment by Barbara Tversky (1968) distinguishes between verbal and pictorial encoding. Her subjects first learned names for eight schematic faces, the names and faces differing along three binary dimensions. These stimuli were then used in a task like that of Posner et al (1968). A first stimulus (name or picture) was shown, followed by a 1-second blank period, followed by a second stimulus (name or picture), and the subject was to respond "same" if the two were (or had) the same name, and otherwise to respond "different." Over many experimental sessions, a variety of intratrial event frequencies were run corresponding to independent variation in (1) the modality of the first stimulus, (2) the subject's expectation of the modality of the second stimulus, and (3) the modality of the second stimulus. The expectations were manipulated by the relative frequencies (80% versus 20%) of the modality of the second stimulus over large blocks of trials. The important result was that reaction time for either response was very much faster if the second stimulus was in the expected (more frequent) modality. Regardless of the modality of the first stimulus, if the subject expected a picture he responded faster to a second picture than to a second word, but the converse occurred if the subject expected a word. Within-modality controls (words presented upright or slanted) were run to rule out a simple surprise explanation. Tversky interprets her findings as indicating modality-specific encoding. Specifically, she suggests that a subject will encode the first stimulus into a modality corresponding to the expected modality of the second stimulus, presumably because template matching is possible only when the representatives of both stimuli are in the same modality. Wallach & Averbach (1955) suggested a similar view of recognition memory. According to this viewpoint, a first name will be converted into an internal facial picture if the subject expects to match it to a picture. This view was supported also by the fact that "different" responses were faster when there were more differing visual features between the expected (imaginal) picture and the actual picture.

There are also indications of specific brain-localization of verbal versus pictorial encoding systems in the work of Kimura (1963) and Milner (1968) with lobectomized patients. The coding systems would appear to be predominantly represented on different sides of the brain. Specifically, removal of the left temporal lobe selectively impairs verbal memory, whereas removal of the right temporal lobe selectively impairs visual (pictorial) memory. Excisions of the parietal or frontal lobes appear not to produce either deficit. Visual memory was tested by recall or recognition of pictures shown earlier. Milner used recall of geometric designs and recognition of photographs of people's faces, while Kimura used recognition of abstract nonsense figures. Verbal memory was tested by recall or recognition of numbers, nonsense syllables, words, word pairs, and stories. The selectivity of the deficit is the significant fact. Patients with right-temporal lobectomies were deficient in visual but not verbal memory; patients with left-temporal lobectomies were deficient in verbal but not visual memory. There is some evidence too that the right-temporal patients are deficient in mnemonic recognition of nonverbal auditory patterns, for example, they fail to recognize snatches of familiar melodies. Milner argues that the right-temporal deficit is specifically mnemonic rather than perceptual since such patients perform almost normally on a variety of simple perceptual tasks.

Natadze (1960) has demonstrated some curious biases produced by prior imaginary experiences of a kinaesthetic or tactile sort. In a typical experiment, a subject is asked to imagine metal balls being hefted in each hand, with the left ball being far heavier than the right. If two equally heavy balls are then actually placed in his hands, he is likely to report a contrast illusion. The ball in his left hand is said to be lighter. A size-contrast illusion was produced by similar imaginings. Since imaginal lifting of a weight often produces recordable muscle-action potentials in that arm (Jacobson, 1932), the effects in such experiments might be attributable to peripheral differences in muscle-tone just before the equal-weight tests.

Another line of evidence concerns the effect of imaginal or mental practice on the development of perceptual-motor skills. A variety of evidence is available (cf. Richardson, 1963) to show that imaginal practice improves some skills (e.g., basketball shooting, mirror-reflected star tracing). Although a mental-practice effect does not necessarily implicate imagery versus rehearsal of verbal descriptions or principles, Start and Richardson (1965) have evidence that larger improvements occur for subjects who have vivid but "well-controlled" imagery.

Another bit of evidence is provided in a mediated generalization study by Laura Phillips (1958). Her subjects first learned to associate five nonsense words with five gray patches varying in brightness. The word for the lightest gray then underwent GSR conditioning. Subsequent tests for GSR to the other nonsense words yielded a smooth generalization gradient according to the visual similarity of their associated gray patches. Presumably the nonsense words arouse sensory imagery which is ordered along the brightness dimension, and for that reason the GSR generalizes differentially to words which are otherwise equally distinct.

The last bit of evidence on imaging is from hypnotic hallucinations. We know that a really good hypnotic subject will report seeing or hearing practically anything the hypnotist tells him to see or hear. The controversy is over whether he is merely role playing. A recent demonstration at Stanford by Graham (1969) appears relatively sham-proof. Graham conditioned his subjects (high school students) under hypnosis to visually hallucinate two gray circles when a buzzer sounded. Then, while they were awake, he sounded the buzzer and had them hallucinate the gray circles as projected upon actual backgrounds of different brightness. For instance, in some tests the left side of the projection card would be white and the right side black. Graham asked his subjects to judge the relative brightness of the two hallucinated circles. A preponderance of their judgments were predictable on the basis of brightness contrast. The gray circle hallucinated against a black background appeared brighter than the other circle hallucinated against a white background. When the two sides of the projection card were white, the hallucinated gray circles were judged equally bright.

The foregoing brief review of behavioral evidence of imagery indicates some conventionally acceptable (i.e., nonintrospective) evidence for the effects of the process we call imaging. At the present time, such results are most readily explained by postulating an information-processing system which has the ability to regenerate a structural representation or analogue of previous perceptual experiences. I will now turn to an account of our experimental work on imaginal mediators in associative learning. As shall be seen, this too provides evidence for the behavioral reality of imaginal processes.

EXPERIMENTAL STUDIES

The Paired-Associate Task

My research group has been concerned with the influence of imagery (always visual) upon ease of associating disparate items of experience. The most elementary associative task is paired-associate learning (PAL) which we have used almost exclusively in our studies of imaginal mediation. Rather than using perceptual events or real objects as the terms to be associated, we use noun words. This is an experimental convenience but it also keeps our work in contact with the verbal-learning mainstream. The use of nouns introduces some special problems, however, because we depend upon the noun, together with appropriate instructions, to arouse some imagery in the subject. Nouns surely vary in their probability of evoking imagery.

How do nouns come to evoke their associated imagery? Psychologists since Aristotle have given roughly the same account: by association (conditioning) of the word to the perceptual imagery (sensory responses) elicited by the referent of that word. Sheffield (1961) or Staats (1968) can be read for recent accounts. Semantically ambiguous nouns (there are thousands) are also imaginally ambiguous, in the sense that *bag* may arouse imagery having to do with containers or with old women. Abstract nouns presumably evoke little or no imagery directly, but may do so indirectly through associated concrete words (e.g., *church* or *priest* as associates to *religion*).

In our typical task, the subject (a university student) is presented with arbitrary pairs of unrelated concrete nouns, like DOG-BICYCLE, and instructed to associate them by imaging a visual scene or mental picture in which these two objects are interacting in some way. The cognitive situation here is unconstrained in several respects: first, we neither control nor measure the specific instances the subject images to exemplify the concepts; second, we do not control the exact scene in which the two objects are placed. After illustrating the types of interactions we have in mind, the subject is left to generate his own imaginative scene. All of the college students we have tested carried out such instructions without the slightest difficulty.

The first results illustrate the imagery effect we shall be discussing throughout the remainder of this paper. Each subject had one 5-second exposure to each of 20 concrete-noun pairs, followed by a cued recall test of the 20 pairs immediately after the study trial. The left-hand word was the cue for literal recall of the right-hand word. Five seconds were allowed for recall, and the subject was informed of the correct response at the end of this test trial. Five successive lists of 20 pairs were tested in this manner. At the end of the session all 100 pairs were tested again. Subjects given imagery instructions were compared to control subjects who received standard PAL instructions: to learn the pairs so the left member could cue recall of the right member.

Recall percentages are shown in Figure 3.1. The salient feature is the clear superiority of the imagery subjects: they recall about one and a half times as much as the Control subjects, and the difference is statistically significant on each list. The delayed recall scores exceed the immediate recall scores, presumably the result of the information provided at the end of the first test trial. There is a small practice effect over the five lists that is of no interest in this context.

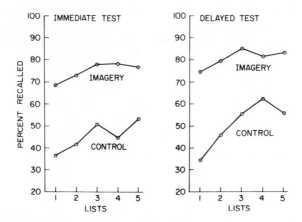

Figure 3.1 Immediate and delayed recall over 5 lists for imagery versus control subjects.

This elementary experiment illustrates the magnitude of the imagery effect. In fact, the effect is probably underestimated in Figure 3.1 because interviews with Control subjects turned up some who were spontaneously using imaginal and/or verbal (sentence-linking) mediators. Paivio, Yuille, and Smythe (1966) found similar control reports. In our later experiments, Control subjects were given explicit repetition-learning instructions. That is, they were told to repeat the word pairs over and over to themselves.

Similar differences arise when imagery versus repetition is varied between pairs being learned concurrently by the same subject. A PAL experiment by John Schnor at Stanford had the following format: concrete noun pairs were shown in one of two locations on a table top. Those shown to the left were to be learned by imagery. Those shown to the right were to be learned by repeating the words aloud three times. Exposure time was controlled at 8 seconds per pair. Within each list, 12 pairs were studied by imagery, and 12 by repetition. Immediate recall tests showed about 80% recall for the imagery pairs and 33% for the repetition pairs. Moreover, on recalled pairs, the subjects were very accurate in remembering whether the pair had been studied by imagery or verbal repetition.

Recall differences like those illustrated above could arise for a number of reasons. Imaginal processing may raise the general availability of the response term (cf. Horowitz, Norman, and Day, 1966). This hypothesis is discounted by an experiment comparing imagery versus repetition instructions, wherein a random half of the pairs was tested for recognition and half for recall. The recognition test was a five-alternative multiple-choice display. The left-hand member (stimulus) of the pair was shown along with five right-hand members (responses) from the prior study list. The subject selected the one response word which he thought had been paired with the stimulus word. This procedure was replicated over three lists of 30 pairs, studied and tested at a 5-second rate. Recall was 87% for imagery and 37% for repetition. Recognition was 97% for imagery and 71% for repetition. The latter difference is significant. This recognition outcome discounts the response availability conjecture, since the imagery-repetition difference still appears strongly when the responses are directly available in the multiple-choice test. Thus an associative effect of imagery is implicated.

Incidental Learning

A further question is whether the superior learning displayed under imaginal elaboration depends upon the intention to learn. Accordingly, intentional versus incidental learning was compared within groups given imagery instructions. The cover story for the incidental learners was that we were collecting norms for the English Literature department on the vividness of word pictures. The subjects were instructed to imagine some interactive scene, and to rate its vividness on a five-point scale, doing this within the 5-second exposure of each pair. Subjects in the intentional condition were similarly instructed, but were also told they had to remember the pairs for an upcoming recall test. After one study trial of 20 pairs (List 1 of Experiment 1), cued recall was 77% for the intentional-imagers and 71% for the incidental-learners. These do not differ significantly. Both scores may be contrasted with that of the intentional controls learning this list in Exp. 1. They recalled 35%, less than half that of either imagery condition.

This outcome for the incidental-intentional comparison is not surprising in the light of the recent literature on incidental learning (Postman, 1964). That literature has shown that the intent to learn is superfluous if the cover task orients the subject to the relevant material and requires him to make differential responses to it. For later recall, the cognitive or imaginal elaboration itself is the important ingredient, not his motivation to remember.

Recall that these subjects rated the vividness of their imaginary scenes at the time of construction. Figure 3.2 shows the relationship between the vividness rating of a pair and its probability of later recall. More vivid scenes are better remembered for both groups. This relation held within each individual: each of the 36 subjects gave a higher mean vividness rating to pairs

he later recalled than he did to nonrecalled pairs. This relation means
that the subject has available, at the time of imaginal elaboration, information predictive of whether he will remember the pair. Suggested factors
might include (a) the strength of the word-image associations, determining
the speed and uniformity of imagery aroused by each word, and (b) the time
required to search for and generate a sensible relation or interactive scene for
the two components. Vivid imagery is stable; faint imagery is elusive, difficult
to fix, and likely to be rapidly replaced by alternative imagery for the words.
This may reduce effective inspection time for any given pictorial coding of the
word pair.

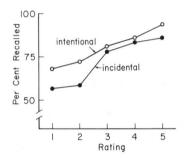

Figure 3.2   Relation between recall of a pair and its rating of imaginal
vividness during study for intentional and incidental learners.

Multiple Associates to Each Cue

In another experiment, we were interested in whether the person could
integrate multiple items in an imaginal scene, and whether the associations
so achieved were as strong as those involving only two items. The first
investigation used a "pegword" mnemonic — a system for converting a non-
cued (free) recall task into a paired-associate task using implicit stimuli
(the pegwords) which the subject can generate from memory. The subject
first learns the pegwords such as one-gun, two-shoe, three-tree, and so on.
He then uses these as imaginal pegs for the successive items of any new list
he is to learn. Thus, the first list-word is imagined in a scene with a gun
(#1), the second list-word with a shoe (#2), and so on. This strategy
solves one of the major problems in free recall: finding a way to remind
oneself of all the things one is supposed to recall.

In this context, our multiple-associates question can be phrased by asking
whether recall suffers with fewer pegwords but more list-words attached to
each peg. Accordingly, different subjects were instructed to use either

1, 2, 5, 10, or 20 pegs to learn a 20-item list. The words were presented serially at a 5-second rate. Subjects learning with k pegs were instructed to sequentially elaborate a grand imaginal scene involving the first peg and the first $20/k$ items, the second peg and the second set of $20/k$ items, and so on. Recall was scored as free recall, although subjects were instructed to try to generate their recall from the k successive pegs they had learned and used at storage. The subjects had one study and recall of each of five lists of 20 concrete nouns, followed by a final recall test for all five lists at the end of the session.

The results of this experiment are shown in Table 3.1 which also contains the scores for a control group given standard free recall instructions. In brief, the number of items per peg has no differential effect, and all imagery subjects recall two to three times more than the controls on the delayed test. With one peg (the 1-20 condition of Table 3.1), it can hardly be said that we have any pegword retrieval cues at all. So the effect in the 1-20 and 2-10 conditions must arise from sequential associations—consecutive chunks of, say, three to five items integrated into progressively developed but over-lapping scenes. The process may resemble episodes in a movie that slowly unfolds. For example, the list "dog, cigar, hat, bicycle, policeman, lady, fence, basket,..." can be integrated into scenes (or sentences) like "A *dog* smoking a *cigar* and wearing a *hat*, is riding a *bicycle* which collides with a *policeman*; the policeman chases the *lady* (who owns the dog) and corners her near a *fence*, but she throws a *basket* at him, and ...". Subjects can easily generate composite imaginal scenes containing a large number of separate items without very much interference from successive items.

TABLE 3.1 Percentage of Words Recalled on Immediate and Delayed Tests for Subjects Learning with Differing Numbers of Pegwords

Number of Pegs	Words/Peg	Immediate	Delayed
20	1	81	69
10	2	85	66
5	4	87	71
2	10	89	77
1	20	87	75
Controls	–	52	28

A later paired-associate experiment modified this conclusion in one respect. The recall probabilities from one cue-term to N response-terms were all high if the N responses were given simultaneously (massed) or in consecutive serial order, so that the subject could integrate them with the cue-term. The recall probabilities were lowered if the N pairs involving the same cue-term were presented singly, well separated in time by intervening pairs involving other stimuli in the list. These results are shown in Figure 3.3, giving average single response recall when the cue-term had 1, 2, or 5 response-terms. These results came from separate lists involving 20 response-terms where the number of stimuli (cue-terms) was 20, 10, or 4 for the different lists. Presentation times were 5 seconds per S-R unit, and subjects received imagery instructions. In the separated condition, recall probability declines with the number of response-terms hooked singly to the cue-term. Introspectively, the massed presentations permit the subject to place the cue and all N response-terms together in one imaginal scene, whereas the singly-presented, separated pairs are more likely to be treated in isolation, with the N response-terms imaged in separate scenes with the cue-term. In conventional terminology, the former arrangement allows for associative mediation among response terms, whereas the latter permits unlearning of earlier pairs by separate attention to the later pairs involving the same stimulus.

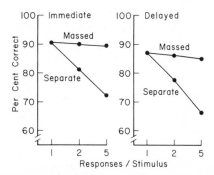

Figure 3.3 Immediate and delayed recall related to the number of response-words attached to each stimulus-word. "Massed" denotes simultaneous presentation of the several responses to each stimulus; "separate" denotes temporally distributed presentations of the several S-R pairs with the same stimulus.

WORD-ATTRIBUTE EFFECTS

Since words are the materials in our experiments on imagery, one is led into a concern for the image-arousing capabilities of the words used, how this varies with other measurable attributes of the words, and how PA learning varies with both. Within the traditional S-R formulation, we would think of the word as a stimulus associated to a number of mediating responses: verbal, imaginal, and perhaps evaluative (or emotional) responses. Verbal associates might include synonyms, opposites, subordinate and superordinate categories, common members of categories to which the word belongs, and syntagmatic associates. Through instruction, the imaginal associates of a word can be primed selectively. The vividness of imagery aroused by a given word would be an index of the strength of the association between the word and some imaginal mediator. Paivio, Yuille, and Madigan (1968) have collected imagery ratings for 925 nouns. They find, of course, that concrete nouns have higher imagery value than abstract nouns. And as the strength-theory expects, latency for image-production is shorter for words rated high in imagery (Paivio, 1966).

The effects of imagery value upon PA learning can be traced with the help of the flow diagram in Figure 3.4. In brief, at the top, words A and B are first given a semantic interpretation which primes or selects particular object images. These are placed into some interactive picture, and a program for generating that imaginal scene is recorded in memory. At the bottom, when cued for recall, word A is interpreted, again leading to an imaginal code for A. The code may retrieve the imaginal composite, from which the subject selects the imaginal code for B. He then decodes this into a report of word B. The multiple arrows represent alternative branches (or competing mediating response) which can be followed, and which may thereby interfere with successful flow of events in the chain.

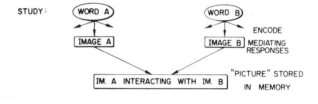

Figure 3.4 Flow diagram of mediating events during the study trial and recall test.

Ambiguity and Similarity of Meaning

Consider first ambiguous nouns as cues. Since the semantic interpretation precedes the imaginal production, recall will be poor if the semantic coding of the noun differs between the study trial and the recall trial. The semantic interpretation of nouns can be altered by context, in particular by qualifying adjectives. Thus, a nylon *slip* is one thing, while a Freudian *slip* is quite another. In experiments conducted in my lab by Samuel Bobrow, PA conditions have been studied in which the cue-term (adjective noun) is either repeated exactly, or the adjective is altered either to preserve similarity of meaning (e.g., lamb chop versus meat chop), or to alter meaning (e.g., lamb chop versus karate chop). Recall percentages in the first two cases are equal and are about double the recall in the latter case, when the critical noun cue has its meaning altered. This occurred despite the fact that subjects knew that the noun was the critical recall cue. Such findings, of course, do not implicate imagery in any way. But they do make two important points: (a) what is stored in most such cases are the meaning relations, not word-word associations; and (b) there is probably no automatic or direct connection from a word to an image. A semantic interpretation is probably interposed, and it controls whatever imagery will be aroused.

Now let us consider synonymic confusions. Synonyms are words which may arouse similar or identical imagery. If synonymous stimulus words are paired with different response words, there will then be two composite pictures retrievable from memory by the single image code of either stimulus word. To the stimulus CAR, subjects may recall the response appropriate to the stimulus AUTOMOBILE. Similar confusions may be expected from priming synonyms on the response side. If the words BOAT and SHIP appear as response terms for different stimuli, the subject may respond BOAT when he should have said SHIP.

One of our experiments compared subjects learning a unique list of concrete pairs to subjects learning a list involving half synonym pairs on the stimulus side (with unique responses) and half synonym pairs on the response side (with unique stimulus terms). Two groups were run: one group received the usual visual imagery instructions, the other subjects were instructed to learn by auditory rehearsal—that is, by listening to the composite sound as they said the word pair over and over during the study interval.

The results of this experiment are shown in Table 3.2. The salient features of these data are first, that imagery subjects recall more, and second, that list-type and learning method interact upon recall. Specifically, the shift from the unique list to the synonym list caused an appreciable drop in recall of imagery subjects, but little change in recall of the auditory-rehearsal subjects. Moreover, the increase in errors on the synonym list by imagery subjects was largely due to synonym confusions of the types mentioned above. Of all recall failures (errors plus omissions), 31% were synonym intrusions for imagery subjects versus only 2% for auditory rehearsal subjects. This experiment illustrates how the coding set used by a subject may affect the learning of different types of material.

TABLE 3.2   Recall Percentages for Different Lists for Subjects Given Different
Learning Sets

Condition	Visual Imagery	Auditory Rehearsal
Unique list	.83	.39
Synonym list	.66	.36
Synonym errors/ all errors	.31	.02

Returning just for a moment to the results of Table 3.2 in relation to
the flow chart of Figure 3.4, it should be mentioned that just because
a response term has a synonym does not imply that the synonym will intrude.
Rather, the synonym has to be primed into availability. The response words
in the unique list above have synonyms, yet these never intruded in recall of
that list. As has been often noted (e.g., Underwood and Schultz, 1960),
some selector mechanism or editor confines recalled responses to the list.
In our flow chart, this means that the response-term image is selected from
the primed or recently tagged verbal labels for that image.

One final point here: with multiple trials on a synonym list, imagery
subjects probably overcome confusions by elaborating differential imagery
for the two terms. Thus, BOAT comes to be imaged as a dinghy, and SHIP
as an ocean liner. Because no two words are really identical, a selection of
differential elements for elaboration can always be done.

Imagery Value

Consider next in Figure 3.4 the effect of variation in the imagery value of
the cue-term of the paired associate items. If imagery rating is an index of
word-image association strength, then we may expect high imagery cues to
be more effective for two reasons: first, the imaginal code occurs quicker, so
there is more time to search for and generate the relational scene, or to study
the cue code-to-response association. Second, recall depends upon reactivating
the same imaginal code (for the cue-term) as was activated during the study
trial. If the cue does not activate the same code, then recall will surely fail
(see Martin, 1968). The strong associations of high imagery cues increase
the reliability of the imaginal code. For this reason, the imagery value of the
cue-term should be especially important.

A number of experiments could be used to illustrate these effects. We
used people's names as cues for a noun paired-associate response. Each
subject answered a questionnaire which enabled us to identify three different
types of names for him: (a) names of 21 of his personal friends, whom he
could picture clearly in his mind; (b) names of 21 historical characters, about

whom he knew some facts but did not know exactly what they looked like (e.g., had not seen pictures or paintings of them); and (c) names of 21 unknown people randomly selected from the telephone directory. These were presented in three mixed lists, seven cues of each type in each list, paired with concrete nouns for one 5-second presentation with imagery instructions. On the test trial following each list, noun recall to the name cues was .93 for personal friends, .66 for historical characters, and .43 for unknown names. Subjects reported being able to do moderately well on historical characters because the few facts they knew about the characters helped them imagine a prototype character, dressed in period clothes, doing his famous thing (e.g., Eli Whitney stuffing his cotton gin).

Although I would like to attribute this effect to differential imagery value of the names, frequency of experience, and verbal associations may be confounded along with imagery. Let me therefore add that a subsequent experiment was done with photographs of front-faces of known versus unknown people as cues for paired associate noun responses. The known faces were of national and campus celebrities, all of whom could be immediately named by our subjects. In this experiment, the recall difference between known and unknown persons shrank to only 10% (65% versus 55% recall after one trial). The difference is of small magnitude relative to the difference between known and unknown names. The argument is that with the picture, the visual (imaginal) cue is immediately available for unknown as well as known characters, so recall differences here are slight. With the names as cues, however, imagery is available for known but not for unknown names, so the recall differences are very large.

Controlled variation of word-attributes in PAL has been researched in great detail by Paivio and his coworkers (cf., Paivio, 1969, for a review). A first important finding is that the image-evoking value (I) of the stimulus term in PAL is a critically important factor in learning rate, even with nonmeaningful response terms. When I-values are simultaneously varied on the stimulus and response sides of pairs, I-value is positively correlated with learning in both cases, but much more so on the stimulus than on the response side.

The results of one of our experiments may be used to illustrate this pattern. Subjects received one study trial and an immediate forward (left-to-right) recall trial on three lists, each consisting of a third of the three classes of pairs as shown in Table 3.3. At the end of the session, a final forward recall test and a backward recall test were given for the pairs from all three lists. Results of these final tests are shown in Table 3.3. Comparing forward recall, one finds a large effect of stimulus I-value (85 versus 56) but only a small effect of response I (85 versus 81). The other feature of interest in Table 3.3 is the relation between forward and backward recall of a pair. With high-low pairs, forward exceeds backward recall; with low-high pairs, backward exceeds forward recall. It thus appears that retrieval of the imaginal association is best achieved by using the high-imagery member of the pair. Lockhart (1969) has reported a similar finding.

TABLE 3.3   Forward and Backward Recall Percentages for Pairs Varying in Imagery. High Denotes High Imagery Concrete Nouns: Low Denotes Low Imagery Words, a Third Each of Abstract Nouns, Verbs, and Adjectives.

		Percent Recall	
Training Function		Forward	Backward
Stimulus	Response	R given S	S given R
High	Low	81	70
High	High	85	85
Low	High	56	71

That stimulus imagery-concreteness correlates with PA learning cannot be taken at face value; other word attributes concerning verbal meaningfulness may be related to I-value, and these may be the truly effective variables. It was to test such possibilities that Paivio and his associates carried out their extensive experiments, first scaling different word-attributes, and second, selecting subsets of words that varied one attribute while controlling others. The chief attribute contrasted with imagery-concreteness was "meaningfulness" (m) of the verbal unit, defined in terms of the number of verbal associates produced to the unit within a fixed time. This is a conventional index that has been found to correlate well with PAL and with serial learning, particularly when nonsense syllable units are used. There is a correlation of .72 in Paivio's norms between the I-value and m of his words, so it is not implausible that I versus learning correlations are really due to m variations.

In a series of experiments (reviewed by Paivio, 1969), I and m values of words were independently varied over equivalent scale ranges on both the stimulus and response sides of PA pairs. The conclusions were that m has little or no effect on PA learning when I-value is controlled or is partialled out of the correlations. The most that has been found for m when I is controlled is an occasional slight *negative* relation between response-m and PA learning rate. On the other hand, for fixed m, PA learning correlates highly with the imagery-concreteness of the stimulus term, and correlates somewhat with the I-value of the response term. The significance of such results is clear: those PA studies reporting learning effects of m-variations with words could all be reinterpreted as displaying uncontrolled variation in I-values. The bulk of studies showing m effects in learning have used non-sense trigrams, and there the m variations are doubtless indexing the extent to which the trigram reminds subjects of a real word.

Paivio (1968) has searched for other word attributes that may be correlated with I-value and which might be causing the correlation between I-value and PA learning. Everyone has their favorite variable to suggest—Thorndike-Lorge frequency, familiarity, associative variety, emotionality, semantic differential ratings, and so on. But these all turn out to correlate only slightly with PA learning, especially when I-value is controlled. It thus appears that imagery-concreteness of the stimulus word is the most potent attribute for PA learning yet identified.

HYPOTHESES ABOUT IMAGINAL FACILITATION

The evidence indicating that imagery facilitates PA learning is of two sorts: (1) subjects who have not been specifically instructed to use a particular learning strategy learn high-imagery pairs faster than low-imagery pairs, and (2) instructions to image relationships improve recall. In fact, we can probably attribute the effect of I-variation in experiments of the first type to the second condition. So the crux of the problem is to explain why imaging is such a powerful technique for learning associations. Several possible explanations will be considered in turn.

Motivation or Interest

A first possibility is that imagery instructions enhance the subject's motivation for learning, making the task more interesting. The imagery-incidental versus intentional-control contrast presented earlier may be offered against this view. But the basic problem with this hypothesis is that it is difficult to test. One might try varying motivation by payoffs; but even if this had an effect, one could not be sure if high motivation caused the subject to rehearse more or to employ more efficient learning strategies like imagery. I consider this explanation useless because it explains nothing, or everything.

Selection from Incidental Redundant Cues

If the nominal stimulus contains a redundant array of possible cues, the subject may select a cue which is easiest to link to the reponse term. The stimulus word may arouse an image containing a large number of incidental cues. For example, my image for the word *boy* might be of my son in a particular setting, engaging in certain activities. Incidental cues might be background objects, things he is carrying or the clothes he is wearing. If the imaginal scene contains many more potential cues than the word *boy* alone, then there is a greater chance that a cue having a strong prior association to the response will be contained in and selected from the former stimulus complex.

If this hypothesis is true, then one should be able to simulate this effect at the verbal learning level, without using imagery, simply by providing more redundant cues in the nominal stimulus. Accordingly, a PA experiment was run comparing the efficacy of a single-word nominal stimulus to a redundant three-word nominal stimulus. All were concrete nouns as were the single response terms. Half of the three-word compounds was unrelated and half was associatively related, the latter to simulate the interconnected components of an image. This amusing experiment was a total bust: contrary to the good-cue selection hypothesis, the pairs involving triad stimulus compounds were recalled *worse* than pairs involving single-word stimuli. The response recall percentages were: single-word cues, 48%; unrelated triad cues, 33%; associatively related triad cues, 35%. So, tripling is crippling. The effect is probably due to a reduction in effective study time for the pairing, and to increased variability of stimulus encoding for the triads.

A further nail in this coffin was provided by results of Jenkins (1967). He found that his subjects learned picture-word PAs faster if the perspective of the photograph (e.g., different snapshots of an elephant) was varied from trial to trial, rather than remaining constant. Since background incidental cues varied in the former case but not the latter, the incidental-cue-selection hypothesis would have predicted the opposite results.

Stimulus Distinctiveness

Another possibility is that imaginal coding facilitates learning because imagery causes the effective stimulus complex to become more distinctive. By *distinctive* I mean that the imaginal complex is better differentiated from the other stimuli in the list, as though a distinctive color had been attached to each cue word. Distinctiveness thus implies less intralist interference, less confusions among pairs, and more accurate recall.

There are problems with this account. First, in Gibson's (1940) original sense of differentiation, practically all moderate-to-high frequency words are already well differentiated stimuli for adults. Second, experiments using predifferentiation of cue words or trigrams have reported small or inconsistent effects upon later PA learning. We might wonder if the highly personalized, idiosyncratic codings elaborated under imagery instructions produce the critical distinctiveness.

We have conducted one experiment to test this hypothesis. During the study trial the stimulus word appeared alone for 5 seconds, followed by the stimulus-response pair for five seconds. Four different groups of subjects were run. In the subject-elaboration condition, the subject was asked to provide a descriptive phrase for each stimulus word that identified a specific familiar example of the word. For example, for the stimulus word SLIPPER, the subject might produce "my mother's pink SLIPPER". After elaborating the stimulus-alone in this manner, the subject was instructed merely to associate the noun-stimulus with the response word when it appeared later.

In a second condition, subjects simply read some context words along with the critical cue word. These stimulus elaborations were of the type generated by subjects in the former condition. The contextual elaboration of the critical stimulus word was provided during the study trial only and not during the cued recall trial. Along with these two conditions of stimulus elaboration, standard repetition and visual imagery control groups were run. The former subjects were told to repeat the stimulus word aloud, and then repeat the S-R pair silently when it appeared. The latter subjects were told first to image an object for the stimulus word and then, when the S-R pair appeared, to image the stimulus-response objects in interaction. Two study-recall cycles were done in this manner on each of three lists of 30 noun pairs, half of the pairs concrete and half abstract.

The question is whether verbal elaboration of a stimulus word makes it more distinctive, thus facilitating recall as much as imagery does. The answer to this question turns out to be distinctly negative. The relevant results are shown in Table 3.4 giving average recall probabilities over the two trials. Verbal elaboration of the stimulus word in context does not enhance recall. If anything, recall is decreased slightly below that of the repetition controls. And as before, the visual imagery subjects recall more than the rest of the pack. The low recall score for imagery subjects here (compared to the earlier experiments) is because half the pairs were abstract nouns. The concrete pairs were recalled one and a half times better than abstract pairs, and the split in this respect was practically identical in all four conditions.

TABLE 3.4   Mean Recall Percentages Over Two Trials for Items Processed in Different Ways ($n = 1260$ per Point)

Condition	Percent Recall
Repetition	53
Imagery	71
E-generated elaboration	47
S-generated elaboration	50

Relational Organization

The former two hypotheses—relating the imagery effect in PAL to *cue selection* or *cue distinctiveness*—relate the effects of imagery to embellishment of the stimulus. The alternative view, which I consider to be closer to the truth, is that imagery enhances the associative connection between the two terms.

A simple experiment suffices to show how this relating or interactively organizing feature of imagery instructions is critical. An incidental learning experiment compared two imagery groups. One group received our standard interaction instructions, namely, to image a scene of the two objects interacting in some way. The second group received *separation* instructions: to image the two objects separated in their imaginal space, like two pictures on opposite walls of a room. One object-picture was not to be influenced in any way by the contents of the other object-picture. Each subject had 10 seconds to do his thing with each concrete-noun pair and to give a rating of how easy it was to visualize the objects. Cued recall was then tested with the result that the interactive imagery subjects recalled 71%, whereas the separated imagery subjects recalled only 46% of the response terms. This is a highly significant difference. But more importantly, the low recall of the separated imagery subjects is about the figure we would expect from repetition controls given 10 seconds per item. Thus, instructions to image the terms *per se* have relatively little effect on associative learning. The important component is the interactive relation between the imaged objects.

We may ask, what characterizes interactive scenes? If one examines the descriptive statements subjects use to characterize their interactive scenes, the phrases usually relate the two nouns as grammatical subject and object connected by a verb or a preposition. The usual scenes for the pair DOG-BICYCLE might be "a DOG riding on (or chasing, or barking at, or urinating on, or running into, or being hit by) a BICYCLE" or "a DOG on (behind, under) a BICYCLE". The subject and object nouns may be embellished by adjectival modifiers (e.g., a mangy old DOG), but the base syntactic form contains either a verb or a prepositional connective. On the other hand, subjects in the separated imagery condition would describe their imaginal scene as "a DOG over here *and* a BICYCLE over there". Again, embellishing adjectives may be added to each noun, but the connective remains the simple conjunction *and*.

There are parallel findings showing the same pattern in PA learning using pictures of familiar objects, and also using words related through different syntactic connectives. Since experiments by Epstein, Rock, and Zuckerman (1960), we have known that two pictured objects are more easily associated if they are shown in some kind of spatial interaction (e.g., lamp in a bottle) as opposed to just showing them side by side (lamp and bottle). Epstein *et al.* (1960) and Rohwer (1966) have shown similar variations in PA recall of noun pairs when, at input, the nouns are connected by a verb or preposition (leading to high recall) as opposed to a conjunction (leading to low recall). To get the facilitation, the prepositional and verb connectives have to make sense for the two nouns; semantically anomalous connectives like "lamp sings bottle" or "lamp how bottle" are of no help in promoting later recall.

This recall pattern with pictures, images, and words is probably being produced by the same relational generating system. An extreme view, to which I do not subscribe, would suppose that the linguistic medium is primary, and that differing pictorial or imaginal scenes have the effects they do because of the different descriptive statements that subjects generate. If one believed this, then one would question how variations in sentence context affect the association between critical words in the sentence. We have done some work along these lines; Rohwer and his associates have done a lot (cf. Rohwer, 1967, for a review), and I will try to summarize it very briefly before returning to the imagery topic.

Sentence Contexts in PA Learning

With primary-grade children, Rohwer finds facilitation of noun PA learning when the nouns are connected by verbs or prepositions, but not conjunctions (and/or). This facilitation is assessed relative to control subjects who merely hear or read the noun pairs without a connective. Among adults, reading nouns in simple declarative sentences produces no net facilitation in learning. If adults are explicitly instructed to overtly rehearse the word pairs, then their recall is worse than that of subjects who study the nouns in the context of declarative sentences. In other experiments, (Bobrow and Bower, 1969), we have reported (1) that studying the nouns in anomalous or nonsensical sentences produces less recall than simply studying the noun pairs alone, and (2) the associative recall between subject-noun and object-noun is roughly symmetrical and about the same over several variations in syntactic form of the sentences studied (i.e., declarative, negative, interrogative, or negative interrogative).

One interesting finding is that subjects remembered sentences they generated much better than sentences we gave them. In the generate condition, subjects were shown noun pairs for 5 seconds, and they had to make up and say some sentence linking the two nouns. In the *read* condition, subjects were shown the two nouns capitalized as subject and object in a sensible declarative sentence, and had to read this aloud and study it for 5 seconds. Later recall (of the object-noun when cued with the subject-noun) is about one and a half to two times higher for the sentence-generating subjects. This difference has held up over four experiments. We now attribute it to a difference in comprehension of the sentence in the two cases. Generating a linking sentence forces the subject to search out, find, and understand the relationship in a more reliable way than does mere rapid reading of a large number of similar sentences.

This led Bobrow and me to do incidental learning experiments in which subjects processed declarative sentences in ways designed to affect their comprehension of the propositions asserted. Comprehension of a sentence establishes a number of cognitive dispositions. So in one experiment we required our subjects to disambiguate sentences, in another to continue the action expressed in the sentences. Incidental recall of such subjects was compared to the recall of others who either searched for spelling errors in the sentences, or who read the sentences aloud three times as rapidly as they could. After processing 45 declarative sentences in this manner (at 7 seconds each), subjects were tested for recall of the object-noun when cued with the subject-noun. The disambiguation and continuation conditions produced about 50% recall whereas the spelling and rapid recitation conditions produced around 20% recall. This 2.5-to-1 difference presumably reflects the effect on memory of comprehension.

Unfortunately, deeper levels of analysis are stymied by the absence of a good theory of linguistic comprehension. There are various sketchy and incomplete proposals in the air. An appealing one is Quillian's (1966) which equates comprehension (of a simple declarative sentence) with finding and tracing a permissible pathway, corresponding to the predicate, between the semantic nodes corresponding to the subject and object concepts. To comprehend a sentence is to find concepts preexisting in the semantic network that are related in ways compatible with the sentential relation. From the standpoint of memory, the process of understanding a sentence involves the construction or tagging of a retrieval scheme, whereby one semantic node points to a path which links it to the node of the other sentential concept. Thus, associative memory (between key concepts) is a by-product of comprehending a sentence.

Problems in Identifying Imagery Effect as Verbal Mediation

The excellent PA recall produced when subjects generate linking sentences suggests that the recall effects of imagery instructions are reducible to sentence generation. That is, subjects may be generating a linking sentence for the word pair. There may be no excess advantage to imagery once the effect of implicit sentence generation is partialled out.

I think this viewpoint is too extreme. A first fact is that if subjects read linking sentences, and also image scenes compatible with the sentences, their later PA recall is higher than it would be if they did not image. In one experiment, this produced a 62% versus 41% difference in recall; in another, a 69% versus 52% difference. Imagery subjects even recall somewhat better than subjects instructed to generate their own linking sentences for noun pairs. In one experiment, the difference was 85% versus 73% in favor of the imagery subjects, in another, it was 90% versus 80%. Although statistically significant, these differences are not very large, so a portion of the imagery effect may still be attributable to implicit sentence generation.

But sentence-generating itself may not be a purely verbal process. Subjects spontaneously report having imagery of the scene described by the sentence. As reported by Yuille and Paivio (1968) and repeated by us, subjects instructed to generate verbal mediators for PAs will recall pairs at a level correlated with the imagery value of the stimulus member of the pair. That is, pairs with high-imagery stimulus terms are better recalled even when the subject is instructed to generate verbal mediators. One might attribute this to lower availability of verbal mediators for abstract pairs, but Yuille and Paivio (1967) found no difference in verbal mediator latencies for concrete versus abstract noun pairs. In fact, abstract mediators were reported slightly faster than concrete ones were. But there was a large difference in later PA learning in favor of the concrete pairs.

Two Interconnected Systems

I think these attempts to reduce imagery effects to verbal processes are unlikely to succeed. The alternative is to postulate two memory modalities, imagery and verbal, with very rich interconnections (cf. Paivio, 1969; Wallach and Averbach, 1955). The interconnections permit us to describe pictures, to describe our imagery, to have words evoking imagery, and so forth. The simplest assumption is that modality can be involved in most of our associative learning. When the learning materials are words, the verbal system is clearly involved in the learning and the imaginal system may be engaged to an extent depending upon both learning strategy and the strength of the connections between verbal and imaginal repertoires. Because adults usually label familiar pictures (if given time), even pictorial information will be partially coded and duplicated in the verbal system. With unfamiliar pictures, like cloud patterns or some abstract paintings, visual information may be stored with only very general verbal information.

According to this view, familiar picture pairs or word pairs under imagery conditions would cause the creation of two connected memory codes, one in the imagery system and a corresponding one in the verbal system. Figure 3.5 provides a heuristic picture. Meaning concepts correspond to nodes in an intricately interconnected verbal-semantic system. These nodes are arranged topologically in organized hierarchies corresponding to different categorizations or semantic markers. For example, *thing, process, manner,* and *quality* would be the highest level semantic tags corresponding to syntactic classes of nouns, verbs, adverbs,

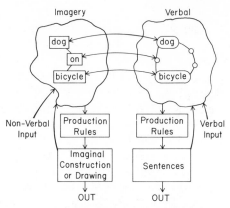

Figure 3.5   Heuristic diagram of the verbal and imaginal coding systems.
Semantic concepts and associated imaginal parameters are denoted
by labeled nodes (list-headings), in a richly connected and
cross-connected system.

and adjectives. A concept like DOG would be the name of a node pointing to interconnected sublists containing such information as:

(a)   *Graphemic* — what the word looks like and how to spell it.

(b)   *Phonemic*   — what the word sounds like and how to articulate it.

(c)   *Semantic*   — definition of its meaning (several if ambiguous), subordi-
                       nate and superordinate categories, verbal associates.

(d)   *Sensory*   — what the object looks like or sounds like. Criteria for
                       class recognition, and lists for subspecies and individuals.

For ambiguous words, sublists of types *c* and *d* would be in coordinate pairs, with each meaning component tied to a particular sensory sublist. Such sublists would be used in stimulus recognition (of object or grapheme or acoustic stimulus) and in response generation. For the present it is immaterial whether we consider the stimulus recognition to be passive (categorizing feature lists) or active (matching generated patterns to those sensed). Illustrated in Figure 3.5 are the nodes and paths that are aroused and tagged by the phrase "a DOG on a BICYCLE." The sensory-information sublists corresponding to these semantic nodes may also be tagged and delivered to a production machine, which will generate an imaginal scene with the specified parameters.

The data suggest that the imagery code (or tag) has a slower decay rate than the verbal code. Perhaps subsequent materials are less likely to disrupt the imaginal memory code. We know from Shepard's (1966) experiments that recognition memory for easily identifiable pictures (e.g., magazine advertisements) is incredibly high, much better than for words. Gorman (1961) found a similar difference in recognition memory for concrete versus abstract words. Concrete words may be coded in both imagery and verbal forms, whereas abstract words may be coded only in verbal form. Free recall is best with lists of familiar pictures (or real objects), next best with concrete nouns, and worst with abstract nouns. Such results imply that the imaginal code decays slower than a verbal code.

This dual-code theory still needs some assumptions concerning associative connections. The experiments on separate-imaging and type of connective (verb or preposition versus conjunctions) point to factors of relational organization. A bare PA learning task presumably activates a relation finding program which searches along associative pathways, fanning out from the two head nodes, looking for intersecting paths. Such associative pathways may be short or long depending on the semantic or phonological similarity (e.g., rhymes) of the key terms or their high associates. For example, a subject who learns the pair K-QUEEN via the path K-king-QUEEN is using the latter sort of route (cf. Schwartz, 1969). When it is successful, the relation finding program tags the associative pathway found, and attaches route information to the key nodes. This route information is usually temporary and is controlled by the set established in the experimental context. A few minutes' verbal learning task does little to alter subjects' store of semantic knowledge (cf. Slamecka, 1966). It should be noted that I am using *associative relation* in a very general sense, not as in tables of association norms. For example, "x rides on y" is an associative relation into which certain terms can be sensibly substituted for x and y. DOG and BICYCLE fit because our semantic network contains the information that bicycles can be ridden by something, and that a dog could sensibly ride on something. So by *associative pathway*, I mean a sensibly possible connection between terms.

There are many varieties of relational associations, from phonological overlap (rhymes) to subject-object predicates. A variety of predicative relations are ruled out by semantic restrictions. Whatever the general principles of relational organization may be, they appear to be similar within the imaginal and the verbal systems. There are similar patterns of associative recall whether the input material is pictorial, images aroused by words, or verbal connections established by sentences.

We may have a common generative grammar that underlies our verbal production of sentences and our imaginal production of visualized scenes or of hand-drawn pictures. In this day of computer graphics, it is hardly novel to suggest that pictures have a "grammar", that scenes can be parsed into subpictures, which can be decoded further into objects and contours. Such decoding contains all the heuristics of Chomskian grammar. Transformations of objects in imaginal 3-D may even be analogous to syntactic transformations. Grammatical picture-analysis (Shaw, 1968; Miller and Shaw, 1967, 1968) is still largely programmatic and experimental, but we can surely expect significant new ideas from this line of research in artificial intelligence.

My speculation is that a base grammar underlies our linguistic and pictorial analysis and generation. In particular, this suggests that Gestalt laws of perceptual organization will be the phrase-parsing rules of the picture grammar.

Pictorial constituents would correspond to perceptual groups, segregated according to the Gestalt principles of spatial proximity and similarity. Kohler (1947) and
Asch, Ceraso, and Heimer (1960) have stressed the various perceptual organizations that lead to strong associations. If one figural component is a constituent
of the other, or is a continuation of the other, or is an integral surface of the
other, or is as part-to-whole with the other, then the figures are easily associated
(cf. Asch, Ceraso, and Heimer, 1960; Prentice and Asch, 1958; and Kaswan,
1957). To illustrate, Figure 3.6*a* shows a constitutive relation (a square constituted of plus symbols) the terms of which are associated more easily than are
those of control (Figure 3.6*b*). Similarly, Figure 3.6*c* shows a part-to-whole relation, the terms of which are associated more easily than are those of its control
(Figure 3.6*d*).

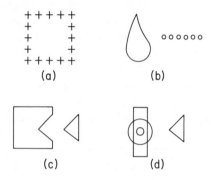

Figure 3.6   Examples of figural-relations. In (*a*), the small plus signs are the
mode constituting a square (unitary figure). In (*b*), a teardrop and a
row of beads (nonunitary figure and mode). In (*c*), the two
parts fit together as part-to-whole; in (*d*), the two parts
are nonfitting.

It is probable that spatial relations like *is a constituent of, is composed of, is
a surface of, is a part of,* and so on are going to be the basic relational predicates
of a picture grammar, appearing as primitives in the most elementary statements
about any scene. Thus, differences in associative memory for the unitary figure
and mode of Figure 3.6*a* versus those in Figure 3.6*b* may be reflected in grammatical complexity of the two strings stored in the imagery system.

 Whether or not these particular suggestions prove viable, I think we are in need
of some heuristic but reasonably formal machinery for talking about relational
organization. I am convinced that associating meaningful terms is largely a matter of relating them in some organization (see also Asch, 1969). And I think the
mnemonic value of interactive imagery or sentence-generating devices arises from
the creative production of relational organizations.

ADDENDUM

In comments on my paper as delivered at the conference, Professor H. Simon asked what sorts of operations on information are possible with mechanisms in the imagery system, which are distinguishable from simple manipulation of verbal symbols. One class of tasks meeting these criteria comprise the major segments of batteries such as the Thurstone spatial abilities test, and the Minnesota paper form-board test (cf. Barratt, 1953). In such tasks, the subject is shown a spatial diagram, has to transform it geometrically in various ways, and must then select the transformed figure from a list of alternatives. Roger Shepard (personal communication) is measuring reaction times of subjects who are judging whether two 3-D rigid, block figures are identical except for rotation either in the vertical plane or in the picture plane. Essentially the subject asks himself, "Can I rotate figure A into correspondence with figure B?" Preliminary results show that errors are very infrequent and that reaction times for same judgments are a strict linear increasing function of the degree of rotation needed to convert figure A into figure B, with a slope of approximately 60 degrees per second of reaction time.

Pilot work has begun in my lab on another task, suggested by Lee Brooks. The subject is first taught a short stroke vocabulary using eight compass directions, for example, north, northeast, east, southeast, and practices drawing segments of unit length (about half an inch) in the appropriate direction when the vocabulary elements are spoken to him. The subject is then blindfolded and the testing begins. A sequence of four to ten strokes is read to the subject (approx. 1 per second) who draws them, connecting them into a continuous figure of line segments. He is asked to visualize the figure as he draws it. Figure 3.7 shows some example figures with the labelled strokes of the vocabulary as generated from left to right.

The subject is then asked to manipulate the information in one of several ways. In one task, he is asked to imagine a line connecting the first point with the last point in his visualized figure, and report how many line segments of the diagram are thus intersected. For the four figures in Figure 3.7, the number of crossings is 0, 1, 2, and 3, respectively. How well subjects perform on this test will surely vary with a variety of factors—the number of line segments, the redundancy or familiarity of the pattern drawn, the input rate of segments, whether the subject actually draws the diagram or merely visualizes it, and so forth. The important point of our pilot demonstration is that some subjects can perform these operations at a level far in excess of chance guessing. Significantly, the problem may not be soluble by a simple symbol-manipulating processor (operating on the list of strokes). Our heads must contain some geometry routines that allow us to treat sequential information as though it were being converted into a spatial diagram.

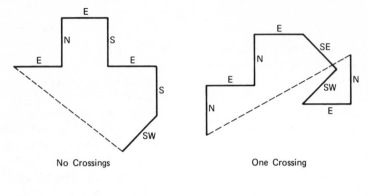

No Crossings   One Crossing

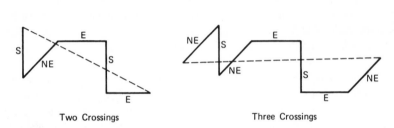

Two Crossings   Three Crossings

Figure 3.7   Examples of diagrams generated by stroke sequences (read
left to right). Dashed line connects first and last points.

Another task that our subjects perform upon the completed diagram is to rotate it 90 degrees clockwise in their heads, and read out the names of the strokes
that now appear in imagery. A final task we are now studying is immediate serial
recall of the sequence of strokes. Half the subjects draw connected diagrams
which they visualize as they draw them. The remaining subjects merely mark
down the sequence of unconnected strokes in a line, and are asked to rehearse
them verbally (rather than visualizing a continuous drawing). The hope is that
those subjects who are drawing and visualizing a continuous, unitary figure will
be better able to recall the stroke series than will those subjects who are simply
recalling a series of compass directions. Preliminary evidence is encouraging,
but many more subjects and conditions must be studied before we are sure of
this conclusion.

CHAPTER 4

John A. Michon
Institute for Perception–TNO
Soesterberg, The Netherlands

MULTIDIMENSIONAL AND HIERARCHICAL ANALYSIS
OF PROGRESS IN LEARNING

If we consider learning as the acquisition of an internal representation of (a part of) the external world, two major questions to be raised at the descriptive level are: how does such a representation develop, and what is it that distinguishes the expert's representation from the pupil's?

Preceding these questions is a third, technical question: how do we measure the internal representation and its development? In this paper we shall discuss these questions in some detail. The examples are taken from several projects which are under way at present, and which are not necessarily aimed directly at the study of learning. All examples may serve, however, to illustrate the main point of describing the development of internal representations.

MEASUREMENT AND DESCRIPTION OF LEARNING PROGRESS

Learning is generally conceived of as the interiorization of originally external events. In this respect the classical approaches to cognition—gestalt, behavioristic and cognitive theory—do not essentially differ.

In gestalt theory the reinforcing aspect of the learning situation with respect to perceived gestalten is stressed in particular. For the S-R theorists, the internal representation is less of a clearcut structure. The internal signs of the external world are primarily seen as covert stimuli, associated with the real world in a S-s-s....r-r-R chain. Although Berlyne's (1965) elaboration on this theory seems to bring in the structure again, (neo)behaviorists in general seem to be more interested in the problem spaces than in the data spaces as a mapping of the real world. The problem space is a mapping of the possible transitions from one state to another. The data space is a mapping of just the present state of the world (Michon, 1968).

Cognitive theory stresses the comparison between the effect of actions in the external world with the effect predicted by operations on an internal representation of that world. If a discrepancy occurs, an alternative choice of action is made, and a revision of the probabilities of certain actions will be made. This approach seems to be capable of handling both the data space and the problem space paradigms.

Learning is most frequently represented in this approach by means of growing networks, where growing means the addition of new distinctive features at new decision nodes. Feigenbaum's Elementary Perceiver And Memorizer (EPAM), is a classical example (Feigenbaum 1959). In order to recognize nonsense syllables presented to it, EPAM will internally grow a network, by sorting a stimulus syllable through its internal representation, until it arrives either at a terminal node containing the exact image of the stimulus—which leads to recognition—or else at a terminal node where it observes a discrepancy with the image. In the latter case EPAM will create a new decision node which takes the observed discrepancy into account. When confronted with the same stimulus, it will be able to make the appropriate distinction. Other examples of growing networks are contained in the work of Baylor (1969), and Quillian (1966).

In all these cases new knowledge is stored in cognitive trees, branching being governed by distinctive features of the stimuli. Under experimental conditions these distinctive features are mostly of a very relevant nature. In practical circumstances this is almost never true: most practical classifications carry many irrelevant features as well. The data processed by clinical psychologists and neurologists, for instance, show that distinctive features are not necessarily informative (Kleinmuntz, 1963, 1968). And as we will see subsequently, teachers may not be able to provide the relevant distinctive features, by lack of analysis of the logical structure of the material.

An entirely different approach to the representative description of learning is offered by some work in the area of attitude change, which by itself is a form of learning. The measurement of changes in opinion and attitudes has of course its venerable history and dates back at least to the work of Thurstone. A well known example in which multidimensional techniques were used, is the work of Osgood and his coworkers on the semantic space. Using the semantic differential technique they were able to show considerable shifts in the attitude pattern of a patient with a multiple personality syndrome (Osgood, Suci, and Tannenbaum 1957). The attitudes towards such concepts as self, father, God, mother, and baby, were found to change with the personality of the patient as shown in Figure 4.1.

Irrespective of the merits of this case, it offers a strategy for studying the growth of an internal representation during a period of learning. This has become even more appropriate with the advent of methodological improvements in multidimensional scaling, such as Kruskal's method (Kruskal, 1964a, b; Roskam, 1968). The multidimensional or cognitive map representation of subsets of the real world has become very popular indeed. Some of the best studied are the color space (Torgerson, 1951, 1958; Indow, 1963), and the vowel space (Hanson 1965, Pols, Van der Kamp, and Plomp 1968). In none of these studies was the influence of learning or experience under concern. One reason for this may be that the stimuli studied are so fundamental, physically or

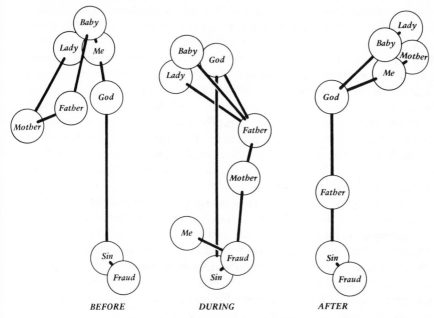

BEFORE DURING AFTER

Figure 4.1 Semantic relations between several existential concepts in a case of multiple personality (after Osgood, Suci and Tannenbaum (1957)).

physiologically, that the perceptual learning involved must be completed at a very early age.

In summary: we may deal with data space in several ways. The hierarchical tree (the strata of the *regna animale et florale*), and the *n*-space (color space, Mendeleyev's table) are three common ways of ordering complex data. Although in principle these structures may be imposed on stimulus sets externally, they may also be imposed by internal cognitive acts. This suggests a distinction between explicit and implicit structures.

EXPLICIT AND IMPLICIT STRUCTURES

Not always do clearcut representations of one or another type suggest themselves when we look at the data. This may be due to a lack of insight in the ordering of the data. Thus, centuries of chemical and physical research passed before the periodic system of the elements emerged. The data may also be too complex for complete representation, or the elementary classes of events or objects may be so intrinsically variable that a taxonomy can be only achieved on a statistical basis.

The availability of an external framework entails questions of (a) whether such explicit networks, n-dimensional spaces or trees are internalized in the way they are structured externally; and (b) what stages can be distinguished in the learning process. In cases where we have an overcomplex data structure, or an intrinsic variability in the taxonomy of the stimuli, learning programs are usually of a rather nonsystematic sort. Instead of a (rote) learning technique to internalize an externally imposed order, we have here learning by apprenticeship. In this learning paradigm, subjects are confronted with examples of data orderings which are in the set of possible states of the world. The apprentice is taught how to operate on these specific examples, and by means of stimulus and response generalization he learns to cope with similar or analogous conditions, not previously encountered.

This learning paradigm is essentially comparable to the Monte Carlo technique in statistics. The major point of interest is how people develop their internal representations without being given explicit reference as to the ordering principles governing the real world. Secondly: is the internal representation that is characteristic of the expert, transferred to the trainee as a consequence of training? And, in the third place, would it be feasible to use the expert's representation—which after all enables him to operate on the real world quite reliably—as a basis for the design of training courses?

These then are some of the questions that we will consider in the remaining part of this paper.

TECHNIQUES OF TESTING INTERNAL REPRESENTATION

Grossly we may divide the techniques, by which information on presence and nature of internal representation can be obtained, into three categories:

1. Direct measures, such as protocol analysis or drawings;

2. Behavior measures, such as reaction times, multiple choice answers, galvanic skin response, etc.

These two forms are encountered in most experimental learning paradigms; in addition they constitute the main body of the usual school examination techniques, if we exclude the psychophysiological measures. Since these approaches are so widely used, we will not deal with them in detail.

3. Psychophysical scaling techniques. As Van de Geer and Jaspars (1966) argued, cognitive theory has had little use for scaling methods thus far. Yet the recent developments in multidimensional scaling techniques have made it feasible to investigate cognitive space by these means.

Two techniques appear to be of particular interest: Kruskal's (1964) multidimensional scaling technique, and hierarchical cluster analysis as exemplified by Johnson's method (Johnson 1966). Since the mathematical assumptions underlying these techniques have been treated extensively elsewhere, we will devote only a few brief comments to their methodological merits.

Kruskal's Multidimensional Scaling Analysis

Extending the work of Shepard (1962, 1963), Kruskal (1964a, b) arrived at a method of converting a similarity or dissimilarity matrix into an n-dimensional space, which rests on mathematically better assumptions than any previously developed method. A matrix of judged dissimilarities—obtained for instance by means of triadic comparisons—may be considered as a table of subjective distances between pairs of stimuli. In general these distances will express only ordinal relations between the stimulus pairs. If the dissimilarities are obtained by triadic comparisons for instance, the order will be a linear sequence from most similar to most dissimilar. For r stimuli an $(r-2)$ space can be constructed which will fully preserve the order of dissimilarities (distances) in the $r \times r$ matrix. Kruskal's analysis is a way of determining if the results will fit a metric n-space of lower dimension than $r-2$, without violating the order of dissimilarities.

Kruskal's program generates such a metric space of lower dimensions by an iterative procedure. The result being evaluated in terms of a stress coefficient:

$$S = \frac{\sum_{ij} (d_{ij} - \hat{d}_{ij})^2}{\sum_{ij} (d_{ij})^2} \tag{1}$$

in which d_{ij} represents the metric distance between points i and j in a given solution, and $\hat{d}_{ij}$ the best obtainable distance between i and j in that solution if the order of distances would not be violated.

This measure thus indicates to what extent the distances in a given configuration of r points in k dimensions will violate the *order* of distances dictated by the results. A perfect fit is obtained when the order of distances in the n-space is a strictly increasing function of the distances in the matrix. The stress is related to the average distance in the n-space, through the denominator in Equation 1. The amount of stress usually increases with a decreasing number of dimensions. The question is, how much stress is statistically acceptable for a particular configuration in order not to be the likely result of a random set of stimulus points.

Kruskal gave a coarse rule of thumb, which did not take into account the obvious relation between number of stimuli (r) and the number of dimensions (n) of the solution. An adequate statistical test was developed by Wagenaar and Padmos (1968), who derived significance levels for various values of r and n.

They used a Monte Carlo technique in which they started from completely random sets of inter-'stimulus' distances. Taking into account the probability that a certain stress level will arise from random arrays as well as various levels of measurement error, they arrived at strict decision criteria as to whether a given configuration would be accepted as the solution (Figure 4.2).

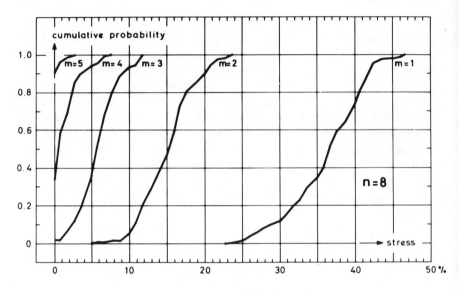

Figure 4.2 Cumulative probability of stress percentages in $k = 1, 2....5$
dimensions for random configurations of 8 points (from Wagenaar
and Padmos, 1968).

Another extension of multidimensional scaling that we shall need, pertains to the matching of several spaces. This problem was first solved by Plomp, Levelt and Van de Geer (1964) for 2 spaces, and later extended to the case of k spaces by Van de Geer (1968). This matching procedure will be helpful to see if and how an internal representation is modified during learning.

Altogether, by using Kruskal's Multidimensional Scaling technique, we are able to determine how subjects map, internally, the external world when it can be characterized by a number of (continuous) qualities, and if and how this mapping alters when the subject becomes more experienced. The technique is applicable whenever psychological distance, as measured by dissimilarity judgments, has a meaning.

Johnson's Hierarchical Clustering Scheme

A different approach, which applies strictly to hierarchical structures, was developed by Johnson (1966). In a hierarchical ordering we have essentially stimuli which are elements of a system of nested sets. In this system each set is in its turn partitioned in a number of equivalence sets, that is, an exhaustive division into nonoverlapping subsets.

From Figure 4.3 it follows easily that from any given point in the universal set U, the distance to all equivalent sets are equal. Distance is here expressed in terms of the number of (valued) set boundaries that must be crossed to reach a given point (or set) from another point.

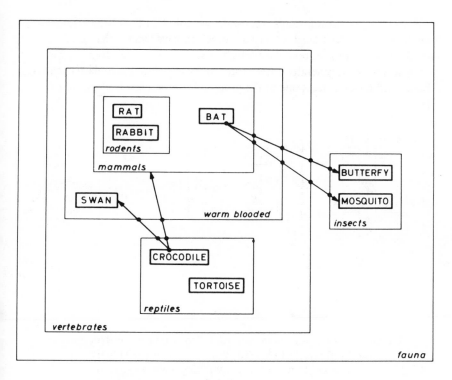

Figure 4.3   Nested set representation of part of the animal world.

A system of nested sets can be represented as a tree structure wherein each set boundary represents a decision node. Equivalent sets are branchings from the same node, and the ultimate elements of the nested set structure are found back in the terminal nodes of the tree. The level at which a branching occurs in a tree is determined by the cost of crossing a set boundary, but the levels usually have only an ordinal meaning.

The mathematical relation underpinning these two representations is the so called ultrametric distance relation

$$d(x, y) \leqslant \max \{ d(x, z), d(y, z) \} \tag{2}$$

This entails a stronger assumption than the normal triangular relation on which multidimensional scaling is based:

$$d(x, y) \leqslant d(x, z) + d(y, z) \tag{3}$$

Without repeating Johnson's arguments, we note that the ultrametric relation defines isosceles triangles, the sides of which have lengths that are determined by the cost of set boundary transitions. On this model, Johnson based an algorithm which generates a tree structure from a given dissimilarity matrix. This algorithm—or at least one of the proposed alternatives—is illustrated in Figure 4.4.

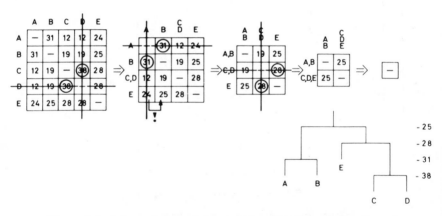

Figure 4.4   Johnson's branch-to-root algorithm for construction of hierarchical trees: (1) Search for most similar individuals; (2) collapse columns and rows by taking highest values of corresponding pairs of cells; (3) repeat until matrix is reduced completely.

The method has been used with very interesting results, for instance by Levelt (1969) who was able to derive linguistic phrase markers (Miller and Chomsky, 1964) of simple sentences, by having his subjects compare all triads of the words in these sentences. These subjective mappings of syntactic relation very much agreed with phrase markers obtained through linguistic analysis. (Notice that Levelt's experimental paradigm may be used for measuring progress in learning a foreign language). Miller (personal communication) used names of parts of the body and obtained the tree shown in Figure 4.5.

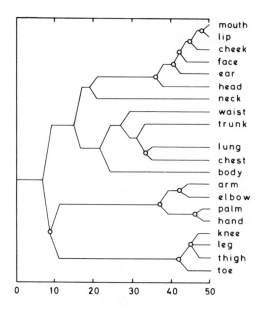

Figure 4.5   Tree for body scheme obtained with Johnson's technique.

This example brings up a methodological issue. It is necessary to distinguish between classification schemes, where the nodes are differentiating tests while only the terminal nodes represent individuals or species, and the pedigrees, which have individuals or species at both branching and terminal nodes. Johnson's method is clearly of the first type and Miller's example shows the inapplicability of this method to pedigree structures.

The Kruskal and Johnson techniques are complementary for the following reasons.

1. If for all branchings that occur at a given level in the hierarchy, the implicit decision to be made is identical, then the representation is in fact multidimensional, each hierarchical level being equivalent with one dimension. Strictly there is no need for these dimensions to be continuous; they may be dichotomous.

2. If the ultrametric (isosceles) relation is violated beyond chance level, Kruskal should be imperative. If the ultrametric inequality holds, Johnson is appropriate.

A test to determine which approach is appropriate has been derived by Miller (unpublished) working from assumptions put forward by Beals, Krantz and Tversky (1968).

So much for the two scaling techniques that were employed in the analysis of some experimental data to be discussed in the following sections.

MULTI-DIMENSIONAL REPRESENTATIONS

The Image of the City[1]

First we shall consider a variation on a theme by Kevin Lynch: "The image of the city". Lynch (1960) obtained mental images of several cities from interviews, drawings and imaginary walks of permanent residents.

Most cities can be described in two dimensions, any pair of points being separated by a certain distance. These distances can be measured as the birds fly, in which case Euclidean geometry is adequate, or as people go (which may be different for pedestrians, cyclists and drivers). In the latter case cityblock geometry is applicable in a most literal sense. Kruskal's method can handle both geometries (Kruskal 1964 a, b; Roskam 1968). In the instructions we have tried to remain as close to Euclidean space as possible. In the experiment subjects were given all possible triads out of eight stimuli, which were landmarks in the city of Utrecht, a map of which is given in Figure 4.6. Subjects were requested to indicate which pair out of each triad they judged to be closest and which pair to be farthest apart.

Twelve subjects took part in the experiment: 3 were life-long residents of Utrecht, 3 were residents of approximately 3 years standing, 3 had lived in Utrecht for less than a year and 3 had had less than 2 months of experience in Utrecht. Each subject compared all $\binom{8}{3}$ = 56 triads twice.

The results of each group of subjects were analyzed separately by means of Kruskal's MDSCAL program adapted for use on PDP-7 computer. The dimensionality was—for obvious reasons—chosen to be 2.

The results are shown in Figure 4.6. The location of the landmarks is shown on a map of the center of Utrecht. Also shown is the optimal Kruskal solution (stress 0.01 percent) obtained from a similarity matrix which was based on triadic comparisons of the real distance relations. Thus the smallest real distance between any 3 landmarks was assigned the value 2, and so on.

---

[1] I wish to acknowledge the cooperation of Mr. C. M. E. Blom in this experiment.

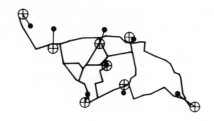

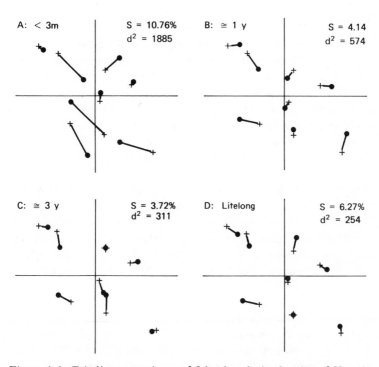

Figure 4.6   Triadic comparisons of 8 landmarks in the city of Utrecht.
Top: relation between geographical locations and Kruskal's
solution. *A-D*: relation between objective and subjective
configurations as function of experience.

It appeared that the optimal solution does not reproduce the actual geographical distances correctly. Therefore the optimal solutions for each group of
subjects was matched with the derived map rather than with the actual map of
Utrecht (Figure 4.6*A* to *D*). The fit of the various groups, as measured by the

stress percentage and the squared distances between the subjects' and the derived objective locations, is seen to improve beyond the level of 1 year experience. No improvement is found between 3 years and lifelong experience.

It would be interesting to check carefully the type of experience (walking, driving, etc.) of our subjects. Also the importance of the landmarks used as stimuli could be varied. Probably all of the landmarks used are important points in a basic grid. Other points might be found that have no such function. Some studies by Pailhous (1968) on the internal representations of Paris taxi drivers show the existence of a basic grid and several secondary grids, which are confined to small parts of the town and are related only to the basic grid.

Word Matrix Learning[2]

A second experiment was based on an experimental technique employed earlier by the present author (Michon, 1968). Subjects were shown the contents of a computer-stored 6 x 6 matrix cell by cell. Each cell contained a short word of 3 to 5 letters, and these words were displayed on an alphanumeric scope display, hooked up to a PDP-7 computer. Each word was shown 2.00 seconds, after which an arrow would flash, pointing in the direction where the next word to be presented was located in the matrix with respect to the displayed word. The arrow was visible for 1.00 second, after which both word and arrow were replaced by the new word, and so on. Using this method a pseudorandom path was traveled, in which each orthogonal connection between all adjacent cells was made an almost equal number of times.

The stimulus words were simple high frequency Dutch words of 4 and 5 letters. Subjects were given a presentation of 100 words in a run, in the way described above, after which they were asked to judge the distances between 7 critical cells by means of triadic comparison. After having completed the 35 triads, they were given another run of 100 words, followed by another set of triadic comparisons. The second time 7 other words were chosen in such a way that the spatial relations of the configuration remained the same. This was achieved by rotating the configuration by 90° with respect to the matrix, and using the words covered by the rotated configuration (Figure 4.7). In this way two goals were achieved at the same time which would be absent had the same seven critical words been used every time: (1) the subjects did not have the opportunity to pay extra attention to the seven critical words of the first comparison trial; and (2) providing a more complete coverage of the internal

---

[2] This experiment is part of a study carried out at present by the author and Dr. B. A. Fairbank, visiting research associate at the Institute for Perception.

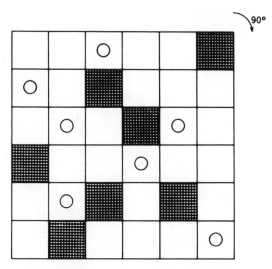

Figure 4.7   Critical cells in 6 x 6 word matrix (shaded cells). By rotating the configuration, other words become critical (circles), while configuration and distances between cells remain the same.

representation while accumulating information on one and the same spatial configuration.

The subjects were given a series of runs plus triadic comparisons up to the point where they felt they were able to draw the correct matrix. The whole session lasted approximately 2 hours. The results of all subjects were pooled in a distance matrix, separately for each learning stage, and these matrices were subjected to a Kruskal analysis. The resulting configurations for a pool of three subjects are shown in Figure 4.8 for all even trials in the series of runs.

The large diagram shows the path of the seven points, described in the two-dimensional Kruskal space within the frame of reference of the 6 x 6 matrix. The position of the grid with respect to the coordinate system was derived from the starting configuration on which the Kruskal analysis was based. The cell in which word (6) was located was given coordinate values (0, 0), whence the eccentric position of the grid. Below the main diagram the successive configurations obtained in the even trials are shown in small grids. The amount of stress is indicated in each case. Only after the fourth trial is there a considerable drop in stress percentage reaching the 5 percent level set by Wagenaar and Padmos (1968). The configuration of trial 2, almost a regular heptagon, illustrates the optimal solution to random data: all distances are made as equal as possible in two dimensions.

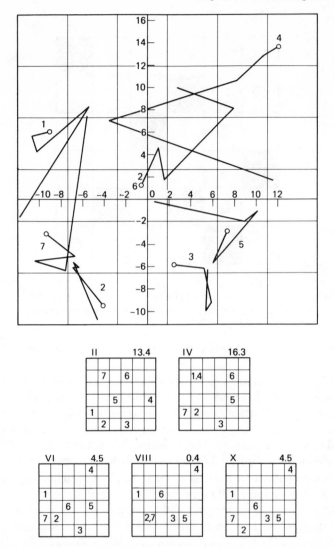

Figure 4.8   Successive (even) trials in word matrix learning experiment.

HIERARCHICAL REPRESENTATIONS

The Animal World

We shall follow a course of arguments which closely traces that of the preceding section. The first example is based on a theme by Desmond Morris

(1967). In *The Naked Ape* he refers to a study of children's preferences for various animals. The animals most liked by young children of age 4-7 years, are relatively small mammals, with flat and expressive faces, furry, rounded, and upright. Later these preferences change and other characteristics of the animals become more important, such as the fun that the animal may provide (dogs to play with, horses to ride on).

The distinctive features indicated by Morris are not, generally, suitable as classificatory principles for the *regnum animale* as adults know it; yet they may serve the child's needs for ordering. It seems worthwhile to study the growth of the internal representation of the animal world to see in how far the external classificatory principles concocted by systematic zoologists determine the subjective model with increasing age.

Schematic drawings of eight animals, given in Figure 4.9 were presented in triads to a girl of 4, a girl of 5, two boys of 7, a boy of 14 years and an adult of some scientific sophistication (though not in biological taxonomy). The latter two subjects were given the names of the animals instead of the drawings. Subjects were asked to indicate which pair out of each three animals belonged most closely together and which pair belonged least together. The experiment was repeated once after a few days. The 2 x 56 triads were converted into a similarity matrix, by assigning 2 points to each pair judged "most", 0 points to each pair judged "least", and 1 point to the neutral third pair. Then Johnson's hierarchical clustering analysis, as described in Figure 4.4 was carried out on these similarity matrices. The resulting trees are shown in Figure 4.10. These trees show that the oldest two subjects have almost a perfect image of the animal world—at least of the rather modest part that was covered by the experiment. On the other hand, the children have representations which not only are vastly different from what official biology teaches, but they are also idiosyncratic. This was already pointed out by Morris (1967). More specifically we may conclude that two types of distinctive features dominate the internal representation of children:

1. Biologically irrevelant phenotypical resemblances like "both have a long tail". A typical example is the resemblance between the ears of the rabbit and the wings of the mosquito shown in Figure 4.9. This occurs only in the youngest children, who obviously have not yet acquired much of an internal connotation of the various animals.

2. Behavioral characteristics, like "both bite" or "they can swim." These mainly occur in the 6 and 7 year old children.

Due to its size, this experiment does not bring out many developmental aspects of the growth of internal representation, and certainly does not add much to what is known from the work of, for instance, Bruner, Ollver, and Greenfield (1966), or Piaget and Inhelder (1964). It serves its methodological purpose

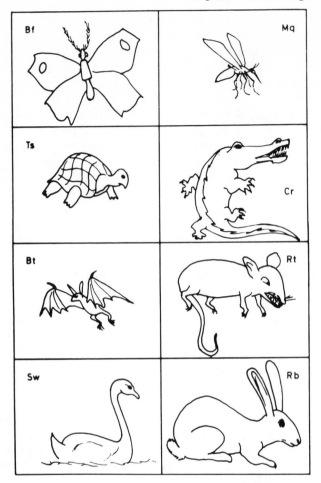

Figure 4.9   Schematic drawings of animals.

however. It shows that one of the 7 years olds is somewhat more advanced than the other young subjects. It is also clear that even for the 4 year old children a hierarchical ordering can be found: the animals stand apart in cognitive space, although the representation is strongly dominated by the properties of the visual stimuli.

Pedigrees[3]

The results of the previous experiment were again based on cross-sectional data, which do not show the growth of the individual representation. A

[3]See footnote 2.

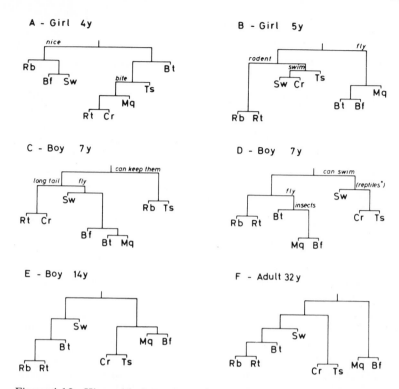

Figure 4.10   Hierarchical structure of animal world as a function of age.

longitudinal example, based on the theme of family relations, will be presented. Family relations have the advantage of having been studied extensively, especially by anthropologists (e.g. Romney and d'Andrade, 1964; Sanday, 1967), so that internal representations of family structure are rather well known. In the present context we are not especially interested in the completeness of the network of family relations, but in the way subjects *learn* the relations within a given pedigree when they are allowed to ask questions about any pair of individuals constituting the family.

Family trees of various shapes were used as stimulus materials in this experiment. Subjects had permanent access to a complete, alphabetical list of the names occurring in a tree. When they asked for the relation between, say, Ben and John, the experimenter would answer "Ben is an uncle of John," or something appropriate. All family relations that have unambiguous denotations in Dutch were used in the answers. These relations are given in Figure 4.11 with reference to Ego. Only relations between male persons were used. If a question exceeded the denotative frame of reference given in Figure 4.11, the

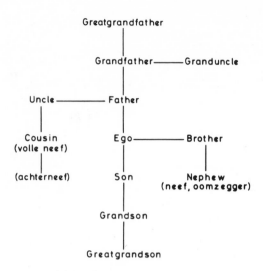

Figure 4.11   Family relations allowed in answering questions of subjects.

answer given to the subject would be "Ben and John are too far apart." Subjects asked 60 questions in succession, upon which they estimated the degree of relatedness of seven of the names in the tree by triadic comparison. These seven names were always terminal nodes of the tree. No internal nodes were chosen, for reasons indicated above with reference to Miller's body scheme experiment. After having completed the 35 triads, another block of 60 questions was asked and answered, followed by a new series of triadic comparisons of the same seven names, until the subject felt that he could draw the family tree without error. He was then given the opportunity to draw it, and if no error was made, the experiment was terminated. The drawings always came after the triadic comparisons. If the subject made an error in his drawing he was given another block of questions, and so on.

From the similarity matrix trees were obtained, again by using Johnson's method. As before, the ultrametric relation was sometimes violated to a lesser or greater extent. For the purpose of demonstration, we have neglected to take these violations into account; the smaller the violation, the fewer ternary or quaternary branchings.

Two of the trees used in the experiments are shown in Figure 4.12. This figure also shows the results of successive triadic comparisons for several subjects. In general we see that in time the trees derived from the similarity matrices become more well structured, more hierarchical, and better representations of reality. Comparison with the drawings indicated that not always will the correct hierarchical structures derived from the scaling results coincide with

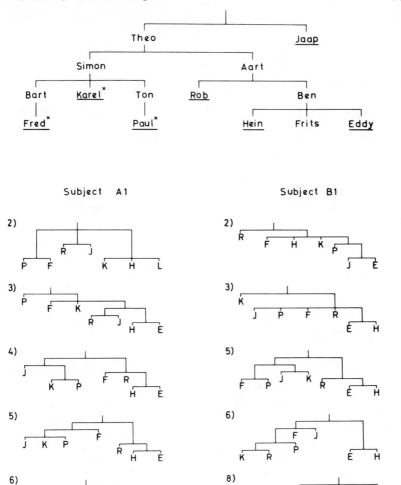

Figure 4.12*a* Tree development during learning of family relations.

correct drawings. Each may be correct while the other is wrong. For some subjects triadic comparisons seemed to be very difficult to reconcile with their actually correct representation—which appears in their drawing. Moreover some subjects complained that the triadic comparisons preceding the drawing added confusion to their pictures. This is probably a simple effect of forgetting in a state where there is no overlearning yet.

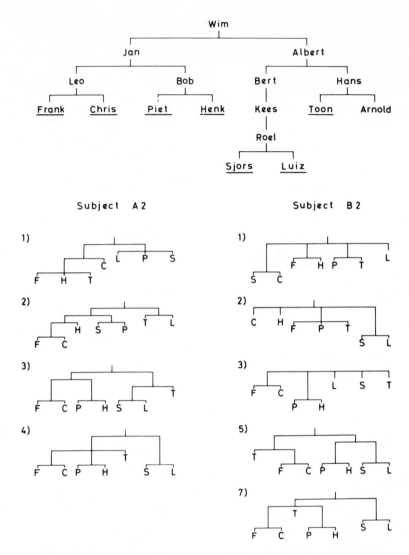

Figure 4.12*b*   Tree development during learning of family relations.

The results show that it is possible to demonstrate growth and differentiation of hierarchical relations during the learning of complex data structures, and that the method used can reveal the presence of a correct internal representation.

Echoes of RASURA[4]

The problem is how to derive a hierarchical representation for a complex perceptual task from the judgments of experts, in order to structure the training program for teaching this perceptual skill.

RASURA is a portable incoherent pulse Doppler Radar System with auditory display. It is mainly used for point control, to detect events at or near road intersections or bridges, for example especially at night. Such events manifest themselves as squeaks, whines, and rattles in the watchkeeper's headphones. Moving objects and moving parts of objects will produce a time varying frequency spectrum, as can be seen in Figure 4.13. The training of RASURA personnel consists mainly of lessons in identifying targets of various kinds under various conditions. These lessons are in part preprogramed on audio-tape, for the other part they consist of field exercises, in which actual objects and men have to be detected and identified.

The difficulties of training RASURA personnel are very similar to those encountered in underwater sound detection (SONAR) training. The sounds are very similar in RASURA and SONAR, and the final performance will be approximately at the same level of 50 to 60 percent in both cases. RASURA may be a little easier because of the greater directionality of the system: at a road intersection we do not expect a flying helicopter or a motor boat. The task being the same, the teaching problems are also very similar. Some of them were formulated by Corcoran *et al* (1967).

Since sound identification will usually be by means of verbal labels, some questions can be raised about training procedures:

"Are the proper verbal labels being used? Verbal labels are used copiously. . . .in order (a) to orientate the listener toward the relevant sound and away from the masking noise, (b) to point out features of the sound which are thought to distinguish it from other sounds, and (c) to aid in the retention of the sounds. Verbal labels may be necessary to train human operators but hazards are involved; for example (a) The trainer may fail to communicate with the trainee or may even give him "incorrect" information by an unfortunate choice of descriptive. (b) The programmer may be wrong in his choice of relevant sound characteristics. (c) Labels may actually impair retention of a sound by causing the trainee to "squeeze" his experience into an inappropriate category" (Corcoran *et al*, 1967, p. 3).

[4] The work on the RASURA training was carried out with the assistance of Mr. E. Alberts of the State University of Groningen, in partial fulfillment of the requirements leading to the degree of Doctorandus of Psychology.

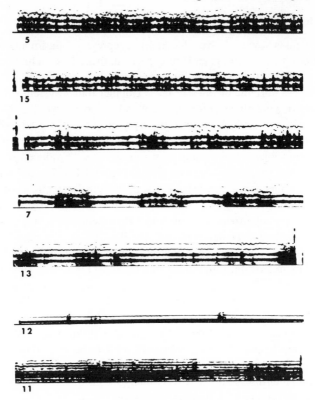

Figure 4.13   Samples of RASURA-Sounds (Sonograph recording)
Numbers refer to Table 4.1.

The present experiment was run as part of a more comprehensive study of
RASURA training, with the aim of checking on the progress of trainees towards
an adequate internal representation. Since we found that the instructors in the
course—who had been trainees themselves only 4 to 6 months earlier—were not
able to state explicitly by which distinctive features they were able to identify
the stimuli, we decided to use their results in the triadic comparison experiment as a basis for structuring the training course. The effect of this decision
can not be estimated as yet since the work on developing a new training course
is only in its planning stage. We will therefore restrict the exposition to the
evaluation of the internal representations that we found in our subjects.

In the experiment 15 stimuli were used, as listed in Table 4.1. This table contains a confusion matrix, displaying the likelihood that advanced trainees will
confuse one target with another.

The subjects were eight trainees and six instructors. Their age ranged from
19 to 25 years, with one exception: one of the instructors was 34 years of age.

TABLE 4.1. Target Designations and Confusions for 15 RASURA-Echoes

presented →	answered 1	2	3	4	5	6	7	8	9	10	11	12	13	14	15	16
1) 1 walking man	48	22	3	7	7	9	1	3	2	-	-	-	2	-	7	1
2) 4 walking men	14	56	4	2	10	10	-	-	4	1	-	-	-	-	10	1
3) 1 running man	3	-	65	20	5	1	1	7	1	1	-	-	2	-	4	2
4) 3 running men	5	9	25	47	4	1	-	-	12	5	-	-	-	-	3	1
5) 1 crawling man	6	7	3	5	36	17	-	-	15	-	-	-	2	-	21	-
6) 2 crawling men	2	8	1	4	14	49	-	-	6	-	-	-	2	-	25	1
7) hand corner reflector	-	-	-	-	-	-	109	3	-	-	-	-	-	-	-	-
8) autom. corner reflector	2	1	1	2	1	-	7	97	-	-	-	-	-	-	1	-
9) light shrubbery	-	5	2	5	3	5	-	-	85	-	-	-	1	-	6	-
10) slow motor vehicle	-	-	-	-	1	-	-	-	-	104	2	-	2	-	-	3
11) fast motor vehicle	-	-	-	-	-	-	-	-	-	-	107	-	4	1	-	-
12) tank	-	-	-	-	-	-	-	-	-	-	1	105	1	4	-	1
13) bicycle rider	-	-	-	-	1	2	-	-	-	5	1	1	97	-	2	3
14) flying helicopter	-	-	-	-	-	-	-	-	-	-	1	4	-	107	-	-
15) herd of cattle	3	6	2	10	3	14	-	-	7	2	-	-	-	-	60	5

All had been tested for hearing losses, and none had been found to be defective. The subjects, four at a time, were seated in small cubicles, equipped with a headphone and a triangular box. Three pushbuttons were mounted on the box, one in each corner. By pressing one of the buttons the subjects could listen to a stimulus sound. Buttons could be pressed only in succession to produce a burst of one of the three sounds that constituted a given triad. The stimuli came from continuous 15 minute recordings of the 15 targets listed in Table 1, recorded on 15 separate magnetic tape cassettes. By simply inserting three of the cassettes in cassette tape recorders triads of stimuli could be presented at a reasonably fast rate. The output of the recorders was amplified appropriately before being presented to the subjects' earphones, and the sound level was approximately 60 to 70 dB, due to variations in the sound characteristics.

Since 15 stimuli would require $\binom{15}{3} = 455$ triadic comparisons, the procedure followed by Plomp, Levelt, and Van de Geer (1965) was used, in which each subject was given only two balanced blocks of 35 triads to compare. This took approximately 2 hours, on consecutive days, instead of an estimated 13 hours for the complete triadic experiment.

The eight trainees judged the 70 triads with respect to similarity before they had any training, and also after they had had an intensive training of 6 half-hour periods on consecutive days. During this training they were given instances of the 15 stimuli in random order, with knowledge of results. Their final performance in a test session reached an average of 70 percent, which compares well with the performance after 10 to 15 hours of training with the conventional try-and-discuss method, currently in use. (The expert instructors reached an average of 82 percent on this test). After the training week the eight subjects did the triadic comparisons once more. The six instructors did the triadic comparisons only once. As before, similarity matrices were prepared and analyzed with the hierarchical cluster analysis. The results are given in Figure 4.14.

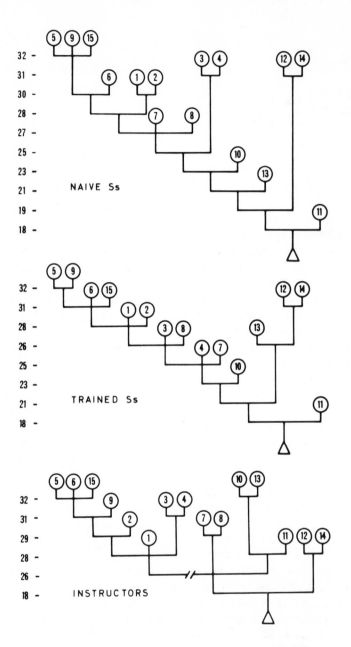

Figure 4.14   Trees for RASURA-targets. Numbers refer to Table 4.1.

Although there is violation of the ultrametric relation, the results appeared to be more interpretable than those of a Kruskal analysis on the same data. The violations occur especially where discriminability is low, as for instance between one or more crawling men and a herd of cattle. This ties in with the confusion matrix presented in Table 4.1.

The results make clear, however, that experience leads to better differentiation in the hierarchical structure. Naive subjects tend to eliminate only one alternative at a time, which means that they need up to 10 decision nodes to reach a decision (which is not necessarily correct, of course). After training a somewhat better tree with only eight decision levels is found, while the instructors need only six levels (four being the minimum for 15 stimuli). It can also be seen that the instructors outperform the trained subjects, for instance, by combining stimuli 7 plus 8, and 10, 11 plus 13, though they have the same difficulty with stimuli 5, 6, 9 and 15. These targets can not be distinguished reliably, and in more recent tape recorded lessons they have been replaced by other stimuli.

Although the expert's tree is apparently not the best of all possible representations, it can serve as a starting point for a training course based on distinctive features. For this purpose the structure of Table 4.2 was proposed as a working hypothesis for further testing. Comparison with Figure 4.14 will make clear to what extent the instructors performance was used in constructing Table 4.2.

TABLE 4.2. Distinctive Features to Serve as a Basis for a RASURA Training Program

Level 0	Level 1	Level 2	Level 3	Level 4	Sound
			few components > 1500 cps		15,9 (not discriminable)
		a-rhythmical			
				no phase shifts	5
			many components > 1500 cps	phase shifts	6
	rough				
				no phase shifts	1
			freq. of rhythm < 1.5 cps	phase shifts	2
		rhythmical			
				no phase shifts	3
			freq. of rhythm > 1.5 cps		
				phase shifts	4

TABLE 4.2. Distinctive Features to Serve as a Basis for a RASURA Training Program (continued)

Level 0	Level 1	Level 2	Level 3	Level 4	Sound
sound					
			regular		8
		modulated			
			irregular	few components > 1500 cps	7
				many components > 1500 cps	13
	smooth				
			many components > 1200 cps	slow changes in pitch	10
				fast changes in pitch	11
		monotonous			
			few components > 1200 cps	irregular bursts with wide spectrum	12
				regular bursts (appr. 10 cps)	14

DISCUSSION AND CONCLUSIONS

This brings us to the end of our examples of the applicability of modern multidimensional and hierarchical scaling techniques to cognitive processes, in particular to the measurement of learning progress. Some critical remarks may be raised at this point.

(1) The work reported here, to the extent that it deals with learning in the wide sense of the word, is entirely at the descriptive level. Its specific aim was to investigate the possibilities of describing the internal organization of complex data structures. No attempt was made to formalize the learning process. The approach is essentially structural, rather than functional. Although we have given no explicit thoughts to this, it appears that the dynamics of both the n-dimensional representations and the hierarchical trees may be open to

quantitative descriptions, if we have the right amount of the right data. The work on EPAM for example shows the possibility of dealing with a psychological tree growing in the functional sense. The state-space approach to group interactions as worked out for instance by Simon (1957) and Coleman (1964), in particular with respect to Homans' model, might be applicable in certain cases. In Coleman's approach in fact cross-sectional are used to derive longitudinal dynamic descriptions of attitude changes.

Such models could possibly show such effects as the trade-off between acquisition of data and stability of the internal representation, or deformations caused by natural forgetting, or provide insight in the process of interiorization—from perception to cognition—in perceptual learning. With respect to computer modeling of the learning process the approach adopted in the present paper may open the possibility to compare the totally covert behavior displayed by the program—for example the net growing in EPAM—with similar processes in man.

(2) Only two representation modes have been selected for our exposition. It is not clear to what extent internal representations take the form of n-spaces or tree structures. We should be warned by Green's comments about quantitative models: should we consider them "as a good description of reality or as fictions contributed by the method of analysis?" (Green, 1968, p. 98). I have been impressed by the clarity and relevance of Green's comments on this matter. Yet I think it is of relatively little importance to psychological analysis—or for any quantitative science—in what language nature is questioned. It will respond in the same language, and as long as we specify our language we should not expect one approach to be more artificial than the other. At best they are complementary.

To illustrate this, an example from a study by Pols (1971) on automatic speech recognition may serve. In these experiments speech sounds were analyzed by triadic comparison. A perceptual n-space was constructed by means of Kruskal's technique. Successive parts of a spoken word are represented by a trace in this space. A newly presented word is analyzed physically and the location of the trace in the perceptual space is calculated. The result is compared with the traces already represented, and if the resemblance is close enough, identification is achieved. Even if we have no real n-space representation in cases where we Kruskalize our data, the model may be psychologically relevant, and provide the basis for an information processing theory describing the phenomena.

Finally, the relevance of other methods to describe the acquisition, use, and decay of internal representations is in no way diminished by the choice of methods in this paper.

CHAPTER 5

Allan M. Collins
&
M. Ross Quillian
Bolt Beranek & Newman, Inc.
Cambridge, Massachusetts

EXPERIMENTS ON SEMANTIC MEMORY AND LANGUAGE COMPREHENSION*

The kind of research we will report here is in part a return to the introspective research of the 19th century [see for example Cattell, (1887)]. It is dressed up in modern clothes, such as microswitches and CRTs, and it is even based on a computer model. But, a major part of this research involves asking people questions like "True or false—A canary is blue?" Then their introspections are gathered up and reshaped into hypotheses, which we try to test with reaction time (RT) experiments. Surely this method of getting inside a person's head violates the vow of chastity sworn by behaviorism, but even though we cheat, the hypotheses sometimes fail. The failures do at least show that the hypotheses can be disproved, which is not always the case in psychology.

THE TEACHABLE LANGUAGE COMPREHENDER

The questions posed in these experiments derive from a computer model called the Teachable Language Comprehender (Quillian, 1969), a program for comprehending written text. The program comprehends text by relating it to memory structures in a semantic network filled with factual information [see Quillian, (1967, 1968)]. A piece of such a network is pictured in Figure 5.1. Though oversimplified, it illustrates most of the basic concepts we need to explain the experiments.

In the network, each word is stored with a configuration of pointers to other words in memory. The word concepts are the nodes, and the pointers are the connections in the network. Consider the word canary, for example. Suppose that stored with canary is "a yellow bird that can sing." Then, as shown in Figure 5.1, there is a pointer to bird which is the category name or *superset* of canary. There are also pointers to two *properties*: (i) is yellow and (ii) can sing.

The research reported in this paper was sponsored by the Training Research Division, Air Force Human Resources Laboratory, Air Force Systems Command, WPAFB, Ohio, under Contract No. F33615-67-C-1982 with Bolt Beranek and Newman, Inc. and also partly by Advanced Research Projects Agency, monitored by the Air Force Cambridge Research Laboratories, under Contract No. F19628-68-C-0125.

We would like to thank Joseph Markowitz, Daniel Bobrow, Tony Bell, Ray Nickerson, Barbara Noel, and Joseph Becker for their contributions to this research.

117

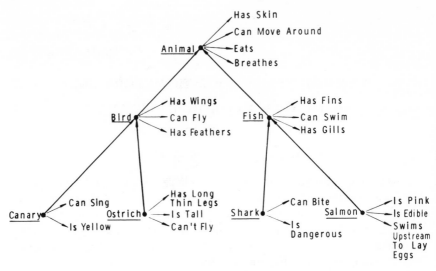

Figure 5.1   Illustration of the hypothetical memory structure for a
3-level hierarchy (from Collins and Quillian, 1969).

Information true of birds in general (e.g., can fly, have wings, and have
feathers) need not be stored with the memory node for each separate kind of
bird. Instead, the fact that "A canary can fly" can be inferred by finding that a
canary is a bird and that birds can fly.[1] By storing generalizations in this way,
the amount of space required for storage is minimized.

According to the model, to comprehend language is to find a path through
the semantic network that interrelates the words of a sentence in a manner permitted by the sentence's syntax. As an example, "A canary has skin" would be
comprehended by finding the path: a canary is a bird, a bird is an animal, and
an animal has skin (see Figure 5.1).

The strategy for finding paths utilizes an *intersection* technique, which can be
described simply for finding a path between canary and fish in Figure 5.1. The
first step is to start at both of these nodes, and trace along all of the pointers to
other nodes in the network. From canary in Figure 5.1 this process will arrive in
one step at (a) bird, (b) sing, and (c) yellow. At each of these nodes a tag will
be left indicating which node led to this tag—in this case the tag will indicate
canary. Similarly for fish, tags will be left at (a) animal, (b) fins, (c) swim, and
(d) gills. On the next step from canary, the intersection routine will arrive at

[1] There are exceptions, of course. An ostrich is a bird, but cannot fly. We assume that
this information is stored with the node for ostrich, just as in a dictionary. Thus the errone-
ous inference that an ostrich can fly is precluded, because the lower level information will be
reached first, given a sentence about ostriches.

animal and find the tag already there from fish. By tracing back along the steps that led to this intersection, the shortest path between canary and fish will be found. When such a path is found, then it must be checked to see if the relation found between the two nodes is permitted by the verb (or other relation) in the sentence. Obviously the path found above would not be a permissible interpretation for "A canary is a fish" but would be for "A canary is related to a fish."

The Teachable Language Comprehender can also be considered as a model of human learning. Most psychological theories of learning have concentrated on how new associations are formed, as when a person learns a list of words or syllables that have arbitrarily been paired. Learning new associations is involved in a child's original learning of the names for things, and in learning new words in a foreign language; but very little human learning is of that kind. Most of what a person learns in school or from books comes in sentences that interrelate concepts he already knows something about. For instance, suppose a person reads a sentence like "There is a kind of ostrich in Australia that can fly." A person reading this has prior knowledge about ostriches, about Australia, and about flying, and learning what this sentence says requires him to use this knowledge to put together a complex new structure. He must use facts like: an ostrich is a bird, birds generally can fly, ostriches cannot fly, and Australia is a place with unfamiliar life forms. To comprehend the sentence he finds paths in his semantic network interrelating these pieces of stored information in particular ways. From these interrelations, in turn, he can construct new pieces of information in the same format as the pieces already stored. Most learning then proceeds by building new structures on the basis of preexisting structures, and not by forming arbitrary new associations.

How fully a person understands a sentence—or any experience he has—depends on how much stored information he relates to it (this is the question of *richness* described in Quillian, 1969). For instance, with the above sentence a person who knows and utilizes the fact that Australia is a continent southeast of Asia understands the sentence more fully than someone who only knows Australia is a place somewhere, and more correctly than someone who confuses Australia with Austria. In general, utilization of any one particular piece of knowledge is not essential for making sense of a sentence. As an extreme example, even the fact that ostriches are birds is not necessary for comprehension of the sentence given. If one knows an ostrich is an animal of some kind, then this sentence can be taken to establish the existence of such flying animals. The essential point here is that there can be large differences between people as to which particular information and how much information they use in comprehending any particular sentence.

This is a summary of some of the basic concepts in the model. The *raison d'être* of the experiments described in the following sections is to determine whether the Teachable Language Comprehender is a valid model of human semantic memory and language comprehension.

HOW PEOPLE DECIDE A SENTENCE IS TRUE

To test the model's applicability to human memory, we have used a true/false reaction time technique. A number of different sentences, some true and some false, are displayed one at a time on a screen. A subject presses one button if he *confirms* the statement as true, another button if he *rejects* the statement as false. The time between the onset of the sentence and his response is his reaction time (RT).

The first experiment (Collins and Quillian, 1969) was a test of some predictions about human information retrieval derived from the memory structure in the model. For example, suppose a person has stored the information in Figure 5.1 in the manner illustrated. Then, to confirm that "A canary can sing," the person need only start at the node canary and retrieve the properties stored there. But, to confirm that "A canary can fly," the person must move up one level to bird before he can retrieve the property about flying. Thus, the person should require more *time* to confirm that "A canary can fly" than to confirm that "A canary can sing." Similarly, the person should require still longer to confirm that "A canary has skin," because this fact is stored with his node for animal, which is yet another step removed from canary. Sentences which refer directly to a node and its supersets—"A canary is a canary," "A canary is a bird," or "A canary is an animal"—should also require decision times proportional to the number of levels separating the memory nodes referred to.

To state our predictions precisely we had to make four assumptions about retrieval, which we will enumerate briefly:

1. It takes time to move through each step (i.e., from a node to a property or from a node to a superset).

2. Where one step is dependent upon completion of another step, the times are additive.

3. Retrieval proceeds from a node in all directions at once, that is to say, in parallel.

4. The average time for any step is independent of which particular level(s) is involved.

Based upon the memory structure of the model and these four processing assumptions, the increases in decision time (or RT) discussed should only reflect the time it takes to move from one level to the next. Therefore we predicted that these time increases would all be equal.

In constructing sentences for this study we used different nouns for each sentence. To illustrate this, one set of sentences is shown in Table 5.1. We have labeled sentences that state property relations, P sentences, and those that state superset relations, S sentences. The appended numbers indicate the number of levels the model predicts it would be necessary to move through to confirm the sentence as true. We used many two-level hierarchies, as well as three-level hierarchies because there were very few three-level hierarchies where we could find common cultural agreement on the proper categorization and the English word to label the category. The false sentences were restricted to reasonable sentences that were always (rather than usually) false. Also the superset/property distinction was carried over from the true sentences. The order of sentences from different sets was pseudorandom.

TABLE 5.1. Examples of the Kinds of Sentences Used in
Experiment 1

P0 An oak has acorns.	P A hemlock has buckeyes.
P1 A spruce has branches.	P A poplar has thorns.
P2 A birch has seeds.	P A dogwood is lazy.
S0 A maple is a maple.	S A pine is barley.
S1 A cedar is a tree.	S A juniper is grain.
S2 An elm is a plant.	S A willow is grass.

The results of this experiment are shown in Figure 5.2. An analysis of variance shows the differences between sentence types and between levels to be significant. Equal RT increases, as predicted by the model, should have produced parallel lines. This prediction held, except that the point for sentences like "A canary is a canary" is out of line. But there is a simple explanation for this exception: subjects indicated that they decided about such sentences without even referring to their meaning—by pattern matching. That pattern matching can shorten RT has been demonstrated by Posner and Mitchell (1967).

It can be concluded, if one accepts the model and disregards the S0 point as distorted by pattern matching, that the time to move from a node to its superset is on the order of 75 milliseconds, this figure being the average RT increase from P0 to P1, P1 to P2, and S1 to S2. The differences between S1 and P1 and between S2 and P2, which average to about 225 milliseconds, represent the time it takes to retrieve a property from the node at the level where we assume it is stored. However, at this point we think that these time differences are highly dependent on the experimental conditions. A later study (Collins and Quillian, 1970a) using only two-level hierarchies found the same difference between S1 and P1 sentences (about 230 milliseconds), but the P0 sentences were moved down to the level of S1 sentences, so that the P0 and P1 difference was much larger. Thus, we were able to replicate the general finding, but not the specific processing time to move from one level to the next.

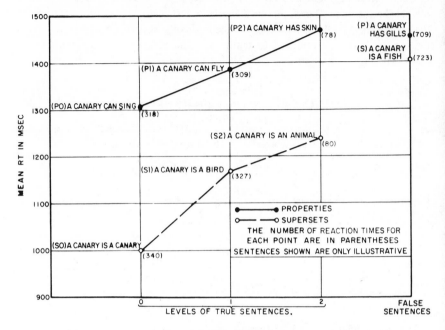

Figure 5.2   Average reaction times for different types of sentences in Experiment 1 (from Collins and Quillian, 1969).

Landauer and Freedman (1968), in a study which they construed as testing the effects of category size, found only a 29 milliseconds RT difference[2] for categorizing an instance, such as collie, as a dog as opposed to categorizing it as an animal. The instances used were always members of both categories. Their procedure was quite different from ours, and it would tend to reduce the differences found. But the fact that their results are in the same direction as the differences we found support the basic model we are presenting. Their explanation of their RT differences is that categories such as animal are much larger than categories such as dog. However, we would argue that their differences result from the fact that an instance, such as collie, is closer in the semantic network to a category such as dog than to a category such as animal. It might be possible to disentangle the two

[2]This paragraph refers only to Landauer and Freedman's results for positive instances in Experiment 1. The experiment discussed in this paragraph is reported in Collins and Quillian (1970b).

explanations by having subjects categorize instances which tend to have animal as their direct superset (such as elephant, mouse, fox) into the category animal, while categorizing instances such as collie, terrier, and spaniel into the category dog. Then any differences found could not be explained in terms of semantic distance, and would probably derive from category size (assuming word length and frequency were controlled). We doubt that there would, in fact, be any differences.

To ascertain whether there were any artifacts contributing to the RT differences we found, we computed for each of the sentence types the average sentence length, weighted averages of the word-frequencies [based on the general count of Thorndike and Lorge, (1944)], and averages of four subjects' ratings of saliency for the properties, with respect to the node where each property was assumed to be stored. None of these produced any consistent differences that could account for the RT differences found, except for the very high word-frequencies of the superset words used such as bird and animal. It has been demonstrated by Howes (see Miller, 1951) that RTs for identifying high frequency words are faster than for identifying low frequency words. Therefore, these high word-frequencies may have tended to lower the RTs to S1 and S2 sentences, which would increase the difference (the 225 milliseconds) between the curves for P sentences and S sentences. Word-frequencies may also explain why false S sentences were rejected some 50 milliseconds faster on the average than false P sentences, as shown in Figure 5.2.

That such a word-frequency effect could indeed contribute to systematic RT differences turned up in a control study we did later. It had occurred to us that if we took all the true sentences in Experiment 1 which made an assertion about a property, for example, "A canary can fly", we could turn them into P0 sentences. By this transformation a P0 sentence like "A canary can sing" would remain the same, a P1 sentence like "A canary can fly" would become the P1-t sentence "A bird can fly", and a P2 sentence like "A canary has skin" would become the P2-t sentence "An animal has skin". In each case the subject noun is the node where we assume the property is stored, as in the original set of P0 sentences. Based on this, our prediction was that all three types of true sentences should have equal RTs. If the transformed sentences were to show the same RT increases as were found in Experiment 1, then it would undercut our explanation of those results. The true sentences were again intermixed with an equal number of false sentences, and the experiment was run on subjects not used in the previous experiment.

The results of this experiment for the true sentences are shown in Table 5.2.[3] As is quite evident, our prediction of equal times did not hold up, but the differences are not in the same direction as those found in Experiment 1. The second group was significantly faster than the first and third groups. We think the reason for this is the high word-frequencies in the

second group, particularly for superset words like bird, which were introduced as the subject nouns by the transformation described above. The
RTs in the three types of true sentences followed the same order as the
average word-frequencies, though by word-frequencies alone we would have
expected the third group to be nearer the second group than the first.
The reason why word-frequencies are critical is probably because they
correspond to the time it takes to find the correct node from the printed
word. For example, a sentence like "A sheepdog is shaggy" may have a long
RT not because the property shaggy takes a long time to retrieve, but
because the concept node for sheepdog takes a long time to identify from the
printed word. In conclusion, it should be emphasized that both kinds of
transformed sentences were faster than the original P0 sentences and these
differences would tend to reduce the increases we found over P0 sentences
in Experiment 1.

TABLE 5.2.   Average Reaction Times for Different Types of
True Sentences in Experiment 2

		RT in Milliseconds
P0	A canary can sing.	1480
P1-t	A bird can fly.	1284
P2-t	An animal has skin.	1443

HOW PEOPLE DECIDE A SENTENCE IS FALSE

The false sentences were included at first only to balance the true sentences,
but it was soon apparent that they too could provide useful insights about
language processing. In considering how people might reject a sentence as
false, we soon concluded there were two basic ways that the memory search
might terminate in a "false" response. One way would be for a person to
search memory for information which confirms the statement as true, but
should he fail after searching for some length of time, or after searching through
some number of levels, he would give up and respond "false" (the Limited
Effort type of hypothesis). The other way would be for the person to find
negative information as he searches, which causes him to cut his search short
and reject the sentence as false (the Negative Evidence type of hypothesis).
There are many hypotheses that can be constructed for either of these types.

[3]The absolute times in this study were much longer, probably because the sentences
were displayed with slides, rather than on a CRT screen as in Experiment 1. For the two
sentence types which were comparable to Experiment 1 (one true, one false), the increases
were 175 milliseconds and 190 milliseconds, respectively.

The first hypothesis we considered (the Contradiction Hypothesis) was the simplest hypothesis of the Negative Evidence type. The hypothesis was that people search memory until they find a single piece of information that contradicts what is stated in the sentence. For example, "A collie is green" contradicts the fact that collies are brown and white, and hence can be rejected as false when this information is found.

We tested this hypothesis in two parts of Experiment 1. First we constructed two kinds of P sentences: one kind with properties that are contradicted by information stored at the lowest level in the hierarchy (e.g. "Coca-Cola is blue") and the other kind with properties contradicted at the next higher level (e.g. "Lemonade is alcoholic"). Here alcoholic was chosen because it contradicted a property of the superset, soft drink. On the basis of the Contradiction Hypothesis it was predicted that the same kind of RT increase found for true P sentences would also be found for false P sentences. The average RTs for these two kinds of false P sentences, however, were only negligibly (7 milliseconds) different.

The other test of this hypothesis was to construct two kinds of false S sentences. This difference was between sentences like "A canary is an ostrich" and "A canary is a fish" (see Figure 5.1). Both nouns in the first sentence are members of the same superset. In the second sentence, one noun is a level removed from the other and in a different branch of the hierarchy. The second kind was rejected somewhat (59 milliseconds, $p < .1$) faster. Under the Contradiction Hypothesis we would have expected the opposite result, because the path between canary and ostrich has one less link than between canary and fish. Therefore, any process that involved finding a contradiction should have involved one less step for the first pair. This result suggests that the closer two nodes are in the semantic network, the longer it takes to decide that they are not related in a particular manner. Such a conclusion parallels the finding of Moyer and Landauer (1967) that the smaller the difference between two digits, the longer it takes to decide which is larger.

At this point we discarded the Contradiction Hypothesis and considered a hypothesis of the Limited Effort Type. In it we assumed that people search memory for a given amount of *time*, responding true whenever they find confirming evidence, and responding false if nothing is found by the end of the time period (a Time Limit Hypothesis). Because the true responses fall out of such a process at different times, the false responses should have less variability in their RTs. However, the standard deviations for false responses on the average were larger than those for true responses in Experiment 1. Therefore, we gave up this hypothesis.

We then developed a more complex hypothesis of the Limited Effort Type, which derived from two basic sources. On the one hand, our subjects often stated that they considered several interpretations of a sentence before rejecting it as false. On the other hand, our computer model searches memory for paths connecting the words of a sentence *before* it considers the sentence's syntax. That is, locating of paths in memory is done by a blindly semantic process, so that each path formed must then be checked to see how the sentence actually relates to it (Quillian, 1969). Therefore, we formed the hypothesis that our subjects search their memory much like the program, and that each path they find and check out amounts to a tentative interpretation of the sentence. If after searching memory for a certain number of levels [or equivalently to a prespecified depth (Quillian, 1967)], they find no confirming path, then they give up and respond "false." This we call the Depth Limit Hypothesis.

This hypothesis would explain the difference in RTs found between sentences like "A canary is an ostrich" and "A canary is a fish" in terms of the large number of properties that are common to two words close together in the network such as canary and ostrich. The more such properties they have in common, the more paths that would need to be checked. Thus it would take longer to reject sentences like "A canary is an ostrich."

In Experiment 2 this hypothesis was explored further. False sentences were constructed differing in (i) semantic anomalousness, and (ii) whether or not there was an extraneous path. Anomalous sentences involve words far apart in the semantic network. The distinction between anomalous and nonanomalous sentences was made on the basis of whether the property was applicable to any instance within a three-level hierarchy such as in Figure 5.1. For instance, "A canary has gills" would be nonanomalous because fish and canary have a common superset (animal) within three levels, whereas "A canary has leaves" would be anomalous because tree and canary do not have a common superset within three levels. While this distinction is arbitrary, it is intuitive that the further away in the superset structure a property applies, the more anomalous the sentence becomes (for instance, compare "A canary has leaves" to "A canary has a dial.") Because anomalous sentences involve words far apart in the superset structure, it was predicted that they could be rejected faster than nonanomalous sentences. This prediction was made on the basis of the RT difference found between sentences like "A canary is an ostrich" and "A canary is a fish," where the distance in the superset structure also was varied.

Extraneous paths relate the words in the sentence in a misleading way. This can be illustrated by reference to the sentences in Table 5.3. For instance in "An almond has a fortune" there is an obvious path through Chinese fortune cookies and almond cookies; in "Madrid is Mexican" through the Spanish influence on Mexico. People, when verbally given these as true or false choices, generally report that they do consider such extraneous paths. One girl said she rejected "An almond has a fortune" as false by interpreting fortune to mean a little piece of paper with a fortune written on it, and then looking inside an almond to see if there is one. We therefore anticipated that such extraneous paths would slow the subjects down, because whenever a subject found one, he would have to spend time checking it out.

TABLE 5.3.   Examples of the Kinds of False Sentences
Used in Experiment 2

	Extraneous Path	No Extraneous Path
Anomalous	An almond has a fortune. A dalmatian has a siren.	A pecan has a castle. A collie has a sparkplug.
Nonanomalous	A newspaper is red. Madrid is Mexican.	An encyclopedia is short. Chicago has mountains.

As can be seen in Figure 5.3, there was essentially no difference in RT between anomalous and nonanomalous sentences. However, the RT difference between sentences with an extraneous path and those without is significant, and approximately the same for both anomalous and non-anomalous sentences.

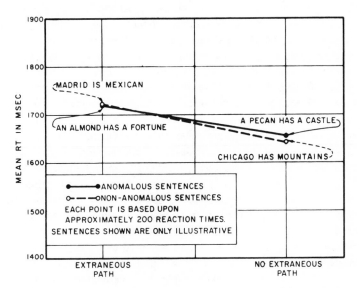

Figure 5.3   Average reaction times to different types of false sentences
in Experiment 2.

These results confirm the hypothesis that people check out very obvious semantic connections of the kind they can recall in their introspections. They do so even when such paths violate the syntax of the sentence, as does the path through fortune cookies in "An almond has a fortune." The construction of this sentence simply does not allow the interpretation of almond as almond cookie or fortune as fortune cookie, and yet people make such interpretations. Thus the results suggest the narrowness of the view of language comprehension which postulates that syntactic processing precedes and directs semantic processing. The construction of paths of the kind found here corresponds well with our computer model of the comprehension process.

The failure to find any difference between anomalous and nonanomalous sentences forced us to rethink the argument that semantic distance (or path length) in the superset structure was the critical variable producing the RT difference found earlier between sentences like "A canary is an ostrich" and "A canary is a fish." When extraneous paths were controlled, then semantic distance (as between anomalous and nonanomalous sentences) turned out not to make any difference. Therefore, it appears that the RT difference between sentences like "A canary is an ostrich" and "A canary is a fish" must result from cases where an extraneous path has to be checked out. Probably the RT difference found does *not* arise with sentences like "A canary is an ostrich" where little confusion exists between the two nouns, but from sentences like "A canary is a parakeet" where the fact that both are songbirds kept as pets would demand extra checking. In constructing sentences of the "A canary is an ostrich" type in Experiment 1, the only restriction was that both nouns come from the same large superset, in this case bird, so that there were probably several sentences included where the two nouns were highly confusable, as are canary and parakeet.

Confusability does, however, have something to do with semantic distance, and what we are saying should not be construed as negating the effect of distance entirely. It is the fact that parakeets and canaries are close together in the network by means of the properties they have in common that makes them confusable. But if the semantic distance between words in the sentence is great enough, so that an extraneous path is not formed, then semantic distance does not matter. Thus, the critical variable is whether or not an extraneous path is formed, and not semantic distance. Semantic distance matters only to the extent that it corresponds to confusability or, in our terms, the formation of an extraneous path.

While the results of Experiment 2 were in accord with the Depth Limit Hypothesis, they in fact supported only that part of the hypothesis that relates to path checking. The fact that people check paths, though, is in itself noncommittal about how a person terminates his memory search in a "false" response. Therefore, this experiment produced no clear evidence either for or against the Depth Limit Hypothesis. There are three aspects about subjects' introspections, however, that led us to give up that hypothesis.

First, subjects almost always report that they decide on an interpretation of the sentence, even for the most wildly anomalous sentences. If they find an interpretation for these anomalous sentences (as they say they do), then that means they are finding a fairly long path through the network. The Depth Limit Hypothesis, though, assumed that people search a certain specified number of levels looking for a confirming path, and respond false only if they fail to find one. It seems contradictory that they find such a path if they stop searching after a certain number of levels.

Second, it turns out that subjects usually can give some reason why the sentences they reject are false. This would seem to indicate that they are in fact finding contradictions in memory, rather than failing to find confirming evidence that the statement is true. The reasons they give often depend on imagery (visual, auditory, taste, etc.), as when a subject says "A limousine has a rudder" is false, because "I looked at the back of a limousine and didn't find any rudder." It is significant that a person looks at the *back*, which is where rudders are found on sailboats. A person has never seen a rudder on a limousine, so that there is nothing in his visual experience that would cause him to put the rudder on the back rather than in front or inside. It is most likely that the rudder is put on the back, because the semantic connection he makes between limousines and sailboats leads to putting the rudder in the corresponding position on the limousine. Thus, there must have been a path in semantic memory before there was a visual image. Imaging and comparing images may be the way that certain kinds of paths are evaluated, at least by some subjects.

The third piece of evidence against the Depth Limit Hypothesis is based on the fact that people almost always realize they have made an error after they make one. The kind of realization that usually occurs can be illustrated by one subject's comments about "A polar bear has hands." When she read the sentence, she thought of the two front paws, immediately responded true, and only afterwards realized that the paws were not called hands. This illustrates two points: (a) that a subject will often respond after finding an extraneous path, and (b) that a subject does not stop processing the sentence when he responds. This last point demonstrates that sentence comprehension (if not interrupted) takes place over a period of seconds, and that the longer a person considers a sentence, the more pieces of stored information he relates to the sentence.

Recognition of errors does not occur just for false sentences where the subject mistakenly responds "true." It also occurs for true sentences where the subject mistakenly responds "false." For example, in Experiment 1 "Gin is wet" was mistakenly rejected by two subjects, presumably upon finding the

path "Gin is dry and dry is the opposite of wet." It was only after responding
that one of the subjects realized that "Gin is liquor, and liquor is liquid, and
liquid is wet." The fact that a person will terminate his memory search by
responding "false," only to realize later that he made a mistake, indicates
that the original search leading to rejection was not very exhaustive. People
apparently do not check out all paths to a certain number of levels before
responding "false," but rather generally respond "false" when they find some
contradictory path. Depending on their willingness to make mistakes, they
may check further when they find a possible interpretation, but responding
either "true" or "false" seems to be based on finding an affirmative or contradictory path. Everything we have found indicates that the processing in
the two cases is symmetrical, but that contradictory paths are inherently
longer.

     If subjects are indeed relying on contradictions to reject false sentences,
why then did the Contradiction Hypothesis fail? In particular, why weren't
subjects any faster in rejecting false P0 sentences like "Coca-Cola is blue"
(where the sentence contradicts a property of Coca-Cola itself) than they were
in rejecting false P1 sentences like "Lemonade is alcoholic" (where the sentence
contradicts a property of soft drinks in general)? Raising this question led us
to reexamine the way we had constructed the false P0 and P1 sentences
originally. Because we had assumed that information such as "A canary is
yellow" and "A collie is brown and white" is stored at the lowest level (i.e.,
with canary and collie, respectively), then any sentences that contradicted
such a property—"A canary is blue" or "A collie is green"—were grouped
together as false P0 sentences. However, these two kinds of sentences are, in
fact, very different, because there exist birds that are blue, but not dogs
that are green. Intuitively, it seems as if "A canary is blue" is somehow more
reasonable than "A collie is green," and therefore "A canary is blue" should
take longer to reject.

     Introspections provided a clue as to why this should be so. It turned out
that two of the people, who were given "A canary is blue" auditorily, pictured
to themselves a blue bird; in one case, a blue parakeet was imagined, in another case a bluebird. When they saw the image, each said to himself "That's
not a canary" and responded "false." For "A collie is green," the same
people did not report seeing any image except a collie. Here again, for "A
canary is blue" there is a kind of extraneous path that occurs. We think that
a person will not find such an extraneous path, if he *first* makes the connection
that "A canary is yellow, and yellow and blue are different values of the
attribute color." (Finding this latter connection first is especially likely if
one has just read about the color of canaries.) Thus, it is only the cases where
subjects find an extraneous path first that need extra processing time.

     In the two cases cited, the extraneous path led to an image, but we doubt
that the image was essential to the confusion. Even a sentence that is not

likely to be decided by imagery, such as "Chianti is carbonated," can produce an extraneous path through a related node (in this case champagne). Therefore, we regard imagery as one way people evaluate semantically-generated paths, but there must be alternative ways of deciding whether a sentence is true or false.

This reconsideration of the Contradiction Hypothesis led, then, to the alternative hypothesis that the time to reject a sentence depends on whether or not there is a neighboring node, which is confusable with the node given in the sentence. Where there is such a node, we predicted that RT would be longer, because the path through that node would need to be checked and rejected. To test this in Experiment 3, we again constructed four kinds of false sentences, parallel to those we used in testing the Contradiction Hypothesis. We constructed two types of false P sentences: (a) P_c sentences where there exists within the superset a neighboring node which has the property specified in the sentence (e.g., "A tiger has a mane"), and (b) P_n sentences where there is no such neighboring node (e.g., "An elephant has a bill"). We also constructed two types of false S sentences: (a) S_c sentences where the superset in the sentence is highly confusable with the correct superset (e.g., "A St. Bernard is a cat") and (b) S_n sentences where the superset in the sentence is not particularly confusable with the correct superset (e.g., "A leopard is a snail").

The results of Experiment 3 are shown in Figure 5.4. The differences between P_c and P_n sentences and between S_c and S_n sentences are both significant. These data show that confusable neighboring nodes do indeed slow subjects down substantially.

The longer times for false S_c sentences ("A St. Bernard is a cat") compared to false P_c sentences ("A tiger has a mane") is the only case where we have found a group of S sentences to require more processing time than an equivalent (or at least somewhat equivalent) group of P sentences. The reason for this may be that the subject must find a distinguishing property of the two nodes specified in the false S_c sentences, whereas the distinguishing property is already specified in the false P_c sentences. For example, two subjects reported that they rejected the sentence "Volleyball is badminton" by thinking of the distinction between the ball in volleyball and the shuttlecock in badminton. The functional equivalence of the ball and the shuttlecock is important; a subject would not think of the racquet in badminton and the ball in volleyball in order to reject the sentence. The essential point, though, is that the subjects had to produce a distinguishing property to reject the sentence. If the sentence had been a false P_c sentence instead (e.g., "Volleyball uses a shuttlecock" or "Volleyball uses racquets"), then one property which distinguishes volleyball from any confusable node (badminton, tennis, etc.) is already specified in the sentence.

These considerations have led us to a hypothesis we call the Conditional

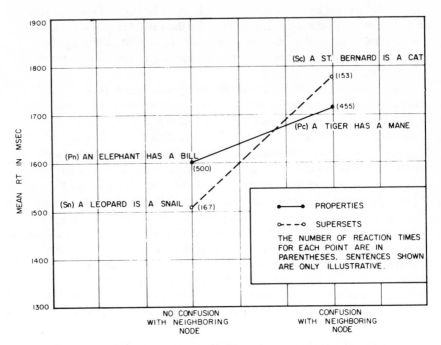

Figure 5.4   Average reaction times for different types of sentences in
Experiment 3.

Stopping Hypothesis. Like the Depth Limit Hypothesis, it assumes that
people perform a blindly semantic, parallel search looking for paths in memory connecting the nodes referred to in the sentence. The intersection
technique generally insures that paths are found in the order of their length.
Thus, for a sentence like "Khrushchev is red" the less common meaning of red
(Communist) is the first meaning which leads to an intersection (though the
subject may later intersect the color red), because it involves the shortest
path between Khrushchev and red. Because people stop after the first intersection if that is satisfactory, it explains why Foss, Bever, and Silver (1968)
found that subjects typically assign only one immediate interpretation to an
ambiguous sentence. The RT to decide whether a sentence is true or false
depends on the number of paths considered, and the length of those paths.
The consideration of more than one path explains why false sentences which
contain misleading associations ("An almond has a fortune") or confusions
("A tiger has a mane" because tiger and lion are confusable) take longer to
reject than sentences without such associations or confusions.
    When a person finds an intersecting path in semantic memory, the

Conditional Stopping Hypothesis assumes there are at least five alternative actions that can be taken.

1. Respond "true" if the path is syntactically acceptable and contains no contradictions (defined below).
2. Respond "false" if the path is syntactically acceptable and contains a contradiction (see below).
3. Project the path in imagery to evaluate its truth value.
4. Continue search for more paths if:

   (a)   The path is not syntactically acceptable.
   (b)   The path is indeterminate in truth value.
   (c)   The path is unacceptable by some other criterion (?) involving, for instance, the subject's interpretation of the task or his willingness to make mistakes.

5. Reconsider a path found earlier if the current path is unsatisfactory as in paragraph 4 and the earlier path was rejected conditionally such as by 4*b* or 4*c*.

The conditions for concluding that there is a contradiction generally involve finding a property for which the attributes match and the values do *not* match. For example, "A canary is blue" could be rejected semantically upon finding an intersection between canary and blue at the node color (canary→yellow→color; blue→color). Because the attribute color has the value blue in the sentence and yellow in memory, a person will conclude there is a contradiction. Similarly, for "Volleyball is badminton" the super-set match at the node game leads to a property search of volleyball and badminton for an attribute (the thing that is hit over the net from side to side) on which the game volleyball has one value (a volleyball) and badminton another (a shuttlecock).

For the cases where an imagery check is utilized in finding a contradiction, there is a property search that parallels the kind of semantic check outlined above. For example, with a sentence like "A rowboat has arms" subjects report that they look along the side of a rowboat for anything that sticks out like an arm (i.e., a particular kind of property). It is very likely in this case that they will picture the oars, and then check to see if they are called arms. Here again there is a contradiction between the value in the sentence (arms) and the value in memory (oars). For a sentence like "A limousine has a rudder" the contradiction is between the null value in memory and the value in the sentence (rudder). It is not very clear to us what the relation between semantic processing and image processing is, but as these comments indicate, they may only be alternative modes which depend on the same basic processes.

We have stated the Conditional Stopping Hypothesis as specifically as we can, although part (4c) is an admission of ignorance. Another aspect of the hypothesis we are unclear about is whether there are cases where a subject finds no path ("A dagger is explosive" may be one), and hence concludes the sentence is false. While the general untidiness of the hypothesis is unsatisfying, it seems to us that a hypothesis at least this complicated is necessary to encompass the results.

A STUDY OF LANGUAGE COMPREHENSION

The last experiment we want to discuss ends on a note of failure, at least for now. This experiment was an attempt to look more directly at language comprehension. It is basic in our computer model that language comprehension involves utilization of information already in memory. For instance, a sentence such as "The man drove to work" is interpreted by people to mean by car, and distinctly not by horse and buggy. However, such assignments are not always made, as was clear from the responses we collected for "She wrote her name." Two people interpreted this sentence as writing with pen on paper. A third, however, made no assignment as to pen or pencil, though he did interpret the writing to be on paper rather than on a blackboard. Even more striking was a response to "The policeman blew his whistle to stop the cars." What was pictured for this sentence was a scene of London bobbies directing traffic. There was no thought of the drivers or the brakes in the cars. As these examples show, there is a basic question as to what kinds of concepts are and are not utilized in language comprehension, which we would like to get at experimentally.

The experiment attempted to see if it would be easier to make a true/ false decision about a concept utilized in comprehending a previous sentence, compared to a concept not needed in a previous sentence. First, we presented a sentence like "The gloves were in his raincoat" where comprehension involves utilizing a piece of stored information, in this case the concept of pocket. Following this initial sentence, we presented a true/false test sentence which involved the concept needed in the prior sentence (e.g., "A coat has pockets"). For this test sentence we recorded the subject's RT. This is called the *primed* condition. In order to ascertain if there was any decrease in RT for test sentences, we presented the same test sentences to different subjects following an equivalent set of control sentences (the *control* condition). The sentences in the control condition were the same as the initial sentences in the primed condition except for a prepositional change (e.g., "The gloves were *under* his raincoat"). Comprehension of the control sentences did not require utilization of the concept (in this case, pocket) that the true/false sentence tested.

Half of the true test sentences seen by each subject were preceded by sentences where the relevant concept should be utilized, and half by control sentences. The false test sentences were constructed in a similar way, but were not analyzed in the results.

To make sure that the subjects read the initial sentence, we gave them a memory test for that sentence after the true/false test sentence. The memory test involved a yes/no decision (e.g., "Did the raincoat have the gloves in it?").

The average RTs for the true/false test sentences are shown in the top curve of Figure 5.5. While the difference was in the right direction, there was so much noise in the data that the difference was not significant, or even nearly so. Subjects intuitively felt that the prior sentence did not influence their RTs to the true/false sentence, because they blanked it out temporarily.

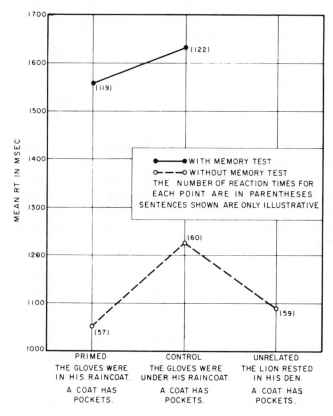

Figure 5.5 Average reaction times for different conditions in the experiment on language comprehension (all RTs are for the second sentence of the pair).

Because this task was so difficult, we decided to eliminate the memory test to see if less strain on the subjects would produce better results. In order to insure that the subjects still read the initial sentences, we asked them to push a button when they had comprehended the sentence. This was done under the guise that we were measuring comprehension time for different sentences. At the same time we decided to add another kind of control sentence, one which was entirely unrelated to the true/false sentence (the *unrelated* condition). For example, in the unrelated condition "The lion rested in his den" appeared prior to "A coat has pockets."

The results of this second attempt are shown in the bottom curve of Figure 5.5. Eliminating the memory test obviously lowered all the RTs substantially, which illustrates how sensitive RT is to different experimental conditions. The difference in average RTs between the primed and control conditions was larger in this experiment, but still not significant. However, the unrelated condition had practically the same average RT as the primed condition. What we think this means is that the longer RTs for the control condition are purely an artifact of surprise. When the subject sees "A coat has pockets" after reading "The gloves were *under* his raincoat," he wonders whether the sentence said "The gloves were *in* his raincoat." Thus, the subject may do a double take which slows him down. In any case it appears that this technique will not yield a way of discerning what concepts are and are not utilized in language comprehension.

There was one interesting sidelight to this last experiment. One subject, when he saw the sentence "The lion rested in his den," pictured a lion stretched out, lying down. He immediately pressed the button to indicate that he had comprehended the sentence. But after he had pressed the button he realized that the lion was regaining its energy. This is another illustration of how language comprehension takes place over time, utilizing more and more stored information as it does so.

We have not given up hope of finding a technique that will get at the question of how people utilize stored information in comprehension. One prospect is that a technique developed by Sachs (1967) can be adapted to this question. She presented to her subjects tape-recorded paragraphs of text, and then asked the subjects if a test sentence was the same as one of the sentences in the paragraph. After several intervening sentences of the paragraph, subjects generally remember only the semantic content or "gist" of the sentence. Therefore, if the paragraph contained the sentence "He drove to work", we would predict a subject could not very easily recognize that the test sentence "He drove his car to work" is different from it. This assumes that the subject in fact supplies the car when hearing "He drove to work." If on the other hand, the test sentence were "He drove his truck to work" or "He drove his Chevrolet to work," the added information should be easily recognized. If we are correct, this technique should indicate just what kinds of information people add in comprehension.

AN AFTERTHOUGHT

Experimental Psychology has left the areas of semantic memory and language comprehension virtually untouched, and so all this is much like tramping around in a new world just discovered. Just about anywhere you go, you find something new, but there is always a good chance of disappearing in the quicksand.

CHAPTER 6

Robert Calfee
Stanford University
Robin Chapman and Richard Venezky
University of Wisconsin

HOW A CHILD NEEDS TO THINK TO
LEARN TO READ*

For the past three years, we have been engaged in the study of cognitive skills related to the acquisition of reading. The primary goal of the research has been increased knowledge about the early stages in the development of the reading process, focusing on those aspects of early reading which involve decoding or translating from the written to the spoken form of the language, as opposed to what is commonly referred to as comprehension.

The plural, *cognitive skills*, is appropriate for two reasons. First, reading is not a unitary ability, but is a collection of abilities which develop rapidly during the primary grades. For example, the first grade child, slowly translating strings of abstract visual symbols into the familiar spoken language, is almost certainly operating in a different manner than a college student scanning a text. Second, each of these abilities requires of the child a variety of prerequisite cognitive skills. As will become obvious, from our point of view cognitive skills are very specifically defined: recognizing that two visual forms are identical, locating a test form in an array, or detecting whether two spoken words rhyme. For other investigators, cognition is virtually synonymous with theory or knowledge; our thinking about cognition has been closer to the approach which has come to be called human information processing.

A second aim of our research project is to use knowledge about the reading process gained through basic research on component cognitive skills to direct the development of more effective procedures for teaching reading. We are not looking for a new and better way of teaching *per se*. The substantial body of research on the relative efficiency of various methods of reading instruction has not produced many exciting results (e.g., Chall, 1967; Bond and Dykstra, 1968). It still takes too long for most children to achieve a reasonable level of competence in reading, and there are still far too many school children who are functionally illiterate. To repeat the point made by

The research reported herein was performed pursuant to a contract with the United States Office of Education, Department of Health, Education, and Welfare, under the provisions of the Cooperative Research Program, Center No. C-13/Contract OE 5-10-154. Special thanks are due to the experimenters who carried out the actual testing: Ella Alexander, Miriam Gelman, Stephen Harrington, Claudia Schellenberg, Michael Vickers, and Nancy Wellman.

Eleanor Gibson (1965), "good pedagogy is based on a deep understanding of the discipline to be taught and the nature of the learning process involved (p. 1072)."

This paper will not concern itself with improving reading instruction, because we have yet to grasp that "deep understanding." For those who like to speculate about how reading ought to be taught, there is adequate stimulation in the technical and popular literature. Instead, this paper will focus on the methodological base from which we are currently working.

Attacking a problem like "how does a child learn to read?" is an interesting challenge to those of us with a bias toward reductionism. Even when the problem is limited to the decoding stage, it is obvious that there are a multitude of task demands—visual and auditory perception, attention, learning, inductive reasoning, and so on—any of which might easily absorb one for a lifetime of investigation. How does a person carry out research that is both extensive and intensive? There are compelling social reasons for trying to locate the most significant "hang-ups" in reading instruction before another generation passes. Yet it is all too easy to deal superficially with these problems. Scanning the literature on reading, one becomes convinced of two things: (a) almost any aspect of a child's intellectual performance correlates to some extent with reading achievement, and (b) almost any remedial effort will be of some help. In fact, the most relevant variable in determining the success of any remedial program would appear to be *time*—the amount of time a teacher spends in one-to-one contact with an individual child (Monroe, 1932, p. 150).

Our research decisions have been guided by certain decisions about the innovative potential of various areas. First, we have decided to concentrate on the initial phases of reading instruction, including reading readiness. Accordingly, we are most interested in the performance of children between 4 and 7 years of age. Second, we have decided that those children with the poorest prognosis represent the greatest opportunity for improvement, although they also pose the greatest challenges in research.

To those readers who are experimental psychologists, these introductory remarks may strike a strange note. Not since Tinker's (1958) paper on eye-movements in reading has there been an article in either the *Psychological Bulletin* or *Psychological Review* concerned with reading. Just as B. F. Skinner bemoaned the "flight from the laboratory," so there might be cause for concern about the absence of learning psychologists from the classroom. This situation has begun to change lately; for example, reading research programs have been established in the last few years under the supervision of hardheaded experimentalists such as Eleanor Gibson, Harry Levin, Richard Atkinson, Harry Silberman, and Robert Glaser, to mention a few. In addition, current research in human information processing, psycholinguistics, and developmental cognitive psychology has had considerable influence on our work on reading as will be pointed out in connection with specific studies to be described below.

TESTS OF BASIC SKILLS

An Assumption and a Strategy

The Basic Skills Test (BST) Package described below was designed as a research vehicle which would facilitate exploratory research. The test package has potential as a diagnostic tool, and could be expanded into an instructional program. At present, it serves as a matrix by which miniature experiments are conducted in areas of relevance to beginning reading instruction. We have thought it premature to concern ourselves with formal aspects of test construction and evaluation until more has been learned about the significance of specific component skills, and the adequacy of alternative methods of assessment.

The principal assumption guiding the research is the existence of separable and independent performance skills which are prerequisite to the acquisition of literacy. The assumption of specific and independent skills is implicit in much that has been written about reading, although the implications of the assumption have rarely been realized in practice. Stern's (1968) report on the UCLA Preschool Language Project is a recent example of this approach, or one can go back four decades to Monroe (1932) who conducted similar research most competently.

An opposing point of view might propose requisite abilities of a more global or maturational nature, as implied by concepts such as *reading readiness* or *critical age*. Under the assumption of specific skills, one is led to try to identify specific deficiencies which are then the focus of remedial procedures, while the assumption of a global factor would suggest the adoption of testing and training procedures of an amorphous type. This contrast can be seen in the comparison between the highly structured preschool program of Bereiter and Engelmann (1966) and enrichment or language-experience programs such as those of Alpern (1966) or Brottman (1968).

Starting from the assumption of separable component skills, we have adopted the following strategy in identification and investigation of specific skills. To start, the skill area is delimited as precisely as possible. Then subtests are designed which surround the skill, the aim being to select convergent subtests which sample the skill in a variety of different contexts (Haber, 1969). For example, in tests of visual matching ability described below, several variations in task format and materials were employed. Single-letter matching tests were administered in simultaneous and successive modes (i.e., the letter to be matched was either present or absent when the test letters were shown), and stimulus materials were varied over a wide range, from real toys which the child could actually manipulate, to groups of letters printed in upper or lower case.

An attempt is then made to identify the underlying psychological processes involved in the ability. It is at this point that the "how" of testing

becomes a major concern. The clarity of the instructions, the quality of
the stimulus materials, the skill of the tester—these and similar general
factors always contribute to a greater or lesser extent to a child's performance. Ideally, the contribution of these general factors should be minimal.

Our approach to this problem has been to establish a basal level of
performance by starting with materials of minimum difficulty for the skill
being tested. If the error rate is too high with these materials, we conclude
that the testing procedure is at fault and must be improved. If the basal
performance is satisfactory, the test is systematically complicated by
variation in materials or task procedure until the children begin to make
errors. Then we look for miniature training procedures which can be
introduced into the testing sequence at the appropriate point to help a
child over the hurdles.

It should not be thought that the approach is to "try everything and see
what works." The original decision to concentrate on the decoding process
has meant that priority be given to investigation of visual and auditory-
phonetic processes, and of learning spoken responses to abstract symbols.
Some areas (e.g., vocabulary) have been selected for study on the basis of
our judgment and evaluation of the work of other investigators.

In summary, the BST package was designed as an indepth test of a limited
set of cognitive skills. Although constructed in the form of a diagnostic
test, the package may also be viewed as a matrix within which miniature
experiments were conducted. Many of the experiments were duds, in the
sense that the basal performance was so poor as to be of no use in isolating
sources of difficulty. From our point of view, such results mean that work
remains to be done to simplify the testing procedure. These tests aim primarily
at uncovering psychological processes, and only secondarily at prediction of
later achievement. Intercorrelations between subtests will occasionally be
reported, mainly to demonstrate the extent of independence of the measures.

General Method, Subject Samples

The BST package covers five areas of cognitive functioning: *matching of
visual forms, auditory-phonetic identification, letter-sound association,
vocabulary knowledge,* and *general achievement.* First, the general procedures
used in administering the test package will be described, then the findings
within each of these areas will be presented and discussed. The entire
series of subtests is listed in Table 6.1. The series was divided into three
sets, each of 30 to 50 minutes duration, and given at one month intervals
between November, 1968 and January, 1969 to kindergartners in Madison,

TABLE 6.1. Basic Skills Test Package, Order of Tests
and Time per Test

Test Name	Session/Session Order		Approximate Time (Minutes)	Notes
	Msn	*Bel*		
Visual Matching				
Matching	I-1	1	5	
Matching-retest	I-9	8	4-6	One group tested after VE training, one group after reproduction training
Oddity-selection	I-5		3	
Memory-matching	III-2		10	
Alphabet Knowledge				
Production	I-2	2	1	
Recognition	I-3	3	2	
Acoustic-Phonetic				
Rhyming	I-6		6	Same-different
Rhyming-retest	II-6		4	Same-different
Initial-sounds	I-10		6	Same-different
Rhyme-production	II-5	5	3	
Segmentation	III-3	9	10	
Letter-Sound Association				
Context-learning	I-11		7	
Letter-word	II-4		10	
Alphabet-learning	III-1		15	
Vocabulary Knowledge				
Picture-naming	I-4	4	8	
Line-drawing-naming	II-1	7	6	
Sorting	II-2		10	
General Abilities				
Word-memory span	I-7	6	2	
Simple directions	I-8		3	"Simon-Says"
	II-3			game

Note. Msn sample was tested over three sessions, I, II, and III in November, December, and January, respectively; *Bel* sample was tested in a single session in March.

Wisconsin. This group of children will be referred to as *Msn*. In March, 1969, ten of the subtests in Table 6.1 were administered in a single session to kindergartners from a school in Beloit, Wisconsin. This group will be referred to as *Bel*. The *Bel* group was tested to replicate some of the more prominent findings from the earlier testing.

The *Msn* sample consisted of 21 subjects, 11 boys and 10 girls, from an afternoon kindergarten class in a predominantly lower-middle class area of the city. The mean age of the 21 subjects in November was 64 months, ranging from 59 to 70 months. The Metropolitan Readiness Test was administered in March, 1969. The *Bel* sample consisted of 22 kindergartners from a predominantly lower-class area. Eleven kindergartners were drawn at random from the morning session, and 11 from the afternoon session. The sample included 10 boys and 12 girls, with a mean age in March of 69 months, ranging from 63 to 75 months.[1] The Metropolitan Readiness Test was administered to the class in May, 1969.

Test variety and total test time were considered in arranging tests for the three different sessions administered to the *Msn* group, and in the selection and arrangement of tests for the single *Bel* session. Within each session, easy and difficult tasks were alternated insofar as possible to sustain attention. The experimenters were male and female graduate and senior undergraduates at the University of Wisconsin, Madison. Detailed scripts were prepared for each of the subtests, and experimenters rehearsed the scripts before giving any of the tests to insure the equivalence of procedures and instructions. Each experimenter tested at least two children for practice. The data from these practice subjects were not included in the results reported below.[2]

Two forms of each subtest were constructed. In some instances, the alternate forms actually comprised different experimental treatments. Children were randomly assigned to form A or B independently for each session with the constraint that approximately equal numbers of subjects were tested on each form. Subjects were tested individually in small rooms at each school. Responses were recorded as unobtrusively as possible. Tests involving spoken responses were recorded with a Uher 5000 tape recorder and a Shure 545L lavalier microphone.[2]

[1] Five of the 22 children in the sample were Negro, reflecting the proportion of Negro children in the school. The data from these children have not been analyzed separately.

[2] A few remarks might be made about testing young children over an extended period of time. First, instructions are always crucial, but especially when success in a test depends upon comprehension of key words or expressions such as rhyme or sound the same. The tester must then rely on indirect tests, examples, gestures, or pretraining procedures for communication. Second, for a test session of half an hour or more, keeping the child's attention is a serious problem. In our experience, attention is best maintained if verbal instructions are kept to a minimum. Constant changes in the format of the tests helps, as does alternation of easy and difficult problems.

Visual Tasks

To read English a child must learn to isolate, differentiate, and identify the letters of the alphabet. He must learn both to identify these symbols in spite of variations in type styles and size, and to disregard structural variations such as upper- and lower-case forms. He must learn to work with ordered sequences of these symbols, noting the elements in such sequences, and treating as equivalent only sequences in which both elements and order are the same.

Method

The visual tasks in the BST package were designed to evaluate relatively low-level skills in this area, using multiple-choice or recognition responses; identification, labeling, and reproduction performance were not measured. Task, instruction, training, and test materials were varied over the several sub-tests.

On *Matching* and *Matching-Retest*, the child was shown a standard stimulus together with a test set of four or five alternatives, and was asked to pick the single alternative that matched the standard. In *Memory-Matching*, the standard was presented alone, removed, and then the test set was presented two seconds later. The child thus had to rely on his memory of the standard in making the match. Finally, in *Oddity-Selection* the child had to point out the odd member in a set of four alternatives.

Materials were varied in the following ways. To determine the difficulty of the matching task itself, small, three-dimensional toy objects were used as the first few items of *Matching*. The remaining items were printed in capital and lower-case letters, first single letters and then letter groups— pairs, triples, and quadruples. The items were printed on strips of tagboard in a horizontal row of letters .5 inches high, with the standard on the left. The test sets always included one or more alternatives designed to be highly distracting. Thus single-letter and letter-pair standards were matched with visually confusing alternatives (e.g., *b* and *d*). For letter-pair standards, the test set always contained an order reversal (e.g., *pq* for *qp*). For groups of three or four letters, the test set consisted solely of permutations of the letters in the standard (e.g., *rmn, mrn, mnr, nmr*). The odd member in *Oddity-Selection* was either visually similar (single letters), or a reversal (letter pairs), or was formed by a permutation of the letter sequence or replacement of a single-letter in the sequence by a visually similar letter (three or four letters). An example would be *VWV, VVW, VWV, VWV*.

Preliminary analyses of matching data from pilot studies had revealed that most errors involved a failure to preserve order (e.g., if *SZ* was the standard, *ZS* was as likely to be selected as *SZ*). Accordingly, prior to the *Matching-Retest*, children were given one of two types of supplementary instructions or pretraining. Either the importance of order was verbally elaborated upon using a single example (V.E.), or the child received a series of seven items in which he arranged individual letters to match a standard, with feedback on the correctness of the reproduction (Repr.).

Results

Single-letter items. Performance on the various subtests is summarized in Table 6.2.

TABLE 6.2. Percentage Correct Responses on Visual Matching,
Related Subtests of BST, and *Metropolitan Readiness*
Matching Subtest

Test/Materials	*Msn*		*Bel*	
	Mean	S.D.	Mean	S.D.
Matching:				
Objects (3) [a]	89	19	–	–
Single letters (10)	83	12	87	11
Double letters (5)	36	36	48	28
3/4 Letters (7)	30	16	35	54
Matching-Retest:				
Double letters (3)	67	26	56	39
3/4 Letters (6)	40	28	33	71
Memory-Matching:				
Single letters (4)	93	24	–	–
Double letters (5)	42	20	–	–
3/4 Letters (7)	42	25	–	–
Oddity-Selection:				
Single letters (2)	86	23	–	–
Double letters (4)	29	25	–	–
3/4 Letters (6)	29	23	–	–
Alphabet-Production:	27	27	33	31
Alphabet-Recognition:	23	77	18	82
Metropolitan Readiness:				
Matching (14)	69	19	49	25

[a]Number in parentheses is number of different items included in each category. Guessing rate is 25 percent except for Alphabet Tests (4 percent), Metropolitan (33 percent), and 8 of the 10 single-letter matching items (20 percent).

The effects of variation in material are quite apparent. Only the *Msn* sample was tested on the toy or "object" materials. On the first two items, the set of alternatives consisted of four very different toys. There were 2 errors out of a possible 42, an error rate of less than 5 percent. On the third "object" item, the standard was a safety pin and the alternatives were three safety pins of varying size and color, and a red whistle. Increasing the similarity of the test set increased the error rate to 25 percent, indicating the importance of the make-up of the test set.

On the other hand, analysis of the single-letter items indicates that for our samples of children, the letters in the English alphabet were not perceived as confusing, though they had been selected as such. Except for the first two items, the single-letter series were constructed to be quite difficult, since pilot testing during the summer of 1968 had produced extremely low error rates on single letters. Typical materials were *G-C Q G D O, b-h d b f k*, and *r-n m w r u*. "Difficulty" was based in part on feature analysis of the upper- and lower-case letters (Gibson, 1965), and in part on findings that right-left and up-down reversals often produce confusions.

The right-left mirror image transformation was the major source of errors. Three single-letter test sets included a right-left reversal of the standard (e.g., *b d*). The error rates on these items were 46 percent (*Msn*) and 41 percent (*Bel*), with selection of the reversal alternative accounting for 85 percent of these errors. For the remaining seven items in the single-letter series there were two errors in both the *Msn* and *Bel* samples out of 147 and 154 opportunities respectively. Dunn-Rankin (1968) asked second and third graders to judge the similarity of lower-case letters; for the two sample sets above (*b* and *r* standards), the perceived similarity of the test sets is about equal from Dunn-Rankin's ratings, but the error rate for the *b* item was 40 percent, whereas the *r* item was correctly matched 100 percent of the time.

Letter groups. The error rate increased sharply when letter groups were tested, particularly triples and quadruples where performance was nearly at chance performance level of 75 percent. For bigrams, one of the alternatives was an order reversal of the standard pair, and two were visually confusable with the standard. Thus, a typical item might be *CQ-OQ QC CQ CO*. Of the bigram errors on *Matching*, 70 percent (*Msn*) and 65 percent (*Bel*) were choices of the reverse order alternative; if the errors had been the result of random selections among the alternatives, only 33 percent of the errors should have been reversal errors.

In the *Matching-Retest*, 52 percent (*Msn*) and 43 percent (*Bel*) of the bigram errors were reversal errors. Unfortunately, the placement of reversal alternatives was not balanced for serial position between the A and B groups, and so a breakdown of reversal errors by treatment groups is meaningless.

On *Memory-Matching,* 54 percent (*Msn*) of the bigram errors were reversal errors.

Serial positions. The items were displayed in a horizontal array with the standard to the left. There were enough errors in the letter-group series for analysis of serial position effects, which showed (Table 6.3) that in the *Matching* and *Matching-Retest* tasks, the children were scanning from left to right. In the *Memory-Matching* task, no pattern to the errors was evident. In the letter-group items, all of the alternatives were highly similar, in the sense that they were constructed of the same letters as the standard. If letter-order information was not preserved by the child, and if the child scanned the alternatives from left to right, one would predict the distribution of errors would resemble the data in Table 6.3. The presence of the standard to the left of the alternatives was important in directing the scanning process, since errors were randomly distributed when the standard was not present.

The data on the right of Table 6.3 provide further information on the scanning process. The percentage of reversal errors in bigram matching are

TABLE 6.3.   Breakdown of Total Errors, Showing Position
Effects in Visual Matching Tests

Test/School	Percent of Total Errors at Each Serial Position				Percent Bigram Reversals[a]		
	1	2	3	4	Training Group	C-R	R-C
Matching							
Msn	63	21	8	8	V.E.	15	67
					Repr.	14	76
Bel	52	23	12	13	V.E.	14	52
					Repr.	14	40
Matching-Retest							
Msn	78	10	6	5	V.E.	15	70
					Repr.	14	27
Bel	50	27	7	16	V.E.	14	55
					Repr.	5	18
Memory-Matching							
Msn	21	27	23	29	- - -	29	33

[a]Percent of reversal errors on two-letter stimuli when correct choice was to left (C-R) or right (R-C) of reversal choice, by V.E.-Repro. training groups; training given just prior to *Matching-Retest.*

shown as a function of whether the correct alternative was to the left of the reversal alternative (C-R), or to the right (R-C). These data are shown for each of the matching tasks, separately for the V.E. and Repr. groups. In *Matching,* if the reversal alternative was to the left of the standard in the test set, it was quite likely to be chosen. This result also held in *Matching-Retest* following V.E. but much less so following Repr. Thus, the training procedure affected the type of errors made by the children, though not the rate of errors. In *Memory-Matching,* the reversal alternative was equally likely to be selected whether to the right or left of the correct alternative, supporting the conclusion that scanning was unsystematic in this task.

Oddity-Selection. Overall performance level on the *Oddity-Selection* task, in which the child was asked to point out "which one of these is not like the others" was comparable to performance of the other matching tasks, which would suggest that these tasks all tapped similar component skills. On the other hand, one child insisted that for 8 of the 12 items, all four alternatives were identical; in 7 other instances a child refused to point out any of the alternatives as different from the others. In the other matching tasks, there were only 2 cases of this sort. There was no evidence of serial position effects in this task.

Metropolitan-Readiness Match. Performance on the *Matching* subtest of the Metropolitan Readiness Tests (Hildreth, Griffiths, and McGauvran, 1964) was somewhat higher than on the BST matching tests. This subtest consists of 14 items, with the same format as *Matching* in BST (horizontal array, standard to the left). A variety of standard items are used in this test—words from four to nine letters long in upper- and lower-case, as well as various kinds of abstract figures. Each test set contains three alternatives which would produce a higher guessing rate than for the BST matching tests. The alternatives are similar to the standard, consisting of letter permutations for the words and minor figural variations for the forms. Also in BST *Matching*, the leftmost alternative in the test set was correct for only 2 of the 12 letter groups, whereas in the Metropolitan *Matching*, the leftmost alternative is correct for 5 of 14 items. Given the previously noted bias for the leftmost alternative, these arrangements would also produce fewer errors on the Metropolitan compared to the BST. Finally, the BST was administered in the fall, the Metropolitan the following spring. Hence, no significance is attached to the higher performance on the Metropolitan Matching test. Comparisons between performance on these various tests will be discussed in a later section on intertest correlations.

Discussion

There are three general considerations in the relation of visual perception to reading. First is the question of *isolation, discrimination,* and *identification of the abstract characters which serve as letters* in the English alphabet. Second is *confusion of left-right mirror images*, which is related to the first question, but warrants discussion as a separate issue. Third is the *perception, analysis,* and *storage of written words.*

Letter perception. Most children in this country encounter printed materials at an early age. Few of the kindergartners we tested "knew their ABC's," but most attempted the letter-matching task without hesitation, and performed quite well, given the confusability of the English alphabet and the fact that they could not label many letters. Whether matching is conceived as a process involving templates or distinctive-features (Neisser, 1967), the single-letter test sets were highly similar, and are judged as such by second-graders (Dunn-Rankin, 1968), and yet error rates were quite low except for right-left reversals.

Gibson, Gibson, Pick, and Osser (1962), in what has become a classic study, investigated the degree to which letter-like standards were confused with various transformations of the standard—perspective, rotation, and reversal, line to curve, and break-and-close. The format of their test was generally the same as that used in BST. There were twelve alternatives in each test set, and the children were instructed to select as many alternatives as they wished from the set, since sometimes more than one copy of the standard would be included.

From the ages of 4 to 6, both right-left *and* up-down reversals produced errors (choice of a transform as equivalent to standard) at a rate of from 50 percent to 15 percent. Kindergartners were also tested on transformations of upper-case English letters, and here the error rate for right-left reversals (*b, d*) was more than double that of up-down reversals (*b, p*) – 19 percent versus 8.5 percent.

Any attempt to identify transformational relations among real letters is risky, but as an example, if it is assumed that C and O are related by a break-and-close transformation, or V and U by a line-to-curve, then the error rates in Gibson *et al.* would lead one to expect much higher error rates in BST matching tests than were actually found. In both of our samples, the overwhelming preponderance of errors made by the children on single-letter tests were right-left reversals; only 10 out of 70 errors could be classified as up-down reversal, close-break, or line-to-curve.

The substantial similarities among English letters are indicated by the difficulty in devising reliable pattern-recognition devices (Uhr, 1966). The Gibson *et al.* investigation suggests that transformational relations may be a useful way of describing perceptual similarity. What remains to be formulated is a model of stimulus structure which can complement feature-transformation analyses. Gibson's (1965) approach took the form of a "feature listing," in which, for example, Z was equal to < straight segment, horizontal, oblique/;

discontinuity, horizontal $>$. This listing provides all the elements or features in Z, but lacks a description of how the elements are structurally related. A more complete list would include features *and* rules of combination. Thus p might be roughly described as $<$ straight segment, vertical, descender; curve, closed $>$. This list consists of writing instructions which are applied from left to right, with semicolons denoting operational breaks.

The point being made is just this: the perceptual similarity of two letters depends not only on the transformational relations between the objects, but also on the structure of the objects. We know that d and b are easily confused by kindergartners, and we have to live with the fact that both are letters in English—but what about S and $Ƨ$, 5 and $Ƨ$ or N and $И$? Is it true in general that the right-left transformation is a source of confusion, or does this hold only for certain structural classes of stimuli? An answer to this question might lead to a better understanding of the nature of b-d and p-q errors.

The matching task has much in common with visual search tasks of the sort investigated by Neisser (1967), in which subjects are presented one or more items to remember, and are then asked to look through a list until they find one of the memorized items. Instructions stress speed—the target is to be reported as quickly as possible. Neisser has shown that increasing visual similarity slows down search rates in college students, and Gibson and Yonas (1966) have reported similar results using subjects as young as second-graders.

The task of reading itself also involves heavy memory and visual loads, and although speed may not be overtly emphasized, the laggard is certainly penalized. There is little research on the effects of item complexity, memory load, visual load, visual similarity, and stress of speed versus accuracy on matching performance. These variables denote, in turn, the choice of letters, words, familiar or nonsense forms as item material; the number of alternatives being searched through; the similarity (transformational or featural) of the alternatives in the test set; and the degree to which instructions require the subject to respond as quickly as possible or as accurately as possible. The Gibson and Yonas study suggests that in speeded search, visual similarity may affect performance. With similar materials, but minimal memory and visual load, and minimal stress on speed; performance was essentially perfect in the BST matching tests of single letters. The difficulty in the more demanding search task would appear to be cognitive rather than perceptual, except possibly for the problem of right-left reversal confusions, to which we will now turn our attention.

Right-left reversals. The fact that children confuse the letter pairs b-d and p-q has been repeatedly documented (see Fellows, 1968, and Benton, 1959, for reviews). The problem is universal, profound, and persistent. Substantially more than half of all kindergarten children confuse these pairs sometimes. In a two-choice test, error rates of 15-25 percent are common. The difficulty may persist until 9 or 10 years of age in the case of children who are nonreaders. The problem has been attributed to various kinds of dysfunction— physiological, perceptual, memorial, or cognitive. Various training procedures have been evaluated, with mixed results (Strang, 1967; Harris, 1969; Jeffrey, 1958). There have been no tests of the long-term effects of such training on reading or reading-related tasks. The degree of confusion appears to depend on the physical arrangement of the stimulus objects. For example, Hutten-locher (1967a, b) presents evidence that right-left reversals occur in a horizontally-arranged display, but when a vertical array is used, up-down reversals are more frequent than right-left reversals.

If it were not for the existence in the English alphabet of the pairs *b-d* and *p-q*, this entire discussion would be of interest only to investigators of spatial orientation (Howard and Templeton, 1966). Various efforts have been made to determine the number of reading errors due to right-left reversals; this is probably a hopeless task. It is clear that children do make such errors, even under optimal testing conditions, and that we do not understand the sources of such errors or how to remedy the problem. One simple solution might be to use only upper-case letters in initial reading instruction, or to adopt some sort of stylistic variation in the typography used in initial read-ing, (i.e., replace *d* with ∂ and *p* with ρ).

Word matching. Next we will consider matching of letter groups. Al-though there is considerable evidence suggesting that experienced readers perceive words as units rather than as letter strings, the manner in which beginning readers or prereaders process words is less certain. Suprisingly, there does not appear to have been a test of the simplest hypothesis—that the probability of error in matching a standard word with a particular test alternative is the product of the error probabilities for the constituent letter pairs—assuming independence of the letter comparison processes. The problem is an interesting one, because there are good arguments to suggest that error rates in word matching should be greater or less than predicted by independent scanning—greater because of the increased information-processing load, less because word configuration cues are another source of information. Although there is anecdotal evidence to the effect that word configuration may be important in scanning by experienced readers, there appears to be little research on the effects of configuration on matching by beginners. (Our data do not provide a sufficient range of tests of single or multiple letter groups for such a test.)

An important source of word matching errors in the BST data and other studies involves confusions between a standard and an alternative consisting of an order permutation of the letters in the standard. A special case of this situation is the right-left reversal of a word—*was* for *saw*. Two of the better studies on word perception in prereaders come from the older literature. Hill

(1936) investigated word-matching ability in kindergartners and first-graders
with a well constructed test designed to evaluate the effectiveness of cues at
different locations within a word. She found that the first and last letters
were more salient than those in the middle, that the error rate was highest
when an alternative preserved the configuration of the standard, and that
the highest error rate was observed when two words differed by a single mirror-
image letter (e.g., *rimd* versus *rimb*). Hill did not test mirror-image word
alternatives, but from her data it is clear that other sources of confusion
contribute substantially to word matching errors. First-graders made fewer
errors than kindergartners, but the pattern of errors was the same in both
groups.

Davidson (1934) compared form and word reversal confusions in kindergartners and first-graders. A five-alternative multiple-choice test was employed,
the child being instructed to select one or more alternatives that were the same
as the standard. For the nonsense geometric forms, one of the alternatives was
a right-left reversal; for the words, one of the alternatives contained the letters
of the standard in reverse order. Confusions were common with both types
of materials; 94 percent of the kindergartners and 62 percent of the first-
graders made at least one form reversal, and the corresponding figures for
words were 83 percent and 33 percent. The percentage of errors, reversal
and others, for forms and words, is rather interesting (Table 6.4). Reversals
account for more than two-thirds of all form errors in both kindergarten and
first-grade children, whereas other errors are in the majority in the word
tests. (Davidson describes the other alternatives simply as "words known
to be easily confused with the key word.") Thus, Davidson's results suggest
that order reversal errors are not necessarily the singular source of confusion
in word perception that mirror-image reversals are in single-letter matching.

TABLE 6.4.   Error Distributions in Visual Matching of Forms
and Words by Kindergartners and First-Graders
(Davidson, 1936)

Grade	Forms (10)[a]			Words (15)[a]		
	Reversals	Other Errors	Total	Reversals	Other Errors	Total
Kindergarten	23	11	34	22	26	48
(*n* = 50)						
First-Grade	13	5	18	5	8	13
(*n* = 120)						

[a]Number of items in test.

Another relevant study is that of Pufall and Furth (1966). In one portion of that study, children from 4 to 6 years old classified pairs of items as same or different. The items consisted of triads of two objects of one kind (*A*) and a third object of a different (*B*) (e.g., *AAB* or *ABA*.) On each trial, the child was presented with a pair of triads which had the same or different sequences (e.g., *AAB-AAB* or *AAB-BAA*). Various types of materials were used—colored marbles, colored cards, familiar geometric forms, line drawings of familiar objects and nonsense forms. Given the high intralist similarity, error rates were relatively low, ranging from 29 percent at age 4 to 0 percent at age 6. The result most pertinent to order errors was the finding that 55 percent of all errors were mirror-image reversals; for example, *AAB* and *BAA* were identified as "same" more than half the time. When the memory component of the task was increased by presenting the two triads successively rather than simultaneously, mirror-image reversal errors occurred at about the same rate, but the rate of other types of errors (e.g., *AAB-ABA*, "same") doubled.

In summary, *word* matching was a relatively difficult task for kindergartners, even though they were able to match the component letters. Words were handled as strings of more or less independent letters, although confusions due to configurational similarity also existed. Children did not appear to match solely on the basis of single letter identity, although initial and final letters were more likely to be correctly matched than middle letters. Permutation confusions are common, and although there is little systematic research on the problem, right-left order reversal confusions appear to occur frequently in word matching, but not so exclusively as right-left mirror-image confusions in single-letter matching.

ACOUSTIC-PHONETIC RECOGNITION

We have argued elsewhere that if a child is to learn to read English, almost certainly he must learn to make use of letter-sound correspondences (Venezky, Calfee, and Chapman, 1969). Learning these correspondences involves analysis and identification of strings of letters and of the phonetic units which correspond to letters. Most literate adults unquestioningly accept a discrete-units theory of phonology, probably because they confuse letters and sounds. Yet research on this problem to be discussed below suggests that prereaders have considerable difficulty performing many tasks which require analysis of a spoken word into phonetic components.

The acoustic-phonetic subtests in BST employed a variety of procedures to evaluate children's competence in this area—recognition of word pairs having the same or different initial or final phonological segments, production of rhymes, and acquisition and transfer tests on a paired-associate problem which could be solved by noticing that the responses were phonological segments of the stimuli (e.g., *FEEL-EEL*).

Method

Three of the tests were same-different tasks—*Rhyming, Rhyming-Retest,* and *Initial-Sounds.* In each, the child was informed by instructions or pretraining that certain features of word pairs would be critical, the final *-VC* segment in the rhyming tests and the initial *C-* segment in *Initial-Sounds.* The child then was asked to respond "Yes" or "No" to a series of word pairs, depending on whether the critical feature was the same or different in the two words.

In *Rhyming,* the child was asked whether or not two words "sounded the same at the end"; a pretraining series with corrective feedback was used to exemplify this concept. The *Rhyming-Retest* was the same as *Rhyming* except for materials, but was preceded by the *Rhyme-Production* task to be described shortly. In *Initial-Sounds* the child was asked whether or not "two words start with the same sound." Three continuants were tested, /s/, /m/, and /1/. To simplify the task for the child, all tests of a given phoneme were administered in a block. Two different testing procedures were used. Children in Group A received two exemplars of the critical phoneme at the beginning of each series. Then a series of test items was presented and the child was asked whether or not each one began with the critical sound. Children in Group B were also required to repeat one of the exemplars together with the target word before the test question was asked.

The *Rhyme-Production* test, designed as another means of testing rhyming ability, consisted of two parts. First, the experimenter gave two rhymes for each of eight words spoken by the child in a picture-naming task. Thus, if the child said "girl" when shown a picture, the experimenter might say "pearl, curl." Then the child was asked to switch roles, to give a rhyme for each word pronounced by the experimenter as the name of a picture. The experimenter told the child he was right if the child produced a rhyme, and gave two rhymes if the child was wrong or gave no response.

The *Segmentation* test consisted of two paired-associate tasks, each task consisting of five study-test trials on a list of three pairs followed by a transfer test on six different but related stimuli. The stimuli were all familiar *CVC* words, and the responses were the final *-VC* segment of each word. For one list (RW), the responses both in training and transfer were real words: [*F(EEL), SH(OUT), P(ILE)*], and for the other list (NS) the responses were nonsense: [*S(OAP), R(IDE), CH(IEF)*].[3] Children in Group A received the

---

[3] The data do not provide an especially strong test of the role of response familiarity, because the responses in the *RW* list, (*-OUT, -EEL, -ILE* or aisle), were not much more familiar to the children (except for *-OUT*) than the *NS* responses (*-OPE, -IEF, -IDE*).

NS list first followed by the RW list. Group B received the lists in the reverse order. The children were urged to give a response on every test, even if it was a guess.

Results

The *Rhyming, Rhyming-Retest*, and *Initial-Sounds* test results are quickly described. In each test, the percentage of correct responses was 49 percent, compared with a guessing rate of 50 percent. In short, none of the children did better than chance on any of the tests. Some variation in performance was apparent in response biases, but it is clear that the children tested could not perform any of these tasks—because of an inability to grasp the concepts of phonetic matching, because the instructions or pretraining were inadequate or other shortcomings of the "same-different" procedure, or any combination of these reasons.

The *Rhyming-Production* test produced the most interesting results. The percentage of rhymes produced were 39 percent (*Msn*) and 37 percent (*Bel*). Some children in both groups refused to attempt the task at all, 5/21 (*Msn*) and 4/22 (*Bel*); for those children who made an attempt, failures to respond were 9 percent (*Msn*) and 26 percent (*Bel*). Some children were quite good at the task; 10/21 (*Msn*) and 10/22 (*Bel*) produced four or more appropriate rhymes in eight attempts. Except for three children who produced a single correct rhyme, the remaining children failed on all eight items, producing noticeably bimodal distributions in both samples. A substantial percentage of the rhymes were nonsensical, 51 percent (*Msn*) and 44 percent (*Bel*), indicating a grasp of the phonological nature of the task. Only a very few of the responses were semantic associates (e.g., *pot-coffee cup*).

In Table 6.5 are the results of analyses of the *Segmentation* test in which children learned two paired-associate lists based on phonological relations between the stimulus and response members and were tested for transfer of this learning. Analysis of variance was carried out on several dependent variables: (a) number of correct responses, (b) phonological errors, (c) stimulus repetitions, and (d) other errors. The independent variables were school, group, RW versus NS, and training versus transfer. Aside from confirming that performance of one of the *Bel* groups was significantly poorer than the other three groups, the most interesting result was a significant ($p < .05$) interaction between RW and NS materials during training and transfer. The details of this interaction are displayed in Figure 6.1. During both training and transfer, about .6 of the responses were either correct or phonological errors. In transfer these two classes of responses occurred about equally often. In training on RW lists, .8 of these two responses were correct, but only .65 of these two classes of responses were correct in NS lists. In other words, RW and NS lists produced equal numbers of phonologically related responses in both training

TABLE 6.5. Percentage of Correct and Phonological Responses
on Segmentation Test During Training and Transfer

Trial	Training					Transfer
	1	2	3	4	5	
Real Word						
Correct	35	44	50	51	60	24
Phonological error	21	15	10	9	9	28
Nonsense						
Correct	27	34	44	44	48	24
Phonological error	25	23	19	19	13	27

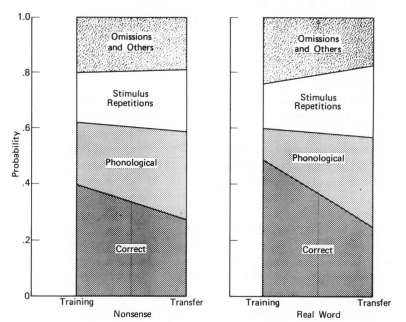

Figure 6.1   Segmentation responses to Real Word and Nonsense Lists on
training and transfer.

and test; RW lists produced a larger proportion of exactly correct responses,
but this was not significantly related to transfer performance.

There were few misplaced responses (e.g., *SHOUT-EEL*) in either the RW
or NS list, except for the response *OUT* which was given incorrectly in the RW

list a total of 34 times (out of a possible 430 opportunities). There were 9 other misplaced responses in RW lists, and a total of 8 misplaced responses in NS lists.

To the extent that the children learn a concept based on the phonological relations between the pairs, one might expect to observe the following: (a) transfer to a new list of stimuli for children who reached criterion on the training list, (b) more rapid learning of the second list compared to the first, (c) errors should be phonologically related to the stimulus word, and (d) the distribution of correct responses should be somewhat bimodal in both training and transfer.

Except for (b) which might be predicted on other grounds as well, each of these hypotheses found support in the data, indicating that many of the children were sensitive to the phonological character of the pairs. (Phonological errors were defined as monosyllabic responses in which the vowel matched that of the stimulus word, excluding repetitions of the stimulus.) Several children responded with an initial consonant substitution rather than a deletion as required by the task. For example, one child produced *WINE, WEAM, WOSS,* and *WAFE* for the transfer items *PINE, TEAM, MOSS,* and *SAFE,* respectively.

The bimodal character of the distributions of correct responses in training and transfer is noteworthy. If a child has grasped the phonological nature of the task by the end of training, most of the responses on the last training trial and on the transfer trial should be correct responses or phonological errors. A strictly all-or-none concept model would postulate that if a subject had learned the phonological concept, only phonological responses would be produced at the end of the training and during transfer; otherwise such responses would occur at a chance rate. This model is certainly too strict; there would be some correct responses due solely to rote learning, and some errors due to attentional lapses even though a child had grasped the concept. The distributions in Table 6.6 showing the number of children making various numbers of correct or phonologically-related responses on the last trial and during transfer, are significantly bimodal when compared, for example, with a binomial distribution. Some children achieved perfect or near perfect scores, and most others made no correct responses, or at most one. Few subjects performed at an intermediate level.

Some children (three in *Msn*, four in *Bel*) persisted in simply repeating the stimulus word. The study-test procedure which has proven an efficient means of teaching paired-associate lists to college students (Battig, 1965) was inadequate in interrupting stimulus repetition errors, perhaps because it did not provide immediate negative feedback to the children. One child (in the *Bel* sample) responded to each stimulus word with another word (e.g., *BOOK, HORSE, CAT*) as though performing a word-association task. Except for the eight subjects just described, there were very few real word responses which were not phonologically related to the stimulus word.

TABLE 6.6. Distribution of Subjects on Segmentation Test; Number of Subjects Making 0, 1, 2, or 3 Correct or Phonological Responses on Final Training Trial, and 0, 1, . . . 6 Such Responses on Transfer Trial

	Number Correct or Phonological Responses						
	0	1	2	3	4	5	6
Final Training Trial							
Real word	6	10	3	24	--	--	--
Nonsense	8	6	5	24	--	--	--
Transfer Trial							
Real word	6	9	2	1	3	5	17
Nonsense	13	2	0	3	3	5	17

In summary, although on the *Rhyming, Rhyming-Retest*, and *Initial-Sounds* children were unable to deal with phonetic segments by identifying words as same or different; on the basis of such segments on *Rhyme-Production* and *Segmentation*, children produced words or word-like units based on phonological segmentation of stimuli. Moreover, there was a definite relation between a child's performance on the *Segmentation* and *Rhyme-Production* tests, as shown in the contingency table in Table 6.7. Also shown in Table 6.7 are the contingency tables for *Segmentation* and *Alphabet-*

TABLE 6.7. Contingency Tables Showing Relation of Performance on Segmentation Test with Rhyme-Production, Alphabet-Production, and Alphabet-Recognition Tests. (Children in Each Sample Partitioned into Those Above and Below Median)

Segmentation	Rhyme-Production		Alphabet-Production		Alphabet-Recognition	
	Above	Below	Above	Below	Above	Below
Above	17	5	15	6	14	7
Below	3	18	7	15	7	15
	$X^2=17.1$		$X^2=6.7$		$X^2=5.9$	
	$p<.001$		$p<.01$		$p<.05$	

Production, and *Segmentation* and *Alphabet-Recognition.* This result suggests that these two tests are convergent, that both are tapping the same set of acoustic-phonetic skills. The relation between Segmentation and the alphabet knowledge tests, weaker than the previous relation but statistically significant, could be taken as evidence that acoustic-phonetic skills are important in later reading achievement, or as a measure of a general performance factor in all the tests, or both.

The possibility that we may have begun to isolate acoustic-phonetic skills in prereaders is encouraging. There remains the problem of relating this skill to other tasks requiring analysis of word sounds, particularly the isolation and identification of phonemes, and of devising and evaluating various training procedures which could be used with children who are deficient in this area.

Discussion

There has been relatively little research on acoustic-phonetic skills in children. Even the simplest problems remain to be fully investigated, such as the types of confusions that occur in phoneme perception. Some work has been done on children's discrimination of minimal pairs using a same-different procedure (e.g., "does /ba/sound the same as /pa/?"; Deutsch, 1967; Templin, 1957). Unfortunately this procedure is difficult for young children, particularly those who are most lacking in general language ability. Studies recently completed in our laboratory (Kamil and Rudegeair, 1969; Skeel, Calfee, and Venezky, 1969) show that under optimal conditions, kindergartners and even younger children could discriminate between minimal phonetic contrasts, even when meaningless CVC's are used as stimuli. One factor in obtaining satisfactory performance levels by prereaders on this task was avoidance of the same-different test procedure. Another factor was the use of repeated test sessions; in the study by Kamil and Rudegeair, the error rate on the second day of testing was about half that on the first day. Half of the errors which did occur involved phonetic contrasts known to be difficult for adults—/f - θ/ and /v - ə/.

An early study by Bond (1935) is perhaps the most complete and informative study of auditory factors related to reading available. His subjects were second and third graders who were reading at grade level (Control) or were below grade level six months or more (Experimental). Half the children had been taught reading by a phonetic method, half by a look-say method. Six different auditory tests were administered, as well as standardized reading achievement tests. The auditory tests were: *AA* (auditory acuity); *SB* (sound blending; e.g., tester says /bə-ai/, student says /bai/); *AP* (auditory perception, a potpourri: (a) giving the letter name for different sounds as in /bi/ for /bə/, (b) giving words beginning with a sound such as /kait/ for /kə/, and (c) giving words ending with a sound such as /kip/ for /-ip/); *AM* (auditory memory measured by digit span and nonsense-syllable span); *AR* (auditory rhyme, reproduction of various tapping patterns); and *AD* (auditory discrimination, a same-different test of minimal pairs such as /res - rez/). Finally, an articulation test was given in which responses were elicited by line drawings of familiar objects.

Bond's analyses showed that on *SB* and *AP* the Experimental Group was significantly poorer than the Control group in both the phonetic and look-say conditions. On test *AA* the Experimental Group was poorer than Control in the phonetic condition only, while on *AM* the Experimental Group was poorer than Control in the look-say condition only. It is tempting to conclude that to benefit from phonics reading instruction it is important to have good hearing, whereas in whole-word instruction it helps to have a good memory. *AD, AR,* and articulation ability were not significantly related to reading performance. *AR* is akin to what has been investigated as *auditory-visual integration,* the ability to match auditory-temporal patterns (e.g., a series of dots and dashes as in Morse Code) with a corresponding visual-spatial pattern. Performance on this kind of test has been shown by several investigators to be correlated with reading achievement. The most complete study of this problem (Muehl and Kremenak, 1966) showed that cross-modal matching (auditory-to-visual and visual-to-auditory) was correlated with first-grade reading achievement (Pearson *r*'s of .52 and .39) but intramodal matching (auditory-to-auditory and visual-to-visual) was not. Bond's *AR* test was essentially auditory-to-auditory, and so both sets of data are consistent in saying that intramodal pattern matching is unrelated to reading achievement.

Muehl and Kremenak also combined the four auditory-visual-integration scores with various reading readiness scores in a discriminant function analysis, and found that the letter-naming readiness score was the only significant predictor of first-grade reading achievement. The predictive value of the child's knowledge of the alphabet in kindergarten is well known. Equally apparent is the diagnostic uselessness of this information. Cross-modal pattern matching ability may be a poorer predictor, but would seem to have greater potential for diagnosis of a specific deficiency.

Two other recent studies have examined acoustic-phonetic segmentation skills in young children. Bruce (1964) had children between the mental ages of 5 and 9 say what would be left if a particular phoneme was deleted. The phoneme was either initial, medial, or final (e.g., BRING, WENT, or EVERY), the underlined letter corresponding to the phoneme to be deleted). Relatively few children were tested at the younger ages, and the stimulus words were quite varied. His pretraining procedures were well designed to guarantee high levels of performance. Nonetheless, children with a mental age of 7 or less were completely unable to perform the task. By age 8, more than half of the responses were correct. Bruce's analysis of errors provides an interesting picture of the development of segmentation ability during the early school years. The details are beyond the scope of this paper, but briefly, from age 6 on, disregarding omissions and stimulus repetitions, more than 90% of the errors are phonologically related to the stimulus word.

McNeil and Stone (1965) first trained kindergartners to hear /s/ and /m/; one group was trained on 24 real words, a second on 24 nonsense words. The criterion test consisted of four real and four nonsense words, for each of which a child was asked, "Do you hear /s/ or /m/ in ___?" Following training on the real words, 58 percent of the criterion responses were correct compared with a guessing rate of 50 percent; following nonsense-word training, 78 percent of the criterion responses were correct. Real words were used exclusively in the same-different tests in the BST package; McNeil and Stone's results suggest that by using semantically anomalous stimuli, children might more easily focus on the phonological properties of the words.

Identification of significant acoustic-phonetic skills is a significant first step, but this must be followed by the development and evaluation of remedial training programs to realize the full potential of this approach. The work of the Russian psychologist Elkonin (1963) is the most interesting effort at training of phonetic or word-analysis skills of which we know. The details of his procedure are a bit obscure, but in general this training procedure taught children to match phonemes with blank tokens which they arranged on a formboard with as many spaces as the word had sounds. A picture representing the word was also present. Gradually, specific identification of sounds was introduced and the formboard removed; the child had to select the appropriate number of tokens, and after repeating the word, break it up into individual sounds. In spite of the scant details, Elkonin's technique looks promising and the results are encouraging.

The investigations above suggest that the problems of kindergartners in acoustic-phonetic analysis are not sensori-perceptual—children can discriminate minimal phonetic contrasts about as well as adults, and can perform some tasks which require phonetic segmentation. Instead, the problems are cognitive, as Vernon (1960) concluded.

> "...The children (backward readers) were familiar with the general shapes of words, and the letters they contained, but their knowledge was quite unsystematic. They knew something about the shapes of letters and letter groups and their associated sounds, and that the letters had to be blended together to form the words; but they were so confused that they had no certainty as to the correct manner of performing these processes, or of coordinating them together.
>
> The most common feature of reading disability is the incapacity to perform the cognitive processes of *analysing* accurately the visual

and auditory structures of words. The backward reader guesses wrong letters, or the right letters in the wrong order....

The fundamental and basic characteristic of reading disability appears to be cognitive confusion and lack of system. Why even quite an intelligent child should fail to realize that there is a complete and invariable correspondence between printed letter shapes and phonetic units remains a mystery which has not yet been solved. It must be attributed to a failure in analyzing, abstraction, and generalization, but one which, typically, is confined to linguistics..." (Vernon, 1960, p. 71.)

LETTER-SOUND ASSOCIATION

This section focuses on tasks which required the children to learn to associate sounds and letter-like symbols. These tasks were analogous in many respects to the early stages of reading instruction. The materials were relatively abstract and unfamiliar. Various task formats were investigated; in some tests a spoken response was given to a visual symbol, and in others the experimenter pronounced a stimulus word and the child had to pick out the corresponding visual symbol. Most of these tasks were quite difficult and learning was slow. Nonetheless, detailed analysis of the data provided some clues to specific sources of difficulty in these tasks.

Method

Alphabet-Learning was analogous to memorizing the names of the letters of the alphabet. Six nonsense forms (after Gibson, et al., 1962) served as stimuli, three paired with a consonant-vowel response (/we/, /ge/, /je/) and three with a vowel-consonant response (/æ t/, /æ d/, /æ b/). These stimuli were chosen to parallel the pattern in the English alphabet represented by such sets as *B, D, G* and *L, N, S*. Except for /æb/, all of the responses were real words.

In this and the other learning tasks, study and test trials alternated. In this particular task, on the first half of each trial, three items were studied and then tested, and on the second half of the trial the remaining three items were studied and then tested. The list was always split on each trial to produce a mixed response set; for example, the /-e/ and /æ-/ subsets were never presented all together. Five trials were administered in this manner.

The *Letter-Word* task investigated the blending of letter-sound combinations. The *Letter* list consisted of three unfamiliar letter forms (capital Greek), denoted *M, N,* and *O,* paired with the sounds /m/, /n/, and /o/. The *Word* list was derived from the letter list by pairing *O* with *M* or *N* to form *MO,*

NO, OM, ON and associated responses /mo/, /no/, /om/, and /on/. Five study-test sequences were given on each list. Half the children learned the *Letter* list first and then the *Word* list, the other half were given the lists in the reverse order. In the instructions it was pointed out that the words consisted of two symbols, but the individual letter-sound correspondences were *not* stressed.

The *Context-Learning* task was directed primarily toward the effect of variability in letter-sound correspondences on learning these correspondences. The test used the capital letters *D, C, A,* and *E* as stimuli. First, the child was shown *A* and *E*, and taught to point to *A* when the tester said /e/, and to *E* when /i/ was pronounced. Then the stimulus pairs *DA* and *DE* were placed before the child and he was told to point to *DA* when (de) was pronounced and to *DE* when /di/ was pronounced. Then a test was administered; the tester said /di/ and /de/, and the child had to point to either *DE* or *DA*. This type of multiple-choice recognition test procedure was used throughout this task. Next, the pairs *CA*-/ke/ and *CE*-/si/ were presented for a study-test sequence. (Thus, all of the letter-sound correspondences were invariant except for *C* which was /k/ before *A* and /s/ before *E*.) There followed a series of five study-test trials on the entire set of four pairs, unless a criterion of two perfect test trials in succession was attained. If the child made an incorrect selection, the tester said "no, that makes the sound ____. Let's try again." Finally a transfer test was given; the set *DAZ, DEZ, CAZ,* and *CEZ* was presented, and the child was asked to point out in turn "which one says ..." /dez/, /diz/, /kez/, and /siz/.

Only the *Msn* sample received these tests.

Results

Alphabet-Learning. Over the five-trial series, the percentage of correct responses to the six-pair list increased from 22 percent to 33 percent; the percentage of omissions decreased from 38 percent to 16 percent; correct responses as a percentage of responses attempted remained constant at around 38 percent. In 28 percent of the attempts, the vowel was appropriate to the stimulus shown. Another 17 percent of the attempts were intrusion errors from the nonmatching sublist (e.g., /æ d/ was given as a response in place of /we/). The remaining errors (17 percent) could not be classified.

From the figures given above, it might appear that the learning was going on in a reasonable manner. Response omissions were decreasing, more than a third of the attempts were correct, and of those attempts which were errors, almost three-quarters gave evidence of response learning. In other respects the data are discouraging, however. First, all of the improvement took place from the first to the second trial, where omissions dropped from

38 percent to 19 percent. From the second through the fifth trials, there was no noteworthy change in any of the measures. Second, not one subject out of 21 reached criterion; in fact, only 5 children made four or more correct responses on the final test of the six-pair list. Third, there was no consistency in the retention of pairs from one trial to the next. For example, of those pairs which were correct on the fourth trial, only 43 percent were correct on the fifth trial. Comparing this percentage with the unconditional percentage of correct responses on the fifth trial, 33 percent, it can be seen that whether or not an item was correct on the fifth trial was only slightly dependent on the response of the previous trial. This indicates that associative learning was not occurring; the children were learning the appropriate response terms, but were unable to connect these terms with specific stimuli.

Context-Learning. The results were similar to those of the previous test. The percentage of correct responses rose from 39 percent on the first trial to 64 percent on the second trial and then remained constant over the remaining trials. Of those items correct on the fourth trial, 68 percent were correct on the fifth trial, compared with the unconditional percentage correct on the fifth trial, 62 percent. Again, whether or not an item was correct on the fourth trial was not predictive of performance on the fifth trial. This was a recognition test, and so the errors can again be attributed to a breakdown in association.

The training series on the consonant-vowel pairs was preceded by pretraining on the vowels, but there was little evidence that the children used this information. A response error could be classified as a vowel error (*DE* chosen for /de/), a consonant error (*CA* chosen for /de/), or both (*CE* chosen for /de/). If the vowel component had been learned, vowel errors should have been rare; a similar argument can be made with respect to consonants. Actually, the even distribution of errors indicates the children treated the items as wholes (32 percent vowel errors, 34 percent consonant errors, and 34 percent both). A similar pattern was found in the transfer data. The percentage of correct answers was 29 percent (compared with a chance rate of 25 percent), and the errors were 39 percent vowel, 36 percent consonant, and 25 percent both. The difference during training between variant and invariant items (*D* versus *C*) was negligible: 56 percent versus 54 percent correct, respectively. This finding is also consistent with the thesis that the stimuli were processed as wholes.

In short, there was little evidence of associative learning either of patterns or components after the first trial, nor was there any substantial amount of transfer. On the other hand, some children performed quite well on the training series; 7 out of 21 reached a criterion of two perfect trials. Moreover, there was some evidence of differential transfer: those children reaching criterion during training were correct 43 percent in transfer, those who failed to reach criterion were correct only 20 percent in transfer.

Letter-Word. Only in this test was there evidence of substantial learning over trials. The results are shown in Figure 6.2. Performance on the Letter and Word lists was essentially the same for both the Letter-Word and Word-Letter orders, and so the data have been combined over orders. As can be seen from the figure, in the Letter list there was a steady increase over trials in the percentage of correct responses, primarily due to a reduction in omissions. Of those pairs which were correct on the fourth trial, 88 percent were also correct on the fifth trial, compared with an overall percentage correct on the fifth trial of 66 percent. In other words, in the Letter list subjects retained previously learned items from one trial to the next, and added to this store of learned items on each trial. The pattern of results for the Word list, on the other hand, was similar to that previously described for the *Alphabet* and *Context* tests. None of the performance measures changed to any noticeable degree over the five trials.

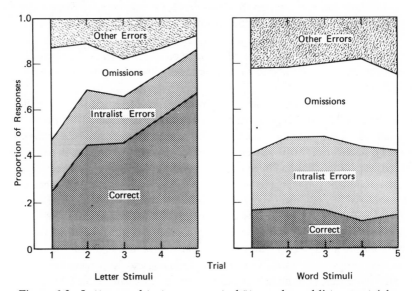

Figure 6.2   Letter-word test responses to letter and word lists over trials.

Summary. The kindergartners tested found it extremely difficult to form associations between the unfamiliar abstract stimulus-response pairs used in this portion of the BST package. The only exception was the Letter list of the *Letter-Word* test. The major distinctions between this latter list and the others were length (three pairs) and the elemental nature of the stimuli and responses (/m/, /n/, and /o/). The effect of list length on paired-associate learning is well known, but in the BST package the variation in length was relatively slight (three pairs in the *Letter* list to six pairs in the *Alphabet* list). Except for the Letter list, the spoken segment comprised two phonemes in these tasks. Moreover, there was repetition of phonetic elements (e.g., /mo/, /no/, /om/, /on/) producing high intralist similarity, which after the fact we feel may be a critical variable in these particular tests.

In any event, if a child does not "know his ABC's," if he has not learned to identify the letters of the alphabet with their corresponding names, it is evident that he faces immediately a paired-associate task of some magnitude in beginning reading. Note that the names of the letters of the alphabet are, by and large, difficult in the same sense that our materials were—they are combinations of two (or more) phonemes used in repetitive combinations producing high intralist similarity.

Discussion

Distinctive feature versus pattern learning. Developmental studies of verbal learning are relatively scarce, given the volume of research in this area on college students. As Flavell and Hill (1969) point out in a recent review, child learning studies have focused on a small number of specific problems—discrimination, transposition, probability learning, and paired-associate learning—and in none of these areas have the studies revealed anything of much interest relative to development *per se*. In fact, Flavell and Hill direct their most critical comments toward this lacuna. They call for research which will in "more direct and sensitive ways assess...the child's knowledge of classes and relations, his attentional biases, his perceptual skills, and his mnemonic strategies...and capacities...(p. 44)."

In a particularly revealing experiment, Ann Pick (1966) taught kindergartners to select standard visual symbols from a set of alternatives which included transformations of the standard. For example, if *b* was the standard, then the set $\{b, d\}$ would involve a right-left transformation. (The letters *b* and *d* are for illustration only; Gibson's forms were used as stimuli.) After a training criterion was reached, a transfer test was administered. In the *Control* group, the transfer task included new standards and new transformations (e.g., select *w* from $\{w, m\}$). In the *Standard* group, the same standard set was used but with new transforms (e.g., select *b* from $\{b, q\}$). Finally, in the *Transform* group, there was a different standard set, but the transformation remained the same (e.g., select *p* from $\{p, q\}$).

It was reasoned that if children had learned to choose the standard by reference to an exact template or image in memory, then the *Standard* group should perform best on the transfer test, since the same templates could be used. If selection was based on transformation of specific features, then the *Transform* group should do best in transfer. If specific inter-item comparisons were learned, then all three groups should perform equally well on transfer. Pick found that during transfer the *Transform* group made 40 percent as many errors as the *Control* group, and the *Standard* group made 70 percent as many errors. These results indicate that young children can abstract transformations of distinctive features and use these apart from the specific context in which they were originally embedded.

Transfer of letter-sound learning. There remains the intriguing question of why such transfer occurs under some conditions and not others. In the *Letter-Word* test in the BST package, there was no evidence of transfer based on combination of elements. Silberman (1964) has recounted his sad experiences in trying to teach kindergartners reading matrices with the structure below.

VOWEL-CONSONANT ENDINGS

	-an	*-it*	*-at*	*-in*
f-	*Test*	Train	Train	Train
r-	Train	*Test*	Train	Train
s-	Train	Train	*Test*	Train
m-	Train	Train	Train	*Test*

In the experimental procedure, the child learned the *Train* CVC's (e.g., $f + at$ = /f æ t/) and then were given a transfer test on the diagonal test items (e.g., $f + an$ = /f æ n/). An initial version of the procedure yielded *no* transfer at all. In the version which finally evolved, the children's attention was directed to the component features (C- and -VC), and then they were taught to amalgamate the elements. A final training segment provided direct practice on transfer to new combinations. After this highly structured program, children performed reasonably well on transfer items (75 percent correct).

It is apparently unwise to assume that transfer will occur naturally, or that a process of induction or stimulus generalization guarantees that children will apply information gained in one situation to other similar problems. This may happen, but it may not. In particular, little transfer occurs when the stimulus-response pairs consist of acoustic-phonetic materials. This conclusion is consistent with the earlier discussion of the integrated character of the spoken language.

Other studies of letter-sound association. A study by Jeffrey and Samuels (1967) bears on "learning the ABC's" and transfer of elements in paired-associate learning involving spoken materials. Jeffrey and Samuels asked whether training on elements or patterns was the more efficient way of teaching reading: is more transfer achieved by teaching words (*MO*-/mo/, *SO*-/so/, *BA*-/be/, *BE*-/bi/), or letters (*M*-/m/, *S*-/s/, *A*-/e/, *E*-/i/) where the transfer set consists of words (*ME*-/mi/, *SE*-/si/, *SA*-/se/, *MA*-/me/)? In the former procedure, the child is trained on integrated word-like units, and must induce the letter-sound regularities, whereas in the latter procedure the regularities are taught but the child has less experience in working with integrated units. The kindergarten subjects were first trained to scan letter groups from left to right and to blend phonically (e.g., (/m/-/i/) equals /mi/). Different groups of subjects were given Word training, Letter training, or were trained on an unrelated Control list of cartoon animals paired with proper names. The stimuli were fairly complex visual symbols (Arabic letters).

Two results from this study are of interest. First, in reaching a criterion of one perfect trial in training, the Letter group required 13.8 trials, the Word group 16.9 trials. Compared with the differences in performance over five trials in the *Letter* and *Word* lists in BST, this is a small difference. The Jeffrey-Samuels materials were of lower intralist similarity, and this may account for the differing results. Second, the number of trials to criterion on the transfer task was 13.5 in the Letter group, 27.2 in the Word group, and 29.3 in the Control group. Thus, training on letter elements substantially facilitated transfer to words in the Jeffrey-Samuels study, although it did not in the *Letter-Word* task of BST. Several differences in procedure between the two studies might be responsible for the different results. First, in the BST *Letter-Word* task, original learning was not carried out to a criterion as in the Jeffrey-Samuels study. This is probably not important because subjects who did reach criterion on the *Letter-Word* test showed no more transfer than noncriterion subjects. Second, in the Jeffrey-Samuels study the child was instructed at the beginning of the transfer task, "You can tell what the word is by making each letter sound. Make the first letter sound, then the next letter sound. Then try to say the word." It would appear that for kindergartners to learn to read words in miniature reading tests, (a) the child should first be taught individual letter-sound correspondences, (b) it must be made explicit that words are to be read as sound combinations, and (c) instruction in phonic blending must be given. These steps are necessary because young children do not tend naturally to break up reading patterns into elements, nor do they naturally induce correspondences in the process of learning specific examples representing particular correspondences.

VOCABULARY

In one guise or another, a child's knowledge of vocabulary is an important predictor of reading achievement. Vocabulary tests often require children to identify uncommon words, or to try to label indistinct or ambiguous line drawings. Performance on such tests reflects the level of general intellectual ability as well as vocabulary skills.

Three different tests of vocabulary knowledge were included in the BST package. Each child was asked to name common objects displayed in full-color pictures, label line drawings, and to sort the line drawings into the most appropriate categorial arrangements. None of the objects was likely to be completely novel to any child, but the names of some were far less common than the names of others.

Method

In *Picture-Naming*, the child was asked to name each of twenty-two common objects. The objects were photographed in color, and the transparencies were seen in a handheld viewer. In *Line-Drawing-Naming*, the child was asked to label objects shown as line drawings printed on 3 x 5 cards. The sketches included some detail and shading. There were five objects in each of six categories and six objects in four categories. The categories were *animals, food, toys, vehicles, articles of clothing, furniture, dinnerware, part of the body, insects,* and *round things*. Within these categories, items were selected on the basis of distinctiveness and familiarity.

The line drawing cards were also used in the *Sorting* test, which consisted of three parts: (a) two categories without exemplars, (b) four categories with exemplars, and (c) four categories without exemplars. In each of these subtests, the child was given a deck of cards containing five cards from each category and asked to sort them into groups that "belong together." A formboard was used to force the children to sort into the desired number of categories. In (b), four exemplar cards were placed at the left of each row of the formboard, and the child was instructed to sort the deck into four groups using the exemplars as a basis.

Results

The error rate on *Picture-Naming* was low, 4.1 percent *(Msn)* and 3.7 percent *(Bel)*. Of the total of 39 errors, 17 were intraclass errors of one sort or another (e.g., *rose* for *flowers, pie* for *cake*), six were omissions, and the remaining 16 were "other" (e.g., *necktie* for *hat, bread* for *apple, cookies* for *pennies*).[4] The errors were widely distributed over subjects—there were 17, 16, 7 and 3 children who made 0, 1, 2, or 3 errors respectively.

The error rate on *Line-Drawing-Naming* was higher than on *Picture-Naming*, largely because the test contained more unfamiliar items. On the

---

[4] The scoring scheme used to classify these responses is admittedly arbitrary in some instances. In general, our classification was conservative; by a more liberal criterion, only two or three of the responses were not related semantically or perceptually to the stimulus. For example, one might argue that *necktie* for *hat* and *cookies* for *pennies* bear some relation to the stimulus, even though we classed them as "other."

eight objects common to the two tests (*apple, cake, chair, car, cat, dog, horse, shoe*) there were actually more errors on *Picture-Naming* than on *Line-Drawing-Naming* (12 versus 4). Overall, the error rate was 15.7 percent (*Msn*) and 20.6 percent (*Bel*) on *Line-Drawing-Naming*. Although the rate was slightly higher in *Bel* than *Msn*, the pattern of errors was the same in both samples, and so analysis will be based on the combined data.

Failures to respond comprised 15 percent of the errors. One quarter of the errors were accounted for by five popular substitutions; more than a third of the children said *wheel* for *tire, dresser* or *drawer* for *desk, baby* for *doll, windmill* for *pinwheel*, or *crib* for *bed*. A closely related error was a coordinate or intraclass confusion, such as *penny* or *nickel* for *half dollar, spider* for *bee*, or *goat* for *cow*. (The distinction between popular and coordinate confusions was based on frequency of intrusion and definitional equivalence.) These accounted for an additional 34 percent of the errors. Another 12 percent were errors of superordination or overgeneralization, such as *money* for *half dollar, meat* for *hot dog*, or *face* for *mouth*. The remaining 14 percent of the errors were classified "other." Most of these latter errors were the result of overdifferentiation of the stimulus (e.g., *bird* to *half dollar*), a few others were incomprehensible (e.g., *leaf* for *ant*, *"boodle allen"* for *deer*).

Seven words (*half dollar, mouth, bee, ant, grasshopper, spider*, and *pitcher*) produced a large proportion of errors marked by considerable variation (e.g., *pitcher* was variously described as *coffee pot, coffee cup, cup, can, kettle, bottle, cream bowl*, etc., *ant* as *grasshopper, spider, bug, fly, flea, leaf, dirt*, etc.). More than a third of the children gave deviant responses to these cards. On 28 of the remaining 38 stimuli, four children or less made responses classed as errors. Thus, the distribution of errors over the stimuli tended to be bimodal: stimuli produced many or few errors. The distribution of errors over subjects tended to be unimodal, contrary to the bimodal subject distributions found in other tests. In *Line-Drawing-Naming*, errors ranged from 1 to 15, with 60 percent of the error scores between 5 and 10. The split-half reliabilities were .53 (*Msn*) and .80 (*Bel*).

Sorting. This test was given to the *Msn* sample only. One performance measure was the number of times the most frequent category in each row was represented. This measure disregarded the cue cards in the four-category-with-exemplar subtest. The guessing rate was 50 percent for the two-category subtest and 40 percent for the four-category subtests. The observed percentages of correct responses were 70 percent, 64 percent, and 63 percent for the two-category, four-category-with-exemplar, and four-category-without-exemplars subtests, respectively. The percentage correct on the second test dropped to 56 percent when correct responses were defined as those sortings which matched the exemplar.

There were substantial individual differences on the sorting task, showing up as a markedly bimodal distribution. About half of the children (10 out of 21) made scores between 37 and 48 correct out of 50 possible, which is less than one and a half mistakes per category. The other eleven children made scores of 27 to 22 correct, or about two and a half mistakes per category.

The distribution of sorting errors over the stimulus categories, on the other hand, was uniform within each of the two four-category sets used in the test, although there was a sizable difference between the sets. The relevant data are presented in Table 6.8. The frequencies along the main diagonals are correct sorts, the number of times that two items belonging to the same normative category were placed in the same stack by a child. The off-diagonal frequencies are category confusion errors; thus, in set 1 there were 63 occasions in which an item from the *kitchen* category was placed in the same stack as an item from the *clothes* category. Also shown in the table are the number of labeling errors for items in each category by children in the *Msn* and *Bel* examples.

TABLE 6.8. Correct Sorts and Intercategory Sorting Confusions in Four-Category Sets

Set 1				
Kitchen (21, 28)	Clothes (9, 12)	Animals (8, 18)	Vehicles (2, 6)	Categories
112	63	70	63	Kitchen
	111	70	69	Clothes
		106	64	Animals
			117	Vehicles
Toys	64			
Food	79	84		
Body Parts	101	77	93	
Furniture	111	90	59	78
Categories	Toys (15, 33)	Food (5, 4)	Body Parts (8, 20)	Furniture (1, 4)
Set 2				

NOTE. Numbers in parentheses are labeling errors in *Msn* and *Bel* samples.

Several aspects of the data should be noted. First, within each set there was little evidence of differences in the number of correct sorts for any category.

There was a difference between sets, which could have resulted from specific category difficulty, or differential intracategory confusability or both. For example, the *toy* category had the lowest number of correct sorts, and was also more frequently confused with other categories, particularly *body parts* and *furniture*. This result could reflect a poorly developed concept of *toy*, or the existence of specific confusions between *toy-body parts* and *toy-furniture*; the data from this study do not permit us to decide between these two interpretations. Second, the distribution of confusion errors is reasonably uniform. As just noted, *toy-body parts* and *toy-furniture* confusions are greater in number than other combinations, but even these maximum deviations from a uniform distribution of confusion errors are relatively slight. Third, there is no discernible relation between sorting performance and labeling performance. In set 1, there were 21 labeling errors (disregarding "populars") for *kitchen* items, and 2 labeling errors in the *vehicle* category; the number of correct sorts in these two categories was virtually identical. Similarly, in set 2 there was a large difference in labeling errors for the *toys* and *furniture* categories, yet only a slight difference in sorting errors. In short, the coherence of a category was not related to the availability of labels for items in the category for the reasonably familiar and concrete items used in this test. The pattern of labeling errors was similar in the *Msn* and *Bel* samples; the Spearman rank-order correlation between labeling errors per category for the two samples was .85.

Discussion

Vocabulary size. Under the conditions used in BST package, the children tested generally gave appropriate names for the common objects in the test. When errors occurred, only rarely were these omissions; most commonly, children produced words that were close to the normative label. To be sure, the test words were concrete objects presented in isolation. The effects of variation in material (abstract versus concrete, verbs and adjective forms versus nouns) and test procedure remain to be fully explored.

Prior to the advent of transformational grammars, estimation of vocabulary size was one of the most popular topics for psycholinguistic investigation (Irwin, 1960; Templin, 1957; McCarthy, 1954). Performance on various types of vocabulary tests was shown to predict intelligence and general school achievement, including reading acquisition. This last relation might be considered unusual in light of the severe limitations on vocabulary size and content in most reading series. Several studies have shown vocabulary size in kindergartners to be substantially greater than the number of different words in most reading series.

It seemed to us that a vocabulary test which used sufficiently direct means of eliciting the names of common objects would not distinguish between good and poor readers. Our assumption was that virtually all children would know the most common words in the language, though they might vary in the extent to which they were familiar with less common words.[5] There is some evidence from BST intertest correlations to be discussed later that this assumption is incorrect, that even in identification of common words the quality or character of a child's label may be related to other cognitive skills which we have assumed to be important in beginning reading.

Vocabulary quality. A variety of techniques have been used to measure vocabulary: samples of free speech, elicitation of words from pictures or line drawings, recognition tests in which the child hears a word and is asked to pick out the most appropriate picture in a set, asking the child to define a word pronounced by the experimenter, free association tests in which the child is asked to pronounce as many words as he can think of in a fixed period of time, or word association tests in which the child is asked to say the first word that comes to his mind when the tester pronounces a stimulus word. The vocabularies being measured by these various techniques might be expected to be quite different.

Templin (1957) distinguished between *use* and *recognition* vocabulary. She measured the former by the Seashore-Eckerson Vocabulary Test in which the child is asked to name a picture, and the latter by the Ammons Picture Recognition Test in which the child is shown several pictures and asked to point to the picture corresponding to a word spoken by the tester. A group of 3 to 5 year olds received the Ammons test, and a group of 6 to 8 year olds the Seashore-Eckerson. Each age group included children from upper and lower socioeconomic levels. There was no substantial difference in performance on the Ammons Test between children from upper and lower socioeconomic levels in the age range from 3 to 5. However, 6 to 8 year olds from a lower socioeconomic level performed substantially poorer on the Seashore-Eckerson Test than an upper socioeconomic group. Although the type of test was confounded with age, the data suggest that the nature of vocabulary test may be an important variable in its own right, again pointing out the necessity of convergent tests.

There are many methodological problems in testing children's vocabulary which have not been systematically examined. We know of no good techniques for testing anything other than concrete nouns, concrete adjectives, and action verbs in young children. The method of elicitation and the choice of whether words are to be tested in a sentential context or in isolation probably affect performance. Finally, the characteristics of the tester are important, especially in testing different social and cultural groups. For example, there is evidence that the speech of Negro children from urban ghettos depends on whether or not they are tested by interviewers of their own race, who may (or may not)

[5] Children for whom English is a second language, or those from extremely deprived backgrounds, might prove exceptions to this generalization.

speak a dialect closer to the child's (Entwisle & Greenberger, 1968; Labov, 1967).

Although a large amount of research had been completed through 1950 on the development of vocabulary size, techniques of analysis were so unrefined that little could be said about the actual process of development, except that vocabulary size increased with age. Most investigators and reviewers have raised the problem of what it means to know a word. If the developing child simply has an increasing number of words at his disposal, that is one thing; however, it has been frequently suggested that not just the number of words available, but the way in which a child is able to use those words changes with age. McCarthy (1954) mentions work by Feifel and Lorge (1950) and by Gerstein (1949) on the form of definitional responses used by children from 6 to 14 years of age in the Stanford-Binet and Wechsler-Bellevue Vocabulary items. "The younger children more often employed the use, description, illustration, and demonstration types of definition as well as inferior explanation and repetition responses. Older children significantly more often used synonym and explanatory responses." (McCarthy, 1954, p. 530.) Unfortunately, when the definitional type of vocabulary test is used, one cannot tell whether or not the observed behavior is an accurate representation of the language system, or whether one is primarily testing the productive system as opposed to the receptive or comprehension system. In other words, younger and older children may understand words equally well, but older children are simply better able to explain their understanding. Communications research by Krauss and Glucksberg (1969a, b) supports the latter interpretation.

Russell and Saadeh (1962) also presented some interesting results on vocabulary quality. They administered a four-alternative-definition recognition test to third, sixth, and ninth grade subjects. The four answers provided as alternatives were classed as *functional, concrete, abstract,* and *incorrect.* For example, *COUNT*: to find the number of things in a group (functional); to find how many pennies are in your pocket (concrete); to say numbers in order (abstract); and to tell numbers one after another (incorrect). The validity of the results in this kind of experiment depends greatly on the quality of the alternatives, of course. The data showed a clear shift from concrete to abstract responses between the third and sixth graders, and this was taken as evidence of improved comprehension.

Word associations. Another lead to vocabulary functioning comes from the literature on word associations. A number of investigators (Entwisle, 1966; Palermo & Jenkins, 1964; Ervin, 1961; Brown & Berko, 1960) have found a shift from syntagmatic to paradigmatic word associations from about 5 to 7 years of age. (Paradigmatic responses are those in which the form class of the response matches that of the stimulus, such as *black-white* or *boy-girl*; syntagmatic responses are those of a different form class which could precede

or follow the stimulus word in a sentence, such as *black-dog* or *boy-hit*.) This
shift can be interpreted as a change in the semantic structure of the child's
language systems, or a change in production ability. Data on this point was
obtained by Ervin (1961) who tested children with both word association and
two-choice recognition procedures. In the latter test, children selected the more
appropriate of two associations for a given stimulus. Certain stimuli were particularly sensitive to the syntagmatic-paradigmatic shift, for example, *ball: bat* or *play*.
In kindergarten and first grade children, the syntagmatic response (*play*) was
selected 67 percent of the time, while sixth graders chose the paradigmatic
response (*bat*) 57 percent of the time. Thus, even when production ability is
minimized, the shift is observed. The corresponding percentages in the productive word-association test were 71 percent and 61 percent.

The thoughtful work of Entwisle (1966) on word associations in young
children is worth noting, especially since it spans the age range of most interest
to us. In her concluding remarks, Entwisle is quite specific as to what word
associations are *not*: they are not simple stimulus-response linkages, they are not
elements of serial chains taken from language samples, they are not representative
of more than limited portion of the child's language, and they do not directly
reflect the semantic space of the child. On the positive side, Entwisle makes five
major points in her summary:

(a) The major shift from syntagmatic to paradigmatic associations around the
first grade was confirmed, but found to be much more complex than previously
realized.

(b) The age at which the shift occurred depended on form class and word
frequency. For adjectives with antonymic contrasts, such as *bright-dark*, the
shift occurs earlier than for those without such contrasts, such as *thirsty-?,* or for
verbs which as a class do not provide many natural contrasts.

(c) There are asymmetries in the form-class relations; adverbs produce
adjectives, but not vice versa.

(d) The syntagmatic responses of children differ qualitatively from those of
adults; for example, noun-verb sequences are used by children, whereas adults
are more prone to produce adjective-noun pairs.

(e) Children give a greater variety of associations than do adults.

Entwisle, following a line of argument also developed by McNeill (1966), feels
that these results, particularly (a), (b), and (c), shed light on the development of
the semantic system; ". . . (they) tend to reveal the formation of word classes or
concepts and so they forecast the individual's potential ability to emit different
combinations of words from those he has heard." (Entwisle, 1966, p. 7.) She
rejects the idea that in associating to a stimulus word the subject finds the word
in a mental dictionary and pulls off the topmost entry in an associative list of
response hierarchy. Instead, it is assumed that a word in memory consists of a
feature list (Katz & Fodor, 1963) containing both semantic and syntactic

features. Hence, *dog* might be described as $\{$ animal, domestic, . . . common noun, regular plural, . . . $\}$. With increasing age, this system of features becomes more fully developed and better organized, so that for an adjective such as *hard*, a subject has immediate associative access to the antonym *soft* because it differs by a single feature. Prior to the full elaboration of this system, there may be confusions among similar words, because the entries in the feature list are not well enough established to permit rapid discrimination of close associates.

An aspect of Entwisle's data of particular interest to us which fits naturally into a feature-list theory is the presence of many acoustic-phonetic or clang associates, particularly in the responses of younger children. If the phonetic description of a word is stored in memory along with the semantic and syntactic features (see Brown & McNeill, 1966), one would expect phonetic associates to occur, particularly if other associations are not readily available. Such associative rhymes were produced frequently by urban Negro children (Entwisle & Greenberger, 1968), by Entwisle's (1966) kindergartners, by Palermo and Jenkins' (1964) sample of fifth grade through college students, in Ervin's (1961) kindergarten to sixth grade sample, and in a free-association study in which college students were asked to produce three-letter words as fast as possible – a sample might be *man, tan, ran, fan, fad, bad, sad* (D. Nelson, personal communication). In Entwisle's (1966) study, for example, the percentages of rhyming responses to *add* (a high frequency, familiar word) by kindergartners, first, second, and third graders were 13 percent, 7.5 percent, 3 percent, and 1 percent, respectively. For *bitter* (low-frequency), the corresponding percentages were 20 percent, 18 percent, 11 percent, and 3 percent. Ervin obtained similar shifts in the rate of phonetic associates from kindergarten to sixth grade. As she remarked, these age-related trends parallel the shift from phonological to semantic conditioning reported by the Russians (Razran, 1939) and by Riess (1946). In the data of Palermo and Jenkins (1964), words such as *the, at,* and *now*, which are frequent but have relatively little semantic content, evoked phonetic associates occasionally even in college students (percentages of rhyming associates produced by college sophomores were 3 percent, 7 percent, and 4 percent, respectively, for the stimulus words given above).

Entwisle and Greenberger (1968), testing Negro children from the inner city of Baltimore, found that the *primary* associations by first-grade Negro children were frequently rhyming responses, such as *bad, fad,* or *mad* to the stimulus word *add*, or *mean* and *bean* as responses to *clean*. These responses usually bore no semantic relationship to the stimulus word, and in many instances the responses were nonsense, such as *fird* to *bird*. In the case of urban Negro children, in 55 of the 96 stimulus words in the Entwisle-Greenberger list, one or more of the three most common associates was a rhyming word. The corresponding count for urban white children was 18 out of 96.

The word association task provides a fruitful method for examining semantic aspects of the language system. The frequency of phonetic associations prior to about six years of age is especially interesting. If it is true that analysis of the acoustic properties of spoken language does constitute a major hurdle to the learning of the decoding portion of reading, and if the preschool child is more inclined than the kindergartner or first-grader to focus on the phonetic composition of words, the teaching of reading (at least that portion concerned with decoding) might be more efficiently introduced at age four or five.

INTERTEST CORRELATIONS

Results

One of our aims in the BST package was to develop clusters of tests which converged on specific skill areas—visual, acoustic-phonetic, learning, and vocabulary. Since performance was poor on most of the acoustic-phonetic and learning tests, few intertest correlations in those areas will be reported. Intertest correlations for the tests with satisfactory performance levels are presented in Table 6.9, grouped according to skill areas. *Alphabet-Production* and *Alphabet-Recognition* have been placed with the visual matching tasks since the latter used real letters as stimuli. Three other variables of general interest—age, Metropolitan Readiness percentile, and word memory span—have been included in the table.

The following conclusions summarize the matrix of correlations. Clusters of tests pertinent to these conclusions are enclosed in block form in Table 6.9.

Visual tasks and alphabet knowledge. The visual matching tests in the BST package did hang together quite well. Of the seven intercorrelations involving tests 2, 3, and 4, six were significant at the .01 level, the other at the .05 level.

There was some relation between knowledge of the alphabet and visual matching. Of the twelve intercorrelations in this set, for six $p < .01$, for one $p < .05$, and the other five ranged from .20 to .36. *Oddity-Selection* and *Memory-Matching* were least related to alphabet knowledge. (*Alphabet-Production* and *Recognition* were significantly related, it will be noted.) The relation of performance within the visual matching tests was closer than the relation between visual matching and alphabet knowledge, which indicates that the visual matching tests tapped a component skill other than general competence or age. This conclusion would be on firmer footing if visual matching performance with nonalphabet stimuli such as Gibson forms were tested.

Vocabulary. The predicted relation among the vocabulary tests in the BST package was *not* found. The absence of a correlation between *Picture-Naming* and *Line-Drawing* may reflect the low error rate on the former test. The fact that labeling and sorting were unrelated was noted in the preceding discussion on the *Sorting* test.

TABLE 6.9. Intercorrelations Among Selected Tests from the BST Package

	2	3	4	5	6	7	8	9	10	11	12	13	14	m	s
1. Age (Months)	36 / -01	40* / -20	22 / --	35 / --	68** / -08	27 / -01	16 / 35	23 / 04	52** / --	24 / 06	28 / 14	-16 / 63**	34 / 24	64 / 69	4 / 3
2. Matching Letter Groups		79** / 72**	58** / --	40* / --	50** / 41*	58** / 67**	36 / 34	27 / 35	01 / --	01 / 54**	17 / 13	08 / 09	36 / 67**	63 / 68	11 / 12
3. Matching Retest			53** / --	52** / --	50** / 34	63** / 75**	60** / 46*	48** / 34	08 / --	09 / 61**	13 / 33	12 / 18	51** / 68**	49 / 42	25 / 32
4. Oddity Selection				63** / --	24 / --	36 / --	33 / --	22 / --	25 / --	25 / --	-19 / --	20 / --	22 / --	26 / --	23 / --
5. Memory Matching					20 / --	35 / --	21 / --	29 / --	27 / --	20 / --	07 / --	05 / --	45* / --	43 / --	19 / --
6. Alphabet Production						61** / 45*	27 / 05	35 / 04	46* / --	26 / 22	48* / 35	04 / -28	42* / 21	27 / 33	27 / 31
7. Alphabet Recognition							34 / 36	59** / 30	15 / --	15 / 52**	29 / 35	17 / 03	46* / 57**	23 / 18	31 / 27
8. Picture Naming								18 / 08	11 / --	04 / 29	13 / 27	17 / -01	10 / 48*	95 / 95	5 / 5
9. Line-Drawing Naming									32 / --	29 / 59**	15 / 54**	15 / 32	67** / 36	82 / 78	7 / 7
10. Sorting										42* / --	24 / --	08 / --	46* / --	61 / --	16 / --
11. Segmentation											54** / 71**	31 / 19	36 / 58**	66 / 59	6 / 8
12. Rhyming Production												03 / 04	25 / 24	39 / 37	40 / 43
13. Word-Memory Span													24 / 14	8 / 8	1 / 2
14. Metropolitan (Percentile)														62 / 41	20 / 27

NOTE. Upper entry in each cell is *Msn* sample, lower entry is *Bel* sample. $N = 21$ for each sample, one *S* in *Bel* not included because test 14 was not available. Decimals omitted. *m* is percent correct except for tests 1, 13 and 14.
*r > .37, p < .05, one-tailed test.   **r > .50, p < .01, one-tailed test.

Acoustic-phonetic tasks. *Segmentation* and *Rhyme-Production* showed inconsistent patterns of significant intertest correlation in the two *S* groups when only correct segmentation responses on trial 5 and transfer were scored. When phonologically related responses were combined with correct (as in Tables 6.6, 6.7, and 6.9), the strongest relation was between *Segmentation* and *Rhyme-Production.*

Other BST correlations. There were 77 other correlations among BST tests (age excluded) for which no relation was predicted; of these, eight were significant at the .01 level, five at the .05 level, and the remaining were not statistically significant. Of the 29 BST test pairs for which both *Msn* and *Bel* correlations could be computed, only one showed significant correlations for both groups. In other words, most of the tests were reasonably independent of one another. In particular, word-memory span bore no significant relation to performance on any of the other tests. (Many of the correlations are between .20 and .35; it may be a general law of behavioral testing that any two variables will jointly account for 5 percent to 10 percent of the total variance.) Age did not appear to be consistently related to performance on most tests.

Metropolitan tests. For comparison, the intercorrelations among the six subtests and percentile rank of the Metropolitan Readiness Tests are shown in Table 6.10. Although each subtest was designed to tap an independent skill, 14 of the 30 correlations were significant at the .01 level and 5 at the .05 level. The remaining 10 were not statistically significant. Of the 19 correlations of Metropolitan Readiness percentile with BST tests, six were significant at the .01 level, six at the .05 level, and seven were not statistically reliable. In short, although the subtests of the Metropolitan were not independent, the test served well as a general predictor of performance in a variety of cognitive skills.

Discussion

Cronbach (1967) has recently raised the possibility of a marriage between differential and experimental psychology. Several contributors to the volume (Gagné, 1967) containing Cronbach's paper take note that these two areas have enjoyed an engagement of long duration, but there is no evidence that the affair has ever been consummated. The failure arises from the difficulty of simultaneously manipulating stimulus variables, training variables, task variables, and subject variables. Without pretending that our effort represents more than a limited step in this direction, some of the results are promising. First, without benefit of factor analysis, the BST data in Table 6.8 do hang together in *à priori* clusters when they hang together at all. The majority of the other intercorrelations are negligible in one, the other, or both samples. Second, distributions of subject or stimulus scores are bimodal in a number of tests, which permits partitioning of

TABLE 6.10. Intercorrelations Among Subtests of Metropolitan Readiness Tests

Test	2	3	4	5	6	7	m	s
1. Word Meaning	60** 56**	06 69**	30 52**	48** 76**	16 51**	68** 70**	63 52	17 16
2. Listening		05 46*	26 43*	35 53*	20 53**	62** 64**	64 59	15 13
3. Matching			05 62**	40* 63**	47* 69**	53** 85**	69 49	18 25
4. Alphabet				50** 71**	-04 58**	56** 84**	85 40	16 27
5. Numbers					26 56**	82** 83**	45 38	12 17
6. Copying						55** 79**	42 60	19 27
7. Percentile							62 41	20 27

NOTE. Upper entry in each cell is *Msn* sample, lower entry is *Bel* sample. $N = 21$ for each sample, one S in *Bel* not included because test 14 was not available. Decimals omitted. m is per cent correct. **$r > .50$, $p < .01$, one-tailed test.

*$r > .37$, $p < .05$, one-tailed test.

181

subjects or stimuli in a relatively simple pass-fail fashion. The questions then follow: (a) why do some subjects perform well and others poorly, and (b) why is the one group of stimuli satisfactorily handled, and the other not? In both instances, the answers will take the form of experimental manipulations—training procedures or variations in materials which produce satisfactory performance. It is important to note that feedback under these conditions is immediate—you quickly find out when a testing or training procedure does not work.

SUMMARY

Even though the BST package is in a preliminary form, and despite the limited number of subjects, certain conclusions are worth noting. First, if skill components are narrowly defined, they appear remarkably independent. This independence is not the result of suppressing variation among individuals; from the bimodal distribution of *S*s in *Rhyme-Production* one might well expect high correlations with other tasks, and yet these are not found except for the *Segmentation* test.

With regard to specific skill areas, it appears that visual perception skills contribute only minimally to matching tests. Few errors are made in the matching of single letters, where perceptual problems should play the primary role. Instead, the problems which arise seem to be of a cognitive nature, such as order and memory for forms. The data suggest that sound matching, segmentation, and association of sounds and symbols are poorly developed skills in most kindergartners. However, testing procedures may be at fault—a possibility which must be evaluated more fully.

Finally, two comments can be made about the relation of the BST data to reading achievement. First, correlational data on this relationship will be available in a year and the relation can be determined empirically. Second, inquiries about the relation of specific component skills to reading achievement may be irrelevant to our purpose because most achievement tests are not particularly sensitive to the decoding process on which BST package focuses.

CHAPTER 7

H. A. Simon
Carnegie-Mellon University

WHAT IS VISUAL IMAGERY?

AN INFORMATION PROCESSING INTERPRETATION

Contemporary directions of research in psychology demand that the question stated in the title of this paper be taken seriously—and even answered if possible. A growing body of evidence is showing that, even in such an austere setting as the standard paired-associate learning paradigm, the semantic and imaginal content of stimulus materials exert a large influence on learning. (See Gordon Bower's chapter in this volume.) If the question of imagery is a pressing one, it is also a disturbing one, for it requires us to reintroduce into psychology terms like *meaning* and *image,* which were banned by behaviorism a generation or two ago because of their introspectionist and mentalist implications.

We must employ such terms, but employ them in a way that is consistent with our standards of scientific method. A conservative course would be to stick to the canons of radical behaviorism: to introduce terms like *image* by defining the specific experimental conditions under which imaging is said to be present, and those under which it is said to be absent. The first section of this paper will show why the solution offered by radical behaviorism is unsatisfactory, and will propose an alternative—defining concepts operationally in terms of an hypothesized processing system and system of internal representations. Of course, if we adopt this alternative, we must satisfy ourselves that our definitions are genuinely operational—that the presence or absence of the postulated constructs can be determined empirically. Hence considerable attention must be given to the kinds of experiments and other empirical observations that might be used to test the veridicality of the hypothesized system.

THE LIMITS OF RADICAL BEHAVIORISM

Let us begin with an examination of what I have called the radical behaviorist position—the position that imaging should be defined operationally in terms of experimental conditions in general and the characteristics of stimuli in particular, and not in terms of processes or structures that intervene between stimulus and response.

In his chapter in this volume, Gordon Bower has surveyed some of the evidence in experimental psychology relating to the behavioristically-defined distinctions between meaningful and rote, and between imaging and nonimaging conditions in learning experiments using the paired-associate paradigm. This evidence will serve both to illustrate the radical behaviorist position (which is not, of course, Professor Bower's position) and to point to its limitations.

Let us consider the following list of (schematized) experimental conditions, in a standard paired-associate learning experiment with common concrete nouns as both stimuli and responses.

1. Standard paired-associate rote-learning instructions.
   S: WHALE   R: CIGAR
   (We will call this condition *verbal-standard*.)
2. Stimulus and response presented in the context of meaningful sentences or phrases:
   WHALE SMOKING CIGAR
   (*Verbal-related* condition)
3. Stimulus and response presented in the context of nonsense phrases:
   WHALE TROTTING CIGAR
   (*Verbal-nonsense* condition)
4. Stimulus and response presented in standard form, but with instructions to subject to join them in a picture.
   (*Imaging-instruction* condition)
5. Stimulus and response presented not in words, but as separate pictures: for example, a picture of a whale next to a picture of a cigar (Figure 7.1 A).
   (*Pictorial-standard* condition)
6. Stimulus and response presented as a picture relating the two objects: for example, a picture of a whale smoking a cigar (Figure 7.1 B).
   (*Pictorial-related* condition)

Epstein, Rock, and Zuckerman (1960), for example, report a whole series of experiments using a range of conditions similar to the above list, and find important differences in speed of learning among the several conditions. Their results have subsequently been confirmed and extended by a number of other workers, many of whose experiments are described by Bower (op. cit.). We can use the list of experimental conditions given above to summarize the main results of these experiments as follows.

Learning proceeds at about the same speed in the verbal-standard and verbal-nonsense conditions (1 and 3), and slower in these conditions than in any of the others. Learning proceeds at approximately the same speed in the pictorial-standard and imaging-instruction conditions (4 and 5), and perhaps half again as fast in these conditions as in conditions 1 and 3. Learning proceeds a little more rapidly in the verbal-related condition (2), most rapidly in the pictorial-related condition (6)—perhaps a third faster in this condition than in conditions

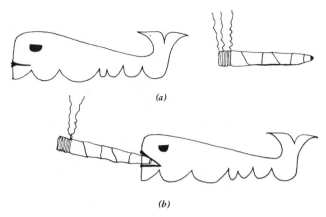

(a)

(b)

Figure 7.1 Pictorial standard (*a*) and pictorial related (*b*) conditions of
paired associates learning.

4 and 5. Even in conditions 1 and 3, of course, the learning of these concrete
noun pairs proceeds two or three times as rapidly as learning of pairs of un-
familiarized, low-meaningful CVC nonsense syllables. Bower's chapter, and the
monograph of Epstein, Rock, and Zuckerman (1960) provide more detail to
fill in this broad picture. Much more parametric work will have to be done,
however, before we can attach much significance to the fine structure of the
data, beyond the broad generalizations I have just stated.

We could follow the time-honored precedent of referring to each of these experimental conditions by its label (e.g., condition 4 is the *imaging-instruction*
condition), and using the description of the experimental condition as the sole
operational definition of the corresponding label. This is the course allegedly
pursued by radical behaviorism. (The reason for the "allegedly" will become clear
presently.) It has a fatal defect. It offers us no theoretical basis for predicting
that two experimental conditions, each with its idiosyncratic operational definition, will both produce about the same rate of learning. Nor does it offer any
theoretical basis for predicting either the sign or the magnitude of the difference
between the rates at which learning will proceed in two different experimental
conditions.

If we follow the prescription of radical behaviorism, to explain the approximate equality of learning speeds in imaging-instruction and pictorial-standard
conditions (4 and 5), say, by labelling both of them as *imaging* conditions is
entirely unjustified. It involves an illegitimate use of the ambiguity obtained by
attaching to the term *imaging* two incompatible operational definitions—the
definitions of conditions 4 and 5, respectively. It is only because the experimenter, on introspecting, adjudges these two conditions to be similiar that he
gives them similar labels. But if we take our operationalism seriously, surely
it is at least as objectionable to inject the experimenter's introspections as the

subject's into the theory. Radical behaviorism demands quite distinct labels for conditions 4 and 5.

Radical behaviorism thus strictly adhered to—as it almost never is—would require us to report our separate experiments as a series of brute facts, forever beyond the hope of condensation into a smaller set of parsimonious generalizations. We would simply have to list our findings in a table, the left-hand column containing the labels for the discrete, and entirely noncomparable, experimental conditions, the right-hand column reporting the learning speeds corresponding to each of the labels.

The only alternative to radical behaviorism that meets the canons of operationalism is to introduce a system of intervening concepts and postulates, sufficiently parsimonious, rich in structure, and rigorous so that it has testable consequences in a wide range of experimental conditions, and, in particular, so that it predicts the relative values of parameters when we compare one experimental condition with another.

OPERATIONALITY OF INTERVENING VARIABLES

Since it is not always understood how intervening variables that are not directly observable can appear legitimately in a theory about empirical phenomena, I should like to make a few comments on this point. To allay unwarranted fears, we note that such intervening variables play an indispensable role even in the hardest of the natural sciences—for instance, in mechanics. Mass, for example, is not observable. Mass ratios of bodies are inferred from ratios of their accelerations. Once inferred, they are used to predict accelerations in new experimental conditions. It is the postulated invariance of mass with time—so that its mass, once estimated, becomes a property of a body—that makes the assignment of a mass number to a body a testable assertion.

It is also easy to see why the trick works. Introducing a quantity that is not directly observable into a theory is like introducing a new variable into a system of equations. Introducing a new law (a relation between quantities) is like introducing one or more new equations (usually an infinite number, if the law is supposed to hold under a whole range of conditions). Assumptions about hypothesized nonobservables can be tested provided that there are *more* equations than variables. Then our various indirect estimates of the nonobservables will be mutually consistent only if the world actually works as the theory says it does; otherwise the theory will be disconfirmed.[1]

We can illustrate the point concretely with the topic under consideration in

---

[1] The issues discussed here have been treated with great thoroughness by econometricians under the heading of "identification." For a simple introduction to the issues, see my "The Axiomatization of Physical Theories," *Philosophy of Science* (March, 1970).

this paper—verbal learning experiments. Suppose that our theory says that short term memory can hold a maximum of seven *chunks*. There is no direct method, we suppose, for determining what components of stimuli are to be counted as chunks. We can, however, reverse matters. We can *assume* that the capacity of short-term memory is seven chunks, and then use the standard immediate recall experiment with various kinds of stimulus material to estimate the number of units of each kind of material per chunk of that material. In proceeding in this manner, we have turned the law stating seven to be the capacity of STM into a tautology—a definition, or an estimating procedure.

Suppose, however, a second proposition in our theory asserts that the length of time required to memorize a set of stimuli is proportional to the number of chunks in the stimuli that have to be associated into new larger chunks. Now let us perform a series of learning experiments using each of the stimuli that we had previously used in our STM chunk-estimation procedures. Since we now have estimated, for each of the stimulus materials, the number of chunks contained in them, we can make no-parameter predictions of the times required to learn any pair of them. These are clearly testable predictions. Thus, the unobservable, the number of chunks per unit of each kind of stimulus material, has provided the link that ties together the two laws of our theory—the one relating to STM capacity, the other to LTM fixation rates—and makes them jointly testable.

Our strategy, then, will be to try to explain the results of the experiments to which we have referred, and others like them, by postulating an information processing system that will behave in the appropriately similar or different ways under the various experimental conditions considered. In conditions 1 and 3, it will learn more slowly than in conditions 4 and 5; but most rapidly of all in condition 2 and condition 6. And the ratios of the speeds of learning will be of the same magnitudes as the ratios observed in the experiments.

EXAMPLE OF A PROCESSING SYSTEM: EPAM

To illustrate more concretely the notions of an information processing system and of internal representation, let us turn briefly to a specific theory that has been proposed to explain certain verbal learning phenomena. Feigenbaum (1961), and Simon and Feigenbaum (1964) developed and tested a theory, EPAM, that takes the form of a computer program written in a list-processing language. Gregg and Simon (1967) and Hintzman (1968) have made further extensions and tests of EPAM. The EPAM theory explains the shape of the serial anticipation curve (Feigenbaum and Simon, 1962); it predicts correctly the quantitative advantage in learning speed of high-meaningful over low-meaningful nonsense syllables, and of familiar over unfamiliar syllables (Simon and Feigenbaum, 1964); it predicts correctly the conditions under which one-trial learning will and won't take place (Gregg and Simon, 1967); it predicts the advantage in learning speed that accrues from presenting subsets of items to be learned in stable groups (McLean and Gregg, 1967; see chapter 1).

The memory organization that enables EPAM to perform has two main components: a *discrimination net* for sorting stimuli and recognizing already familiar ones; and *images* of recognizable structures, containing partial or complete information about those structures. (The present description refers to the version known as EPAM III, employed in Simon and Feigenbaum, 1964.) Images are stored at the terminal nodes of the discrimination net, and are retrieved by means of the stimulus cues used for recognition in the net. Each node corresponds to a *chunk*, as that term was used in the previous section. Learning, in EPAM, consists in elaborating the discrimination net to recognize additional stimuli, and assembling and storing new images, constructing these from component chunks that had been stored previously. The whole system can be viewed as a large, self-modifying lexicon, in which the discrimination net provides the index entries, while the stored images are the individual lexical entries. Every lexical entry is a chunk, and every chunk a lexical entry.

The structure of images in EPAM III is extremely simple. An image is simply a short list of symbols (two or three symbols), each of which is either a primitive symbol (not further analyzable) or the name of some other image. Thus, we might have: $I1 = <I2, I3>$, $I2 = <I4, P1, P2>$, and so on, where the I's are names of compound images, or chunks, while the P's are names of primitive symbols.

In order to fixate a new chunk consisting of two previously available chunks (<WHALE, CIGAR> from WHALE and CIGAR, say), and to store the new chunk so that it is available in response to the stimulus chunk, EPAM elaborates its discrimination net to recognize WHALE as the stimulus part of a new chunk, generates the new structure <WHALE, CIGAR> and indexes it by attaching it to the new node in the net.

In the interpretation of EPAM, a stimulus element is regarded as fully meaningful if it consists of a single chunk—for example, is recognizable as having a lexical entry. It is regarded as less meaningful if it consists of several chunks, hence lacks its own lexical entry. The relative speeds of learning more or less meaningful syllables are predicted (correctly) by

EPAM as resulting from the different amounts of new net-growing and chunking that are required to enter them into the lexicon.

EPAM is a rigorously defined, if relatively simple, system. It permits us to define the term *meaningful,* without vagueness or embarrassment, in terms of the internal representation, and not just in terms of experimental conditions. Hence, it permits us to compare different experimental conditions, and to predict differences in behavior under these varying conditions. It predicts, for example, that low-meaningful CVC syllables, which contain about three chunks per syllable, will take nearly three times as long to learn as very high-meaningful CVC syllables, or familiar English words, which contain only one chunk per item.

EPAM, being a precise theory, is also a refutable theory. Specifically, in its present form it does not predict correctly the outcomes of the experiments in the six verbal learning conditions defined above. We might suppose that the advantage of almost two to one in the rate of learning in the verbal-related, as compared with the verbal-standard, condition could be attributed to the higher meaningfulness of the pair in the former condition. Unfortunately, *meaningfulness* does not mean the same thing here as it does in the experiments discussed in the previous paragraph. The subjects we are likely to encounter in the laboratory have had no previous experience of whales smoking cigars—have not likely even entertained the notion—and hence do not possess a corresponding lexical entry in their memories. WHALE SMOKING CIGAR corresponds to three chunks in an EPAM memory, not one.

In the EPAM theory, a chunk is a chunk is a chunk. The task of associating CIGAR to WHALE, whether in words or pictures, whether with or without verbal context or instructions to image, is for EPAM the same task; and the theory in its present form would predict essentially the same learning speed in all six conditions.

INTERNAL REPRESENTATIONS

With the background of the EPAM theory, let us view the problem of representation in memory from a more general standpoint. In these learning experiments, we are concerned with the formation of associations, and with the ways in which associations can be represented in an information processing system.

To respond correctly to a stimulus in a paired-associate learning task, the information processing system must have stored internally an *image* of the response term, and an *index* whereby this image can be found and retrieved when the stimulus term is known. Here the term *image* is used simply to mean any stored information that is sufficient in kind and amount to enable the response term to be generated; the term *index,* any stored information sufficient to get from the stimulus to the stored image. In EPAM III, as already indicated, the image takes the form of a two-element list containing the stimulus and the response. The index in EPAM is a discrimination net that, in the case of the paired-associate item, indexes the S→R image to a structure of the form (S→*) (where * is a blank symbol).

The EPAM association is therefore the simplest kind of relational structure—a pair of elements joined by the relation we have symbolized as →, and which might be read "S and then R", or "R is next to S". Not all schools of psychology have agreed that such a relational structure is adequate to handle all the memory phenomena that we ordinarily regard as associational. In particular, Ach and Selz made a very strong case for considering *directed associations* as well as simple associations (Humphrey, 1951; chapters 3 and 5). In their research, the Würzburgers showed that a given stimulus does not have a unique associate. Instead, any one of a number of responses may be produced when the stimulus is presented, and which one is produced can be controlled with contextual cues. Thus, in the context of SUPERORDINATE, the response to DOG may be ANIMAL; while in the context of SUBORDINATE, the response may be TERRIER; and in the context of COORDINATE, CAT.

If we follow the Würzburgers in considering this wider range of relational structures—encompassing not only the simple asymmetric relation we have symbolized as →, but also a general class of two-termed relations, which we may symbolize as $R(A,B)$—we open up new possibilities for the ways in which information can be represented internally in an information processing system, possibilities that may have distinct implications for observable behaviors. Let us put aside the experimental evidence for the moment, and view matters from an abstract standpoint.

Whatever information about a visual stimulus is stored in the head, that information is not stored as a picture in any literal sense. That is to say, if a memory is stored of the visible line segment ABC, the memory of B is not stored—in a brain location that lies midway between A and C on the line joining them! There is no reason to believe, either, that the information is stored in English words and sentences, although its content might be described in language somewhat as follows:

> L is a line segment made up of equal contiguous subsegments L1
> and L2, meeting at point B. The endpoints of L are A and C.

Using the standard notations of logic and mathematics, we could reexpress the information as follows:

SEGMENT (L); SEGMENT (L1); SEGMENT (L2)
POINT (A); POINT (B); POINT (C)
ENDPOINTS (L1; <A, B>); ENDPOINTS (L2; <B, C>)

LENGTH (L1) = LENGTH (L2)
L = L1*L2

Except for its telegraphic style, there is little to distinguish this formalized statement from the English language description that preceded it. (The formalized statement contains 30 words, ignoring punctuation; the English statement, 25 words.) In storing the formal statement in memory, however, we can induce additional structure upon it as follows: We consider a memory that contains a discrimination net, *à la* EPAM. We establish terminal nodes for each of the recognizable objects: L, L1, L2, A, B, and C. Each terminal contains a *description* (image) of the corresponding object. A description consists of a list of *properties* belonging to the object, and a list of *relations* connecting that object to other objects. Thus, the description of L1 might look something like this (Figure 7.2):

L1:   LINE-SEGMENT, LEFT-RIGHT, 1 UNIT;
       PART-OF (L); RIGHT-COLINEAR (L2);
       RIGHT-TERMINUS (B); LEFT-TERMINUS (A)

and the description of A might look like this:

A: POINT; LEFT-TERMINUS-OF (L);
     LEFT-TERMINUS-OF (L1)

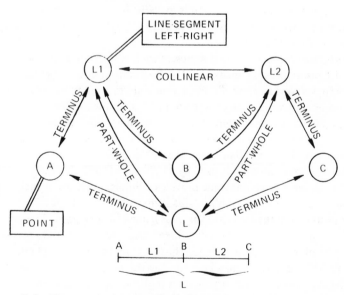

Figure 7.2   The terminal image of the line segment *ABC* that maintains pictorial properties.

The proposed representation makes use only of predicates that describe properties (expressions of the form "P(X)") and two-termed relations (expressions of the form "R(X, Y)"). While the two previous representations were unredundant—no statements could be deleted without losing information—the new representation is highly redundant. For example, it contains explicitly both the information that A is the left terminus of L1 and that L1 is a segment whose left terminus is A. But having paid the price of redundancy, we find in the new representation pictorial properties that are absent from the others. The new representation may be regarded as a model of the situation it describes.

First, *all* of the information about any component of the stimulus that has been recognized is directly accessible at the node for that component. It is contained in the description stored at that node. Recognition of the node is analogous to looking at that component in the stimulus. Second, from any such component it is possible to go directly to any other component that has been recognized as related to it in a specified way—from a point, we can find the lines on which that point lies (see the description of point A above) and from a line, the points that lie on it (see the description of L1). Thus, not only does the internal representation contain all of the information that was extracted from the visual stimulus, but it contains it in a form that permits simple retrieval operations to be performed on it that are more or less isomorphic to the retrieval operations performable on the visual stimulus. Considering, in memory, a particular element of the representation corresponds to fixing that element in attention in the original external stimulus; moving to a directly related element corresponds to shifting attention to the latter.

The proposed form of internal representation also handles satisfactorily stimuli of more than one dimension. A representation of this sort for a chessboard was developed successfully by Newell and Prasad, and has been incorporated in an operative chess-playing program for a computer (Baylor and Simon, 1966). In particular, this representation has been used in a program to simulate the noticing processes of a skilled human chess player looking at a board position for the first time (Simon and Barenfeld, 1969).

A similar representation was used by T. Williams (1965) for the visual display in tic-tac-toe. Since this game provides a simpler example of such a representation than does chess, I will describe its main features (Figure 7.3). Each of the nine positions in the tic-tac-toe array is named by a symbol. In addition, there are names for the three vertical, three horizontal, and two diagonal arrays. Associated with each position is a description—a set of two-termed relations of the form $Ai(Pj, Vij)$, which may be read: "Attribute i of position j has the value Vij." The attributes associated with each position include the mark (X or O) in that position, the positions (if any) in the directions N, S, E, W, NE, NW, SE, and SW from the given position, and the horizontal, vertical, and diagonal (if

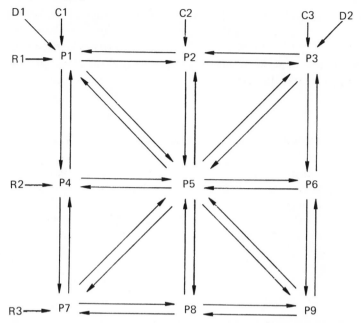

Figure 7.3   The representation of the visual display for tic-tac-toe.

any) arrays to which the position belongs. A similar description is associated with each of the arrays.

Using this representation, it is easy to define simple processes for scanning arrays to determine the marks in them, for determining the position at the intersection of two arrays, and so on. In other words, operations can be performed on the representation that are the counterparts of the operations that can be performed ocularly on a visual array. Notice that in this representation, unlike an external visual stimulus, direct scanning can only be performed in particular directions—those directions that have been encoded in the representation. Whether this is also true of the human internal representation of visual stimuli is a question to be determined by empirical evidence.

There is no need to pursue further the specifics of this particular representation. Enough has been said to show that, starting with a relatively parsimonious information processing system—consisting of the EPAM recognition and imaging mechanisms augmented by the storage of properties and descriptive relations at nodes—we can define a variety of internal representations, and hence indicate, at least in principle, how different representations might be used to encode information obtained through different sensory modalities. Notice that if this approach is followed, it is not necessary to postulate any mode-specificity in the underlying *mechanisms* available to the central storage system. Mode-specificity corresponds to specific variation in *organization* of a common set of mechanisms. There is nothing more mysterious in this than in the fact that twenty-odd amino acids suffice as building blocks for all proteins, or the fact that ninety-odd elements suffice as building blocks for all molecules.

EVIDENCE FOR MODAL SPECIFICITY

To avoid generating metaphysical entities—or nonentities—we need to return periodically to the firm earth of experimental data. What kinds of empirical evidence would lead us to conclude that information stored in memory is stored in structures exhibiting organizational isomorphism with specific sensory modalities? At least three kinds of experiments yield relevant evidence of this kind.

Similarity and Confusion

Norman (1969, chapter 7) summarizes the evidence showing that confusion among stimuli can be attributed to specific modalities. Conrad (1964) showed that in short-term memory experiments most confusions were attributable to acoustical similarity, even when verbal material was presented visually. Subsequently, Baddeley (1966) showed that errors in recall from long-term memory depended mainly on semantic rather than acoustic similarity. The important point, however, is that in both kinds of experiments the modality of the information stored was deducible from the nature of the confusions.

In a similar vein, R. Shepard (forthcoming) has used multidimensional scaling techniques to measure judged similarity among items. The nature of the similarities then permitted inferences to be drawn as to the modality of the information stored.

Aphasias

Data on the performance of aphasic subjects, when the locus of the brain lesion is known, provide evidence that information in different modalities is stored, at least to some extent, in different brain locations. In particular, aural storage of verbal information appears to be localized in one hemisphere, but visual information in the opposite hemisphere.

The aphasia data are particularly significant in indicating a definite distinction between *semantic* and *visual* storage, a point to which I shall return.

Implicit Information

The speed or ease with which subjects can retrieve certain information that is implicit, but not explicit, in information given them, may give indications of the structure of the stored information. Several examples will show how this can be done.

1. The subject is asked to visualize the following situation: A 3-inch cube is painted blue on one side. Two other sides, adjacent to the blue side but opposite each other, are painted red. The cube is now diced in smaller 1-inch cubes. How many of the 1-inch cubes have exactly one blue and one red side?[2]

There are several interesting features of subjects' performance in this task. The subjects have to perform a calculation to obtain the answer, but their subjective report of the process is not that it is a calculation in the ordinary sense, but that it involves visualizing the cube and slices and counting, in the visualization, the smaller cubes having the desired property. That is to say, they report a process that is isomorphic to the one they would perform if they actually painted a cube as required, then marked it along the lines of the slices.

A second interesting point is that if the subject is now asked, "Which side of the cube did you color blue?" he can always give an answer. Since the problem statement does not specify any particular orientation of the cube or of the sides to be colored, this information must have been supplied by the subject at the time he constructed his internal image.

A third interesting point is that if the subject is now asked to "rotate the cube so that the blue side is on the bottom," he will be able to report— even though the rotation is only ambiguously defined by the experimenter— the new orientations of the red sides that result from the rotation.

All of these performances illustrate the ability of the subject to supply information, in order to make the situation more concrete than the one defined by the experimenter; and his ability to draw inferences to obtain new information implied by the information given. But the inference process is described by subjects as a visual perceptual rather than a deductive process.

2. The subject is given—in writing or orally—the following algebra story problem, and asked to set up (but not solve) the appropriate equation:

> A man cuts a board into two parts. The first part is two-third's the whole length of the board. The second part is four feet longer than the first. How long was the board before it was cut?

[2]Mr. George Baylor called this task to my attention, and is using it in his doctoral research to study the nature of visual imagery in memory. I am indebted to him, through conversation and access to drafts of his study, for most of the ideas in this section.

Some subjects set up the equation, $X = 2/3X + (2/3X + 4)$, which if solved, gives the nonsense answer, $X = -12$ feet. Other subjects, however, say, "Isn't there a contradiction?" and point out that the second piece, only 1/3 the length of the board $(1 - 2/3 = 1/3)$, cannot be four feet longer than the first, which is 2/3 the length of the board. But to notice the "contradiction," the subject must supply the information (1) that the whole board is the sum of the two pieces, and (2) that 2/3 is greater than 1/3.

It follows that the subjects who notice the contradiction cannot simply be applying a syntactic process to translate the original sentence into an equation. Their process must include a semantic component—whether verbal or pictorial. Their subjective reports indicate that the semantics were usually, in fact, pictorial—that they visualized the board and noticed that the first piece was longer than the second.

3. I have elsewhere (Simon, 1969, page 76) described a game, number scrabble, that is logically isomorphic with tic-tac-toe. Number scrabble is played with nine chips, numbered from 1 through 9, placed initially, face up, in a central pool. The players draw in turn, their aim being to form, from among the chips they have drawn, a triad of chips whose numbers sum to 15 (e.g., if a player has drawn 5, 9, 2, and 1, then he can form the winning triad (5, 9, 1)).

By numbering a tic-tac-toe array appropriately (e.g., row-by-row: 2-9-4, 7-5-3, 6-1-8), the isomorphism can be seen immediately, for drawing a number in number scrabble is precisely equivalent to marking the corresponding square in tic-tac-toe. Nevertheless, subjects who know perfectly well how to play tic-tac-toe are unable to carry their skill over to number scrabble; and even when they learn of the isomorphism, are able to exploit it only by superimposing the number scrabble representation on the usual visual representation of the tic-tac-toe array. From this example we obtain striking behavioral evidence of the effects of differences in representation.

In evaluating these examples, we must be careful, of course, in the kinds of evidence we accept; and these demonstrations and experiments provide varying amounts of nonintrospective evidence for semantic processing and for a specifically visual storage modality. The number scrabble evidence is particularly convincing, however, not merely in pointing to semantic processing, but in showing how translation to an encoding that uses isomorphs of visual linear arrays to provide the (implicit) information as to the winning combinations causes a striking change in performance. Just as the collinearity of positions can be determined on an external tic-tac-toe array by visual scanning, so collinearity can be detected on any array in the "mind's eye" by an apparently isomorphic process of internal scanning.

All of the evidence for internal modalities, introspective and other, amounts to evidence that certain information is stored in such a way that it can be retrieved by internal processes isomorphic to the external processes that are used to retrieve information in the corresponding modality from external sources. Operationally, this is what *internal modality* means. In the previous section we showed how an information processing system having basic capabilities for handling properties and relations could be organized to store visual images.

SEMANTIC AND VISUAL ENCODING

I have several times alluded to the distinction between internal representations that are semantic in some general sense and those that are more specifically visual. This distinction is important to our understanding of the verbal learning experiments, and we need to address it directly.

An internal representation of a verbal (oral or written) stimulus is regarded as semantic if it preserves the meaning of the stimulus without necessarily preserving the exact form of words in which that meaning is encased. Many experiments, beginning with Bartlett's (1932), have shown that memories frequently preserve semantic information while losing syntactical details. Even when this occurs, the internal representation might still be basically verbal—for example, more or less isomorphic to structures compounded of words.

In terms of one of the currently popular theories of transformational linguistics (Chomsky, 1965), the verbal stimulus may be processed by extracting the deep structure (meaning) from the surface structure. A single deep structure may correspond to many surface structures—different sentences that are "different ways of saying the same thing." The deep structure is a relational structure (representable in terms of descriptions like those we introduced earlier), whose elements are entries in a lexicon— hence isomorphic to words.

From these considerations, we must admit the possibility of an internal representation being both semantic and verbal. (Whether the lexical items preserve either the auditory or visual characteristics of words—whether they are encoded in one of the sensory modalities—is irrelevant to the present discussion.) We must not assume the converse: that a semantic representation *must be* verbal. On the contrary, meanings may be held in structures that are isomorphic to two-dimensional visual stimuli rather than in structures that are isomorphic to verbal strings. We must be prepared to explore both possibilities, and others as well.

It should not be supposed, however, that it will always be possible to discriminate sharply between semantic encodings that are verbal in character and those that are in a visual modality. On the contrary, in the case where the visual stimuli represent relatively simple scenes, they may be encoded in a way very similar to the way in which a verbal input describing the same picture would be encoded—and it will not be easy, in such cases, to determine which form of internal encoding is employed.

There are theoretical reasons for expecting such ambiguity to occur. One of the important functions of language, particularly simple language of the kind used by a child, is to describe external configurations of objects or events. The encoding of such descriptions would be greatly facilitated if there were a high degree of isomorphism between encoded visual images and encoded language (that is, between images and linguistic deep structure).

I can give a very concrete illustration of the difficulty that may be encountered in maintaining the distinction between linguistic-semantic and pictorial-semantic internal representations. It arises from an attempt to create a computer program capable of translating pictures into words, and vice versa. Laurent Siklóssy (1968) in his doctoral dissertation describes a processing system that is capable of performing the language learning task presented by the I. A. Richards books, *Language Through Pictures*. The idea of these books is that a foreign language should be learned, not by translation from one's native language, but by direct learning of the association from sentences in the new language to their denotations or meanings. Each page of *Language Through Pictures* illustrates some simple situation, and, directly beneath the illustration, prints a sentence that means the same as the picture.

In practice, the *Language Through Pictures* books present a number of difficulties. The most serious is that it is often not clear what the picture is about, and which aspects of the picture the sentence refers to. To take one of the more ambiguous examples, an early page in the book may picture a human stick figure standing inside a circle, and pointing to itself (Figure 7.4). The sentence underneath may say, in the appropriate language, "I am here." The reader must infer that the pointing means self reference, that the circle designates location—and specifically the location "here"— that the sex and age of the stick figure, as well as all details of its construction, are irrelevant, and so on.

In the present context, I am not concerned with the efficacy of *Language Through Pictures* for language learning. I would recommend them only to puzzle-solvers, who might find them fun. Our present interest, however, is in Siklóssy's use of this idea. The *Language Through Picture* books simulate, in a certain sense, the procedure whereby a child learns a language. He hears sentences in the presence of situations, and learns to use these sentences to denote these or similar situations. Moreover, he learns how to recombine the lexical units he acquires into new sentences expressing new meaning and denoting other situations.

Figure 7.4 "I am here."

In order to build a processing system to learn in this way, Siklóssy had to define an internal representation for the pictures. Now the pictures—at least the simpler ones—belonged to a relatively small number of types. There were pictures attributing a property to an object: LARGE(HOUSE). There were pictures showing an action: RUNNING(BOY). And there were pictures showing a transitive action: RIDES(BOY,PONY). There were others, of course (e.g., BIGGER(THIS HOUSE, THAT HOUSE)). But the three types mentioned will suffice for purposes of illustration.

In designing an internal representation for these pictures, Siklóssy found it convenient to use just about the same apparatus that one would use to represent internally the deep structure of a sentence in natural language. Thus, if a picture represented an action of one object upon another, it seemed natural to represent it internally as A(X, Y), where A is a symbol to denote an action, and X and Y are symbols denoting the actor and the object acted upon, respectively.

A sentence describing the picture might have, in English, the form, X A's Y. But a natural way to represent the deep structure of this sentence is, A' (X', Y'), where the primed symbols are the internal names of the corresponding words of the sentence. Hence, there is a direct one-one correspondence between the internal representation of the picture and the internal representation of the English sentence describing it.

In cases like this, it would appear to be exceedingly difficult to distinguish between a verbal (semantic) and a pictorial (semantic) representation of a simple visual scene. To detect the difference between the modalities experimentally, we should consider more complex visual stimuli—more like those involved in the tic-tac-toe example—where the stored visual information cannot be simply represented as a sequence of deep structures obtained from natural language sentences.

THE VERBAL LEARNING TASK AGAIN

We can now return to the verbal learning task and ask what light is cast on it by our discussion of representations and modalities. Assuming that there exists a representation for concrete nouns in an aural modality, and a representation for their meanings in both verbal-semantic and visual modalities, we can conjecture that the processes employed by the subjects in the six experimental conditions might be somewhat as follows.

1. Verbal-standard condition.

   Store <WHALE, CIGAR> as list (pair) in aural mode.

2. Verbal-related condition.

   Encode sentence into picture in visual mode;
   Store copy of encoded visual image.

3. Verbal-nonsense condition.

   Store <WHALE,CIGAR> as list (pair) in aural mode.

4. Imaging-instruction condition.

   Encode each word in visual mode;
   Generate picture relating the two visual images;
   Store copy of encoded visual image.

5. Pictorial-standard condition.

   Encode each picture in visual mode;
   Generate picture relating the two visual images;
   Store copy of encoded visual image.

6. Pictorial-related condition.

> Encode combined picture in visual mode;
> Store copy of encoded visual image.

The processes have been described above in ordinary English, to make them as readable as possible. They could without marked difficulty be translated into formal programs for an information processing system capable of executing them. Our earlier analysis of how various representations can be achieved through organizations of simple relational structures should make reasonably clear how this can be done for the "encode" processes, and the "generate picture" processes that are required by the scheme.

If we now examine these hypothetical processing schemes, we see that the processes for conditions 1 and 3 (verbal-standard and verbal-nonsense) are identical. Conditions 4 and 5 (imaging-instruction and pictorial-standard) are very similar—the only difference being that in 4 the input to the encoding process is verbal, while in 5 it is pictorial. Conditions 2 and 6 (verbal-related and pictorial-related) are also similar—differing in essentially the same way as 4 and 5 differ. Moreover, conditions 2 and 6 dispense with a process (generating a picture containing the related S and R images) that is required for 4 and 5.

When we compare conditions 1 and 3—those in which learning is slowest—with the others, we see that their distinguishing characteristic is the encoding of <WHALE,CIGAR> as a pair in the aural mode. If we were willing to make the *ad hoc* assumption that storing an aural list is a slower process than storing a visual image, we would conclude that 2 and 6 would permit the most rapid learning, followed by 4 and 5 as the next most rapid, and 1 and 3 as the slowest—exactly the order exhibited in the empirical data.

Such an *ad hoc* assumption, however, would deny a main thesis of this paper: that all internal modalities employ basically the same kinds of relational structures for storage; and that their differences are differences in organization which enable them to be accessed by processes paralleling the processes of the corresponding sensory modalities. Since the new assumption is *ad hoc* we will prefer an alternative explanation that allows us to dispense with it.

The difficulty in which we find ourselves derives, at least partly, from our implicit assumption that the differences in the learning speeds are derived from differences in the fixation processes. But we have already seen that this is not the whole story—that the lower rate of learning in the pictorial-standard condition, for example, relates to the extra image-generating step required there. This suggests that we should look carefully at the steps that must be taken prior to holding in STM the structure that is to be fixated—that is to say, at the noticing processes that extract information from the stimulus and store it temporarily in STM.

NOTICING PROCESSES

For any save the very simplest visual stimuli, the information extracted from the stimulus is a partial—and very incomplete—selection from the totality of information in the stimulus. The *noticing* processes play a decisive role in determining what will be extracted at each step. The noticing processes, in turn, will be responsive to cues implicit (or explicit) in the stimulus itself.

The information extracted from a visual stimulus will not only be an abstraction of the information actually present, but it will always (except for very simple stimuli) be limited to some restricted area of the full stimulus. Suppose, for example, that a stimulus consists of the two English words, WHALE CIGAR, arranged side by side. Since contrasting white-black boundaries are one of the cues to which the visual apparatus is highly sensitive, it is quite likely that WHALE may first be recognized and encoded, and then CIGAR. If the stimuli are encoded into an internal aural mode, the order information (CIGAR follows WHALE) would likely be preserved, but if they are encoded into a pictorial mode, this information may be lost. In either case, the noticing process, cued by the space between the two stimulus words, may produce two independent structures internally— hence no relation between stimulus and response. Thus, it is still necessary to generate a single S→R image internally before that image can be fixated.

Consider, on the other hand, the case where the stimulus is a picture of a whale smoking a cigar. The information that is noticeable in the picture includes not only a whale and a cigar, but a relation (of smoking) between them (Figure 7.1B). In this case, the information cannot be encoded as three separate and independent structures, for these would simply be: WHALE, CIGAR, and SMOKING (,   ). There would be nothing in such a set of structures to convey the information of who was smoking what. A process able to acquire this relational information must be capable not only of recognizing the three elements (the two objects and the relation), but also of recording in a single structure (say, SMOKING (WHALE, CIGAR)) that it is precisely *these* two objects, a whale and a cigar, that stand in the given relation and not some others.

Let us postulate, then, that the noticing processes *extract* information from the stimulus, *recognize* certain components of the stimulus, and relations among them, and, as a result, *store* certain relational structures or sets of relational structures in STM. It is these structures, in turn, that are fixated. Thus, if WHALE and CIGAR are stored separately in STM as the product of the noticing processes, an additional generational process is required to produce a relational structure R(WHALE,CIGAR) in STM before the two components can be associated. If SMOKING(WHALE,CIGAR) is already in STM, as the product of the noticing processes, then fixation can proceed at once without this additional generational step intervening.

To make the explanation complete, one additional observation is necessary. In the imaging-instruction condition (4), appropriate relations for use in building up a structure are already available in LTM (e.g., SMOKING(,)), and can be retrieved for that purpose. In the verbal-standard and verbal-nonsense conditions (1 and 3), in the absence of an imaging cue, the stimulus and response may reside in STM for a considerable interval of time before any relational structure is generated to embed them.

Thus, what gets associated and fixated as a single structure in memory may depend primarily on what gets *noticed* as a single structure. Fixation processes may be partly or completely under the control of noticing processes that are deeply rooted and not easily susceptible to conscious control by the subject. The imaging instructions (or the presentation of a picture actually embodying the relation) enlist appropriate, and already available, noticing processes in behalf of the task while the standard instructions leave the subject without any simple, easily controllable means for establishing a structure relating S and R.

The present hypothesis has a distinctly less *ad hoc* flavor than the one previously considered. It starts with the observation that *some* process must determine what relations present in a visual display are noticed and what ones are not. It adds to this observation the hypothesis that when two objects are noticed in relation to one another, that relation becomes the basis for the association between them that is fixated.

At least one important piece of evidence, mentioned earlier in another context, gives support to the hypothesis. In the experiment of Gregg and McLean (1967), during the process of memorizing a permuted alphabet, subjects grouped together letters that were presented together on the same card, and the several cards served as boundaries for the first-level chunks that were fixated.

CONCLUSION

The findings of contemporary experimental psychology have revived the need to introduce, with proper operational safeguards, concepts like *meaning* and *image*. The preceding pages have attempted to sketch and illustrate how this can be done, drawing upon what has been learned over the last decade or two about information processing systems and the forms of internal representation of symbols in the memories of such systems.

Using variants of the standard paired-associate learning paradigm as a central example, I have tried to demonstrate both the necessity and the possibility of explaining and predicting the differences in learning speed among different experimental conditions in terms of the way in which stimulus information is noticed, represented, and processed by the subject.

In the course of this exploration particular attention has been given to defining unambiguously what is meant by saying that certain information is stored in a particular modality—say, aural or visual. Modal specificity inheres in partial mappings between the processes available to the system for extracting information from external stimuli and the processes available for retrieving the information when it is held in the internal store in the corresponding modality.

Perhaps the most significant new notion that emerges from the exploration relates to the close interdependence that appears to exist between the noticing processes used in extracting information from external stimuli, and the fixation processes used to store the information internally.

CHAPTER 8

William G. Chase
Carnegie-Mellon University and
Herbert H. Clark
Stanford University

MENTAL OPERATIONS IN THE COMPARISON OF SENTENCES AND PICTURES

In this paper we would like to describe our efforts to understand the mental processes people use in deciding whether or not a sentence is an accurate description of a picture. In studying this issue, we have chosen a restricted but revealing set of problems in which people are timed while they decide on the match or mismatch of a sentence and picture. We have asked our subjects, for example, to read the assertion *plus isn't below star*, look at the picture $\overset{+}{*}$ and decide whether the sentence is true or false of the picture. The mental processes of tasks like this are particularly difficult to introspect about. Indeed, people often notice when it is that they have difficulties in these tasks, but they are quite unable to pinpoint the reasons why. What we would like to demonstrate is that with the proper theory and methodology it is possible to tease apart the mental operations which make up these processes.

It is our conviction that the processes investigated here are far more general than they might appear, for they suggest a particular way of looking at *meaning* as it is applied to sentences, to pictures, and even to visual imagery. So we will devote the first part of the paper to the sentence-picture task and its underlying mental operations, the second part to the implications of this work for previous studies on mental comparisons, and the final part to some speculations on how one might extrapolate from this work to the role of visual imagery in cognitive functioning.

THE COMPARISON PROCESS

The basic experimental paradigm we have used in developing the theory consists of measuring the latencies of true-false (match-mismatch) judgments for 16 different sentence-picture displays. The eight sentences, all in the pattern of *plus isn't below star*, are formed by combining (1) *star* or *plus* as subject, (2) *is* or *isn't* as verb, and (3) *above* or *below* as preposition. Each sentence is paired with one of two possible pictures, a star above a plus $\overset{*}{+}$ or a plus above a star $\overset{+}{*}$. For example, the display containing the sentence *star isn't below plus* and the picture $\overset{+}{*}$ has *star* as subject, is negative, has *below* as preposition, and is false. What we had our subjects do was to look first at the sentence, then at the picture, and then indicate whether the sentence was true or false as quickly as possible by pushing a "true" or "false" button. There are several plausible models that might be proposed to account for the extensive data we have collected using this experimental paradigm. Here, we will present the favored model and compare it to some models that also have a bearing on the role of imagery in such tasks. A more elaborate description of the model, its motivation, a comparison with other theoretical efforts, and a more extensive empirical justification can be found in Clark and Chase (1972).

We decided to analyze latencies for several reasons. First, errors are usually not informative because they are not very sensitive to the independent variables under consideration. Second, verbal reports are not detailed enough or consistent enough to yield a complete picture of the process. In fact, one might say that people *retrospect* rather than introspect about their processing because the judgment is over so quickly. The powerful methods of protocol analysis (Newell, 1966) cannot be brought to bear because people are unable to tell us what they are doing or about to do in these tasks. Perhaps the verbal reports suffer from memory limitations, or—because part of the process may be one of the high-speed automatized control processes—perhaps the judgment is not available to consciousness in the first place. We will say more about the verbal reports later. Third, and most important, we hoped that the latencies could be used in the classic Donders' sense. Donders' idea was that the time between stimulus and response is occupied by a series of stages where certain operations are performed, and, with the appropriate subtractions, these stages could be uncovered. Recent applications of Donders' subtractive technique have been quite successful in uncovering some important mental operations (Posner and Mitchell, 1967; Sternberg, 1969a, b).

The model we have developed for this task consists of a series of additive stages with real-time characteristics in the sense described by Sternberg (1969a). In particular, it consists of two gross additive stages, a stage for Encoding the display, and a stage for Comparing the internal representations of the sentence and picture. Within the Encoding stage, there are two additive substages for the encoding of the sentence and picture, respectively, and within the Comparison stage there are two additive substages consisting of a series of mismatch-and-translation operations. Finally, there is a Response stage that converts the output of the Comparison stage—an implicit *true* or *false*—into the appropriate response. But it is the Comparison stage that is the most important. It receives the output of the Encoding stage, translates the representations of the picture and sentence into a common format so that they are symbolically equivalent, and forms a match-mismatch (true-false) judgment on the final result. The ability of the

Encoding and Comparison stages to predict verification latencies depends on quite specific assumptions about (1) the nature of the internal representations set up at the Encoding stage, and (2) the series of mental operations carried out at the Comparison stage.

The Encoding Stage

The sentences used in this task are assumed to be interpreted in terms of their deep structure propositions (cf., e.g., Chomsky, 1965; Clark, 1969; Lyons, 1968; Miller, 1962). A simple sentence like *A is above B* is represented something like $[\,[A\,]_{NP}\,[above\,B\,]_{VP}\,]_S$ in which the labeled brackets denote the tree structure of a sentence (S), composed of a noun phrase (NP), and a verb phrase (VP). The negative sentence *A isn't above B*, however, consists of a positive proposition embedded within a denial and would be represented as $[[[[A\,]_{NP}[above\,B\,]_{VP}]_S]_{NP}[false\,]_{VP}]_S$, which might be read as *it is false that A is above B*. For simplicity, we will use the notation (*A above B*) and (*false (A above B)*) to represent the positive and negative sentences, respectively, and we will take these representations to mean the deep structures shown in the tree diagrams of Figure 8.1.

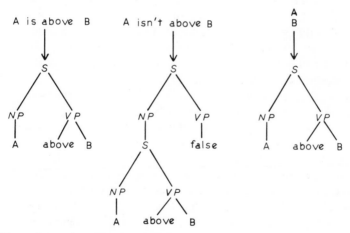

Figure 8.1   Deep structure representations for a positive sentence, a negative sentence, and a picture.

But *above* and *below* are not primitives in these representations. Rather, we want to capture, somehow, the fact that *above* and *below* are converses: that whenever *A is above B* is true then *A is below B* is false and *B is below A* is true. This relation can be specified by considering the meanings of *above* and *below* to consist of sets of features such that *above* and *below* differ on only one or two features. It can be shown, within this framework, that *above* should be more simply represented than *below* (cf. Clark and Chase, 1972) in much the same way that *higher, better, taller,* and other unmarked comparative adjectives can be more simply represented than their marked opposites (cf. Clark, 1969).

The complexity of the encoding of these sentences then allows us to predict that positive sentences should be represented at this stage more quickly than negative ones, and sentences with *above* more quickly than ones with *below*.

It is also necessary to evaluate each sentence as true or false. For this purpose, we consider each sentence to have associated with it a *truth index*, an index whose values are either *true* or *false*. At the beginning, the truth index is set at *true*—for example, subjects suppose *a priori* that the sentence is true unless evidence proves it false—and the operations of the Comparison stage change it to *false*, and even back to *true*, depending on what mismatches are found. The final value of the index serves as the basis for the output of the Response stage.

Second, it is assumed that pictures are ultimately represented in the same way as sentences. When the sentence is viewed first, the picture encoding is contingent on the sentence coding; the picture $\frac{A}{B}$ is ultimately encoded as (*A above B*) when the sentence contains the preposition *above*, and as (*B below A*) when the sentence contains *below*. When there is no previous sentence, however, the picture is normally encoded as (*A above B*). This characterization of encoding is in agreement with several independent pieces of evidence (cf. Clark and Chase, 1972). First, a linguistic analysis of the description of verticality in English shows that *above-ness* is normal and *below-ness* is not. Normative data bear this out by showing that *A is above B* is greatly preferred to *B is below A* as a description of two vertically arranged objects. People have a normal tendency to scan visually from the top down (Yarbus, 1967), and Sutherland and Bowman (1969) have shown that even goldfish discriminate figures by features of the top of figures! Also, when people draw pictures, geometric shapes, stick figures, and the like, they invariably draw from the top down. In short, verticality is normally encoded as (*A above B*). But when the sentence encoding precedes picture encoding, the picture coding is made contingent on the sentence coding and, as we shall see, one stage is eliminated from the Comparison stage.

The Comparison Stage

The Comparison stage consists of a series of two tests, and if a test fails, a translation operation is required. *Operation 1* compares the subject noun of the sentence and picture, and if they match—if they are both plus—then the process goes on to Operation 2. If not, *Operation 1a* changes the truth index associated with the sentence into its opposite. Operation 1, then, checks to see that the inner string of the sentence and picture are synonymous; if they are not, it tentatively marks the sentence as false. *Operation 2* compares the embedding strings of the sentence and picture, and if they match—if the sentence does not contain *false*—then the process stops. If not, *Operation 2a* changes the truth index, and then the process stops. Operations 2 and 2a, then, insure that if only the embedding strings mismatch, the sentence is assigned the value *false*, but that if both the embedded and embedding strings mismatch, the sentence is correctly assigned the value *true*, altered from the assignment of *false* by Operation 1a. These operations are illustrated in Figure 8.2.

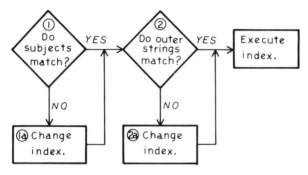

Figure 8.2   Mental operations in the Comparison stage.

The Basic Experiment

The times for these mental operations can be estimated from the latencies for the 16 sentences described earlier. The internal representations, mental operations, and observed and predicted latencies from Experiment I of Clark and Chase, 1972) are shown in Table 8.1.
The predicted and observed latencies are also compared in Figure 8.3. The latencies are based on 10 or fewer correct responses from each subject and are averaged across 12 subjects and the subject of the sentence (*plus* or *star*). The eight conditions are determined by whether the sentence (1) contains *above* or *below*, (2) is true or false, and (3) is positive or negative. The estimates for the two mismatch-and-translation operations were 187 and 685 milliseconds for 1-1a and 2-2a, respectively. These two mental operations, plus the *above-below* difference in encoding time, accounted for 99.8 percent of the variance between the means of the eight basic conditions.

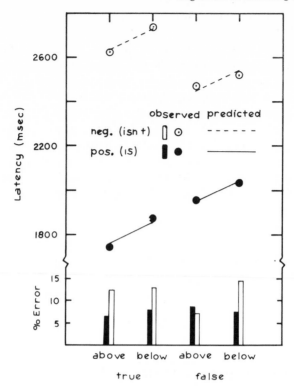

Figure 8.3 Observed and predicted latencies and error percentages from the basic experiment (from Clark and Chase, 1972).

We can now return to the times consumed during the Encoding stage. First, *above* took 93 milliseconds less time to encode than *below*, in agreement with our *a priori* expectations. Second, it should be noted that it is impossible to make an independent estimate of the extra encoding time for negative sentences, since that time is confounded with the time required for Operations 2-2*a* of the Comparison stage. Other evidence, however, can be brought to bear to show that Operations 2-2*a* do consume time. This implies that the 685 milliseconds extra time for negative sentences can be divided into an extra encoding time *and* the time for Operations 2-2*a*, both of which are additive with the other times in the model.

Verbal Reports

When subjects give verbal reports about what they are doing in these tasks, they are often able to give at least partial reports. These reports sometimes provide converging operations on some of the processes, but sometimes they can be misleading about the role of images in these tasks. Subjects, for example, point out that they read and understand the sentence and then look at the top or bottom part of the picture depending on whether the sentence contained *above* or *below*. The model we proposed is in agreement with this kind of report, since the model supposes that the encoding of the picture is contingent on the encoding of the sentence in just this way. But the Comparison stage is more difficult to report about. Once subjects have noted what they have attended to in the picture, their reports trail off with something like "...and so it is true." They do not report Operation 1*a* directly at all. Their reports do, however, suggest that the Comparison stage is divided up into two ordered comparison operations. Subjects report, for example, that for the false sentence *A isn't above B* they first note in the picture that A *is* above B and since the sentence says that A is *not* above B it is contradictory, and therefore false. This implies that the outer string (*false*( )) is checked after the inner string has been verified. Overall, then, verbal reports indicate the skeleton of the comparison process, although subjects are unable to retrospect fully about the operations themselves. Sometimes the verbal reports are couched in terms of visual images and scanning strategies; for example, some subjects say that they construct a visual image from the sentence and then scan the picture from the top down. Nevertheless, we have assumed a more abstract model than this, since we have data to show that a simple scanning model makes incorrect predictions, and since it is impossible to capture the negative embedding proposition in a picture. We will say more about these two points below.

Modification by Instructions

It is important to note, however, that certain alternatives can be ruled out because of the verbal reports. One thing that subjects claim they never do, at least in our experiments, is translate negative sentences like *A isn't below B* directly into positive ones like *A is above B*. Evidence internal to the first experiment in fact shows that they could not be doing that. But, we thought, since this aspect is open to introspection, it might also be open to instruction. Therefore, Young and Chase (1971) instructed subjects to convert negative sentences directly into positive ones *before* making a comparison. The subjects were given either one of two instructions: (1) change *A isn't above B* to *A is below B* and *A isn't below B* to *A is above B*; or (2) change *A isn't above B* to *B is above A* and *A isn't below B* to *B is below A*. In one transformation, the preposition is changed while in the other the subject and object are interchanged, and in both cases, Operations 2 and 2*a* are eliminated from the Comparison stage. The subjects found these instructions quite possible to follow. Notice, incidentally, that either instruction still produces the correct answer to the 16 problems.

The results of these two instructions for a single subject are shown in

TABLE 8.1. The Internal Representations, Mental Operations, and Observed and Predicted Latencies From Experiment I of Clark and Chase

Displays			Sentence Code	Picture Code	Mental Operations 1a	Mental Operations 2a	Latencies Observed	Latencies Predicted
pos.	true	above	(A above B)	(A above B)	- - -	- - -	1744	1762
		below	(B below A)	(B below A)	- - -	- - -	1875	1856
	false	above	(B above A)	(A above B)	true→false	- - -	1959	1950
		below	(A below B)	(B below A)	true→false	- - -	2035	2044
neg.	true	above	(false (B above A))	(A above B)	true→false	false→true	2624	2636
		below	(false (A below B))	(B below A)	true→false	false→true	2739	2730
	false	above	(false (A above B))	(A above B)	- - -	true→false	2470	2448
		below	(false (B below A))	(B below A)	- - -	true→false	2520	2542

Figure 8.4. With the proper transformations in Table 8.1 and from their consequences on Operations 1 and 1*a*, it can be seen that the theory predicts the outcomes in Figure 8.4 extraordinarily well. For this subject, the negative-to-positive transformation took 310 milliseconds, the *above-below* difference was 167 milliseconds, and the one remaining comparison operation took 46 milliseconds; these three parameters accounted for 98.5 percent of the variance between the 16 means. Furthermore, the 310 milliseconds negative-to-positive transformation took far less time than did Operations 2-2*a* (517 milliseconds for this subject), which, of course, is now eliminated from the process. And also, it was not that the printed word *above* is easier to read and discover than *below*, but rather that the encoded word *above* takes less time in the process than *below*. That is, in the conditions where *isn't below* is transformed to *above*, the *above-below* difference exactly reverses; it is the final encoded preposition, not the printed word, which determines the encoding difficulty. The

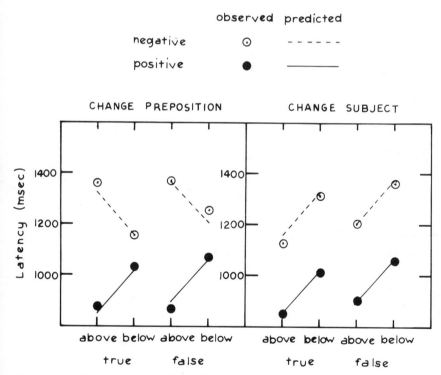

Figure 8.4 Observed and predicted latencies for one subject under instructions to convert negative sentences to positive sentences by either changing the preposition or the subject (from Young and Chase, 1971).

extraordinary thing about the results of the first experiment, then, is that subjects used the negatives in their true sense and did not bother to translate them immediately into viable positive forms. Subjects report that the negative-to-positive transformation seems to take longer, although in fact, it saves time. It appears that subjects do not like to spend an extra 300 milliseconds on the sentence before looking at the picture. Rather, they like to encode the sentence immediately and handle the negatives in the Comparison stage.

Encoding the Picture First

When we asked subjects to view the picture first and then the sentence,

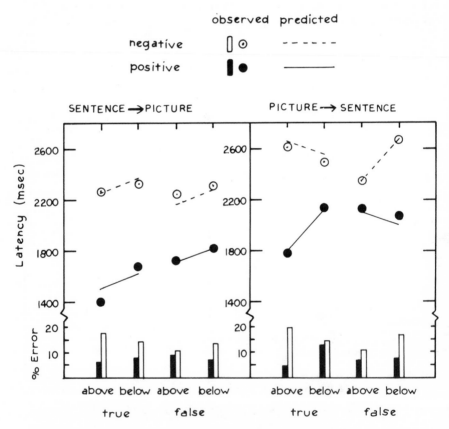

Figure 8.5   Observed and predicted latencies and error percentages under instructions to either encode the sentence first or the picture first (from Clark and Chase, 1972).

the pattern of latencies changes in an informative way. We asked 24 subjects to judge the 16 sentence-picture displays under instructions to (1) view the sentence first and then the picture, or (2) view the picture first and then the sentence. Figure 8.5 compares the means for the eight basic conditions under the two sets of instructions. These results show first that the picture-first condition takes longer, and second that the picture-first pattern is quite different.

These results can be accounted for by the model we have proposed with the addition of one operation to the Comparison stage and a slight alteration of the operations. First we assume that when subjects attend to the picture first, they encode the picture as (*A above B*), and then when they attend to the sentence, it is encoded as before. Since these are two independent codes, the first problem is to make them equivalent. In this case, *Operation 1'* first compares the subjects of the sentence and picture; if they are not identical, *Operation 1'a* translates the picture code by the rule (*A above B*)→(*B below A*). Now *Operation 1* can check to see if the inner strings of the picture and sentence match, but now this comparison is altered to compare the prepositions. If the prepositions do not match, *Operation 1a* changes the truth index to indicate the nonsynonymy of the embedded strings. Operations 2 and *2a* are as before. These operations are illustrated in Figure 8.6 and Table 8.2.

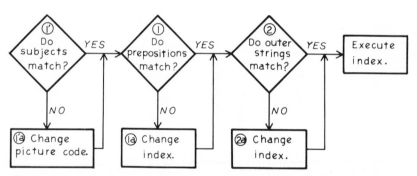

Figure 8.6   Mental operations in the Comparison stage when the picture is encoded first.

When we fit this model to the data, the *above-below* difference was 117 milliseconds, Operations 1-1a took 148 milliseconds, and Operations 2-2a took 556 milliseconds; these parameters are in good agreement with the other experiments. The additional Operations 1'-1'a took 212 milliseconds, which is close to the extra time (296 milliseconds) it took to process the picture-first displays. These four parameters accounted for 98 percent of the variance between the 16 means.

TABLE 8.2. The Internal Representations and Mental Operations for the Picture-First Condition

Displays		Picture Code	Sentence Code	Mental Operations 1′a	Mental Operations 1a	Mental Operations 2a
pos.	true above	(A above B)	(A above B)	- - -	- - -	- - -
	true below	(A above B)	(B below A)	(A above B)→(B below A)	- - -	- - -
	false above	(A above B)	(B above A)	(A above B)→(B below A)	true→false	- - -
	false below	(A above B)	(A below B)	- - -	true→false	- - -
neg.	true above	(A above B)	(false (B above A))	(A above B)→(B below A)	true→false	false→true
	true below	(A above B)	(false (A below B))	- - -	true→false	false→true
	false above	(A above B)	(false (A above B))	- - -	- - -	true→false
	false below	(A above B)	(false (B below A))	(A above B)→(B below A)	- - -	true→false

216

We have also tried another variation on this experiment in order to control the way subjects represented the pictures. In this variation, we asked subjects to view the picture first, then read the sentence, under instructions to (1) view the picture as a whole, (2) attend to the top of the picture, or (3) attend to the bottom of the picture. Since the picture subtended a visual angle of only .8°, there is no question that both figures were well within the fovea: the question is how subjects will *encode* the display under the different attention instructions. We supposed that subjects would be forced to encode the picture as (*A above B*) when they attended to the top, but as (*B below A*) when they attended to the bottom. Figure 8.7 shows that the model fits these results quite nicely. First, the results for Instruction 1, "view the picture as a whole," were very similar to those for Instruction 2, "attend to the top." Second, the results for Instruction 3, "attend to the bottom," were quite different, but in exactly the way predicted by the model. Here the results of Operation $1'$-$1'a$ were in exactly the opposite direction since now the complementary subset of conditions requires the transformation (*B below A*)$\rightarrow$(*A above B*). This can be seen by substituting (*B below A*) as the picture code in Table 8.2, and working through Operations $1'$ and $1'a$. The parameter estimates for this experiment were 84 milliseconds for *above-below*, 196 milliseconds for Operations $1'$-$1'a$, 145 milliseconds for Operations 1-1a, and 660 milliseconds for Operations 2-2a—all in good agreement with the previous experiments. These four parameters accounted for 97.4 percent of the variance between the 24 means of this experiment.

These results show why viewing the picture first is more difficult—because there is an extra mental operation involved. When people view the sentence first, almost all the encoding is contingent upon the sentence. The super-structure of the picture code is already set up—for example (? *above* ?) or (? *below* ?), depending upon the sentence preposition. When subjects then view the picture, all that is required is to recognize a pattern and fill in the nominals. Subjects in fact say that they do not code the object, so that the final structure may look something like (*A above*), which is not inconsistent with the model we have developed. At any rate, when subjects view the picture first this conditional encoding cannot take place, so two independent codes must be compared. The problem here is that (*A above B*) compared to (*B below A*) is true, but this cannot be discovered directly by a match-mismatch comparison. People therefore first make sure that the subjects of the picture and sentence representations are identical, and so the additional Operation $1'$ is required. Notice that in both picture-first and sentence-first conditions, the first comparison is with respect to the subjects. This operation insures that the first comparison operation will discover a contradiction in meaning between (*A above B*) and (*A below B*). The comparison operations are then carried out, in order, from the embedded to the embedding sentences. The results are also clearly

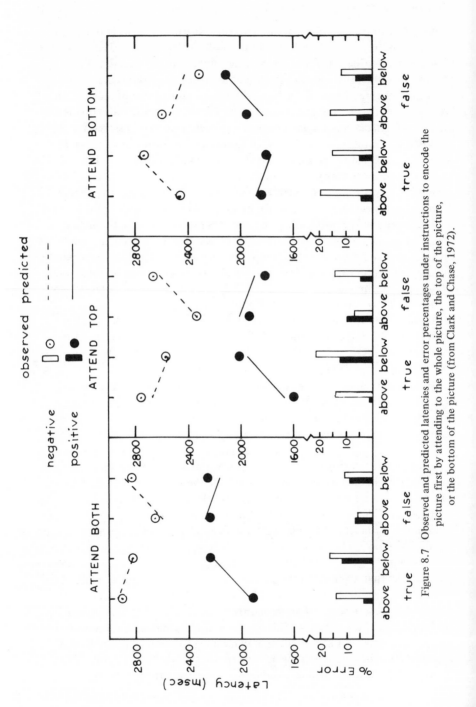

Figure 8.7 Observed and predicted latencies and error percentages under instructions to encode the picture first by attending to the whole picture, the top of the picture, or the bottom of the picture (from Clark and Chase, 1972).

218

consistent with the premise that the normal code for pictures is one thing above another.

The theory we have presented has been given reasonable support in the several experiments we have reported. But it is not simply an explanation for judgments of sentences with *above* and *below:* it is more versatile than that. With modifications, it also accounts for judgments of *present-absent, larger-smaller, front-back, ahead-behind,* and other such pairs. Moreover, the basic assumptions of the model—for instance, that the encoding and comparison stages are separable, that sentences are encoded in terms of their deep structure propositions, and so on—are identical or similar to the assumptions of a more general theory of sentence comprehension (Clark, 1969, 1970). This latter theory accounts, for example, for certain results in deductive reasoning and in the comprehension of negation. In these instances, there are no perceptual processes, and the theory deals entirely with abstract linguisitic relations. If the present theory is this general, then it has something important to say about the perception of properties of objects and relations between objects. The important point we wish to make here is that the perception of relations and properties involves an abstract mental code that is, ultimately, in the same representational system as the meaning—the deep structure propositions—of a sentence.

OTHER APPROACHES TO SENTENCE-PICTURE COMPARISON

The account of the sentence-picture process we have just given does, of course, have its challengers. The particular alternatives we will consider here are ones that postulate a more concrete comparison operation—an operation that is carried out on a less abstract internal representation of the picture. These theories all talk about an image of one sort or another. The images are more or less abstract, but they are always less abstract than the deep structure representation we describe. The theories we will consider here are Seymour's (1969) top-down scanning, DeSoto, London, and Handel's (1965) spatial paralogic, and Posner's (1969) generation of visual information.

Top-Down Scanning

Seymour (1969) suggests that *above* is faster than *below* in experiments like the ones we have just described because subjects invariably scan images from top down. In an experiment similar to ours, he found that subjects took less time to judge that the word *above* correctly matched the position of a small circle drawn above a large reference square than they took to judge that *below* matched with the circle below the square. Seymour proposed that the subjects first generate an internal representation of the display from the word *above* or *below* and then scan this internal representation and the display simultaneously from the top down until they locate the circle in both the model and the display. Seymour claimed that his internal representation was not necessarily an image, but it does have the interesting property that it can be scanned from the top down. This top-down scanning property is the critical part of the theory: the assumption is that, as a consequence of scanning from the top down, subjects are able to verify the critical upper part of the circle-above display more quickly than the critical lower part of the circle-below display.

In a series of Experiments (Chase and Clark 1970), we have examined Seymour's hypothesis more closely, since it seemed to us that his hypothesis required much too concrete a comparison operation. In one experiment, we replaced the words *above* and *below* by two small arrows that meant the same thing as *above* and *below*. In this case, the asymmetry disappeared altogether. The top-down scanning process is therefore not obligatory. Here too, the meaning overrides any scanning process: Is the arrow pointing *toward* or *away from* the circle? In a second experiment, we made it impossible for the subject to scan the picture by covering up either the top or bottom position in the display. When only the top was visible, the same *above-below* asymmetry occurred; and when only the bottom was visible, the *above-below* difference also occurred, though within an entirely different overall pattern. Since these displays could not be scanned, the explanation of the *above-below* difference must lie in the semantic interpretations of the words and displays. It cannot lie in an image-scanning process. The appropriate application of the present theory predicts these results correctly.

We should also note that the scanning strategy, if taken literally, would be impossible to use in the experiments we have discussed previously. It is impossible, for example, to form a visual image, or an image surrogate, for the sentence *star isn't above plus*. This sentence is consistent with pictures of a star and a plus side by side, a star in front or in back of a plus, a star below a plus, and so on. The multiplicity of possible referents is a general property of negatives: they specify what something is *not*, and only rarely does this specify uniquely what that thing is. Although it was possible in our experiments to predict that the correct image for *star isn't above plus* was always going to be a plus above a star, this would not be generally so, and there is no reason to think that people cannot verify *star isn't above plus* in general. Furthermore, if we assume that our subjects *did* generate an image of a plus above a star for the sentence *star isn't above plus* and did scan according to Seymour's hypothesis, the negatives would come out exactly the reverse of the data. A scanning hypothesis seems difficult to support under these empirical considerations.

Spatial Paralogic

Imagery, or spatial paralogic, has also been called upon to account for how people solve deductive reasoning problems like "If Pete is better than Dick, and Dick is better than John, then who is best?" DeSoto, London, and Handel (1965) were the first to suggest that people solved these problems in a paralogical way by placing the three terms (*Pete, Dick,* and *John*) in a type of visual image and then searching the image to find the answer. DeSoto *et al.* noted, for example, that people often report constructing a visual image with the best person on top, the next best in the middle, and the worst on the bottom. The relative difficulty of the many forms of these problems is predicted by two assumptions: (1) It is easier to build (or scan) these images from the top down than from the bottom up; and (2) it is easier to build (scan) the images from the extremes inward than from the middle outward. The first assumption, for example, predicts why the problem *A is better than B, and B is better than C* is easier than the problem *C is worse than B, and B is worse than A*. The second assumption predicts why the problem *A is better than B, and C is worse than B*, is easier than the problem *B is worse than A, and B is better than C*.

In contrast to this image-scanning theory, Clark (1969) has proposed that in order to understand how these problems are solved, one must look at the linguistic processes involved in the comprehension of the sentences themselves. For example, *better* is lexically unmarked and *worse* is marked, and it is this difference, rather than the top-down building or scanning of some visual image, that accounts for the success of the first assumption of DeSoto *et al*. The critical test for the paralogic versus linguistic theory lies in the consideration of so-called negative equative sentences. For example, the paralogic theory predicts that the problem *A isn't as bad as B, and B isn't as bad as C* should be easier than the problem *C isn't as good as B, and B isn't as good as A*, whereas the linguistic theory correctly predicts the reverse. The linguistic theory also compares favorably with a variation of the paralogic theory proposed by Huttenlocher (1968). The point here is that, although subjects sometimes report visual imagery in this kind of task, the difficulties they experience in reasoning appear to lie not in the imagerial processes themselves, but in the logically prior and more abstract process of comprehending the sentences and searching through this comprehended information for the answers to the questions.

The Generation of Visual Information

Perhaps the best evidence for visual images in match-mismatch judgments comes from a series of experiments by Posner and his colleagues. In these studies, two letters of the alphabet are presented in succession, and subjects have to say whether the two letters are the same or different. The first result (Posner and Keele, 1967) is that with no delay between the first and second letter, the latency for the "same" judgment is faster if the letters are identical than if they have the same name (e.g., AA versus Aa), but this difference disappears if the second letter is delayed a second or two. The second result (Posner, Boies, Eichelman, and Taylor, 1969) is that if subjects are uncertain as to whether the second letter will be a capital or a small, the latency for a physical match increases with the delay of the second letter, but if subjects know the physical form of the second letter, the latencies do not increase. Further, if the first letter is auditory, the latencies *decline* with the delay of the second letter. Posner's explanation of the first result is that if the second letter comes soon enough after the first, subjects can match visual information of the first letter with the second letter. But if the second letter is delayed, the visual information decays so that the comparison must be based on the name of the letter. The second result occurs, according to Posner, because if the subjects know that the second letter is a capital, they can rehearse the visual information of the first letter if it was visual, or they can generate visual information from the name of the first letter if it was auditory. Posner (1969) refers to generation as the subject's ability to go from a general code to one of greater specificity, which is quite similar to Seymour's (1969) model described earlier.

There are two possible interpretations of the term *generation* that we would like to consider. The first interpretation is that the subject begins with the name of the letter and locates in memory all the specific information about it, such as font type, sharpness of angles, radii of curvature, and so on. In this extreme interpretation—which Posner meticulously avoids—the subject in effect generates in the mind's eye a full-blown image, replete with detailed metric information about the letter's physical form. This interpretation must be rejected for several reasons. First, it suggests template matching, and this brings with it a number of unsavory consequences. For example, template matching requires almost perfect physical matching of the image and picture, since any near-match might miss just that feature that would prove that the image and picture actually did not match; this requirement appears to be impossible to satisfy in general. Second, this interpretation suggests that pattern recognition generally requires all the detailed information of the letter that is being recognized. The *sine qua non* of pattern recognition, it seems to us, is *abstraction*, not generation in this sense. The problem is to abstract the relevant features (the letter's abstract representation) from the morass of metrical and structural details (the surface structure) of the physical stimulus.

The second interpretation of *generation*, which we will tentatively accept, is that the code is changed with no, or very little, increase in the informational content of the internal representation. When the subject hears the word "A," for example, he can generate, from memory, a representation that specifies the distinguishing features of the letter A, such as, that it consists of three lines that join in a certain configuration. The perception of the physical *A* on the page also consists of constructing (abstracting) a representation that specifies the same distinguishing features, that it consists of three lines in a particular configuration. A match is made by comparing the two representations—the one generated from memory and the one abstracted in perception—to decide whether they differ on a *significant* feature. The comparison here is carried out on the same abstract level as we have described earlier. The reason physical matches are so fast, according to this view, is that the featural representation of the first letter can be compared directly to the featural representation of the second letter without any intervening processes—that is without so-called figural synthesis. Name matches are slower since the first featural representation, say for *A*, must be used to derive a category—"A"—from which an alternative feature representation, for *a*, can be generated for comparison with the featural representation of the second letter *a*.

Visual confusions are possible under this interpretation, but now they depend on the internal representations of the particular letters. Evidence suggests, however, that neither visual nor acoustic confusions occur very easily. Chase and Posner (1965), for example, found neither visual nor acoustic confusions with successive visual presentations, and even with simultaneous pairs, the latencies were unaffected by visual similarity. On the other hand, Chase and Calfee (1969) found that if the pair was presented in different modalities (auditory or visual) the latency of the comparison was affected. Posner *et al.* (1969) present further evidence that the image of the first letter is more abstract than Sperling's (1960) icon because (a) the visual information is protected from pattern masking, but (b) the visual information is not protected from an intervening task where subjects have to recognize a pair of digits during the delay between the first and second letter. This evidence suggests that the comparison is based on modality-specific features which are abstract enough to be resistant to visual noise and visual or acoustic confusions, but are susceptible to occupancy constraints on a limited capacity short-term memory.

There is at least some suggestion in this explanation why latencies for a physical match should increase with a delay of the second letter when subjects are uncertain of whether the second letter will be capital or small. We might describe the process as follows. When the first letter is capital *A*, subjects immediately abstract a featural representation of the letter. But when given time, and since they know that small *a* could also occur second, they continue on to find the concept "A" that corresponds to their featural representation of *A*, and to generate the second featural representation appropriate for "A", specifically the one for *a*. Therefore, if the second stimulus comes soon enough, the representation for *A* is ready, but not the one for *a*. In this case the physical match would be fast. But if the second letter comes after a long enough delay, both the *A* and *a* representations are ready, and both would be matched against the featural representation of the second letter. Making both tests would make this process take longer. On the other hand, whenever there is no uncertainty about the physical form of the second letter, then only one feature representation is needed. If the first letter is visual, the correct representation is already set up and the latencies do not change with delay, but if the first letter is auditory, the latencies will decrease as the featural representation of *A* is set up. According to this explanation, the increasing latencies over time for a physical match are not due to decay of visual information, but rather to a change in testing strategy. This explanation has the advantage that it retains an abstract feature-test for the comparison process and it still accounts for Posner's results.

THE ROLE OF VISUAL IMAGERY IN COGNITIVE FUNCTIONING

If comparisons *are* carried out at such an abstract level, then what is the role of imagery in these tasks? Is imagery nothing more than an introspective conscious side-effect that mirrors the mental processes actually occurring at the symbolic level? Or is imagery necessary for certain cognitive functions that have to be carried out on an internal blackboard? What *is* clear is that imagery is reported in abundance in almost every problem-solving task. But in the few cases where it is possible to compare hypotheses that say that imagery is the cognitive work-horse with those that say that there is a more abstract work-horse (cf., e.g., Chase and Clark's (1972) study of sentence-picture comparison and Clark's (1969) investigation of deductive reasoning), then the more abstract hypothesis appears to win out. One might be led to conclude that thinking is neither visual nor verbal, and that the comprehension of both pictures and sentences utilizes the same cognitive apparatus. So glib a conclusion, however, is forestalled by the data of Brooks (1968), described in Bower's chapter in this volume, which suggest that some cognitive operations are easier when the modality being processed is different from the response modality. Although we do not have pat answers to the questions we have posed, it may serve a useful purpose to speculate, on the basis of our results, about the role of imagery in cognitive functioning.

A Common Underlying "Meaning"

Our results suggest that the comprehension of both pictures and sentences must ultimately be represented in the same mental symbolic system. We do not mean by this that the ultimate representation of pictures and sentences is identical to linguistic descriptions of deep structure, but rather that there is a deep or conceptual structure that is common to both sentences and pictures. In this paper, we have made use of linguistic deep structure because it is a handy, empirically well-founded symbolic system for representing some kinds of ideational content. But it appears to be too restrictive, since it leaves unspecified two- and three-dimensional properties of visual perception that must be represented (cf., e.g., Michon, this volume; Shepard and Metzler, 1971; Watt, 1966, 1967a, b). And motor schemata probably also have their characteristic structures. The point is, however, that all these cognitive structures would be best handled at some stage in the same representational system.

We should point out here that essentially the same argument has been put forth by Watt (1966, 1967a, b) on the basis of his linguistic and iconic analysis of Nevada cattle-brands. On formal grounds alone, he has shown that cattle-brands are systematically related to each other in that they can all be generated from a single well-defined set of deep structure rules. Moreover, the same rules can be used to generate either the visual symbol—the cattle-brand itself—*or* the name the ranchers give to that symbol—for example, "Flying A Lazy D." That is, the brands and their corresponding names have a common underlying structure. And, as Watt has demonstrated, there is no simple or direct way of translating from the brand to its name or from the name to the brand; the brand's deep structure is necessarily involved.

Our results suggest that it is legitimate to speak of the meaning of both pictures and sentences. Our conception is that meaning is to be found in a modality-free symbolic memory, but can be converted into modality-specific images when this is wanted. For example, from the meaning of the sentence *Go to the bank*, we could generate the auditory image of the sentence by saying it to ourselves or we could generate a visual image of ourselves going to a bank. In one case, there is a linguistic system that fills in all the surface structure details of the auditory image; in the other case, there is an imagerial system that fills out the visual image. But auditory and visual images such as these are different in kind from their meanings. The particular auditory image "Go to the bank" might be interpreted with *bank* as a river bank, a savings bank, or the like. Thus the images themselves are normally of no importance, for it is their interpretation that serves as the basis for action: we go to a river bank or a savings bank depending on how the auditory image is interpreted. The point is that it is the meaning or interpretation of sentences and pictures, hence also of auditory and visual images, that serve as the basis for most mental decisions.

This point can be made in quite a different way. It is possible to store information in a modality-specific memory. For example, we could attempt to store a sentence—if it is not too long—in an echoic memory, the place where auditory images seem to reside (Waugh and Norman, 1965). Or we could attempt to keep a visual configuration in the mind's eye in some sort of visual storage (Hochberg, 1968; Parks, 1965). But both auditory and visual images of this sort are easily lost or interfered with (Conrad, 1964; Brooks, 1968), and they are extremely limited in their capacity (Miller, 1956; Baylor, 1969). The more usual and durable way to remember information is to derive the underlying representation of the sentence or picture and to store the representation instead. The durability of memory for meaning has been shown for words (Anisfeld and Knapp, 1968; Fillenbaum, 1969), for sentences (Fillenbaum, 1966; Sachs, 1967; Clark and Card, 1969), as well as for pictures (Bartlett, 1932). Again, the reason why meaning, rather than auditory and visual images, is the normal mode of remembering is that it is the meaning, not the surface structure details, of today's events that is important for tomorrow's actions. We act on meanings, not on uninterpreted perceptions.

The Image as a Working Model

Assuming that this conception is correct, then what function do images serve if they are not used in comparison operations or in more durable memory? We suggest that they are used to devise new structures. The mind's eye is a working space, if you will, for generating new concepts and relations. Suppose, for example, someone were to describe the initial moves in a chess game: "Pawn to king's four. Pawn to queen's four. Knight to queen's bishop three. Knight to king's bishop three." This surface structure can be used for deriving the deep structures shown in Figure 8.8b. We are said to comprehend the sentences in one sense; we understand the meaning of four isolated moves in sequence. However, in order to play the game, we must understand the situation in another way, and so we generate the visual image illustrated in Figure 8.8c, and from this image we abstract the new structure shown in Figure 8.8d. This structure contains the pieces, their color and location, and the important relations between pieces: *attack* and *defend*. This image might be further elaborated to incorporate other important aspects of the position, such as the defense of the center pawn by black's queen, the other squares controlled by the pieces, and the color of the squares for example.

If one looks at eye movements while a human player scans the chess board, one can see the development of these structures out of more primitive relations. The initial five seconds or so of noticing behavior is critical to the subsequent

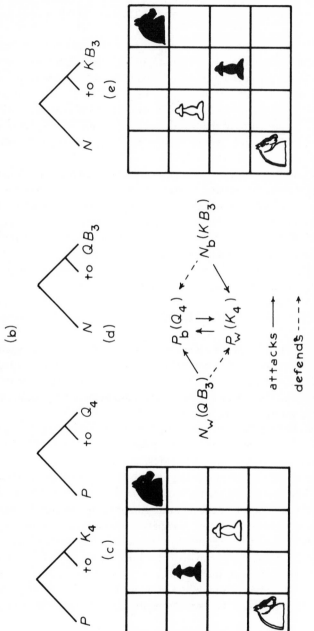

Figure 8.8 (a) The first four moves of a chess game; (b) the deep structure representations of these moves; (c) the visual image generated from these moves; and (d) the new deep structure abstracted from the visual image. (e) A center configuration from Simon and Barenfeld (1969).

processing that takes place (DeGroot, 1965), for it is here that the initial perceptions are formed for subsequent analysis. The same problem arises here as with our sentence-picture judgments: the initial few seconds are so rich in processing but over so fast that people cannot report the full extent of their analysis. However, Simon and Barenfeld (1969), in their PERCEIVER program, were able to simulate these initial eye movements by building in four very simple relations involving an attended piece and its neighbors: (1) *attacks,* (2) *defends,* (3) *attacked by, and* (4) *defended by.* The simulation involves an initial fixation on a piece in the center of the board, and then the program either remains fixated on the piece or moves to another piece which has one of these four relations.

Simon and Barenfeld, upon comparing the noticing behavior of their program with the eye movements of expert human players, discovered a surprising similarity in the noticing patterns. Both the program and the human showed "almost complete preoccupation with the 10 critical pieces." In fact, the particular middle game position they analyzed contained a configuration quite similar to that shown in Figure 8.8*c* except that the white and black pawns were reversed (shown in Figure 8.8*e*). The first thing the program did was fixate on the black pawn. The sequence then proceeded as follows: (1) NOTICE: *attacked by* white knight, (2) NOTICE: *defended by* black knight, (3) $FIXATE_1$: black knight, (4) NOTICE: *attacks* white pawn, (5) $FIXATE_2$: white pawn, (6) NOTICE: *defended by* white knight, (7) $FIXATE_3$: white knight, (8) NOTICE: *attacks* black pawn, (9) $FIXATE_4$: black pawn, (10) NOTICE: *attacked by* white queen, (11) NOTICE: *defended by* black knight, (12) $FIXATE_5$: black knight, . . .The sequence then moved off to other critical pieces. The human eye movements, although not identical, showed a similar interest in these central pieces.

It seems fairly clear from these data that abstract relations, like that shown in Figure 8.8*d*, are built up from more primitive *attack* and *defense* relations, which in turn are based on the actual physical moves which can be executed on the board. These same processes are also at work during the subsequent analysis. For example, in the position analyzed by Simon and Barenfeld, a rook move is needed to defend a pawn. And it turns out that the human expert's eye movements trace this imaginary move backwards from the endangered piece to the critical defending square and from there to the desired rook. The PERCEIVER program also discovered the correct move in this way. In short, the eye movements indicate that people shift pieces about the board in their mind's eye, and the simulation of these eye movements using *attack* and *defense* relations reveals the mental operations which guide these imaginary moves.

It should be noted that even when the chess board is in front of the eyes, a complete retinal representation of the board does not exist; only that part of the board fixated by the fovea is clearly resolved by the visual system. Under normal playing conditions, only about one square can occupy the fovea and the ability to see pieces in the periphery falls off so sharply that pieces lying more than two or three squares away cannot be resolved; peripheral vision for forms is notoriously poor (Williams, 1966). Indeed, a complete representation of the chess board, if such a thing exists at all, must be *constructed* out of a series of partial images (cf. Neisser, 1966, chapter 6). It is not surprising, given the complexity of the game of chess and the severe short-term memory limitations, that people rarely see more than three or four moves ahead or that blindfold chess is so difficult.

We might suppose, then, that a player's search through the problem space must proceed in the mind's eye. When the player looks at the board, a new position is generated by picturing, in the mind's eye, a piece moved to a new location, with perhaps a captured piece hypothetically removed from the board. From this image, new relations might be abstracted out (static analysis). New higher-order structures might be constructed by generating moves which interconnect pieces (via *attack* or *defense*) between two isolated structures.

We might further suppose that these visual-imaginal processes are quite common in other problem-solving tasks which require spatio-mathematical reasoning. If this speculation is correct, then the mind's eye serves an indispensable role in cognitive functioning. Imagery is used, for example, in solving Baylor's cube-dicing and board-cutting problems (described in Simon's chapter in this volume). The subject himself can make surface structure changes in the imaginary cube by painting a side or rotating the cube or making a slice. Once he has carried out these operations within the constraints of the image, he can then observe and derive new relations from that image. This view is consistent with the subject's reports that they are using visual-perceptual rather than deductive methods in this task; the subjects are in fact abstracting new information from the visual image in much the same way they would from a physical stimulus. The surface transformations of the image are probably analogous to actual physical transformations of a perceived object, except that the image may be incomplete because of memory limitations. The actual comparison operations, like those in our experiments, are conducted at the abstract level. Only generation, surface transformations, and abstractions are assumed to occur in the mind's eye.

People probably use imagery in many kinds of tasks. It is quite possible, for example, that people scan mental images in deductive reasoning problems like Clark's (1969); yet difficulty in reasoning seems to stem not from the difficulties of scanning images, but from the difficulty of comprehending the sentences and retrieving the more abstract semantic representations. In other more complex problems, as in geometry proofs, for example, the mental imagery required is much too complex to do in the head, and we must resort to pencil and paper. The process, however, is probably just the same. And we often talk to ourselves in order to test out a new turn of phrase, an impertinent answer, and so on. Composers and artists regularly report hearing and seeing the works they are about to compose or construct.

Imagery instructions may facilitate paired-associate learning via the generation of a new structure that is exactly relevant to the two members of the pair. To take Simon's example, *whale* and *cigar* (Figure 7.1) are initially two isolated structures, just as the four moves in the chess example are isolated. But under imagery instructions, the subject may generate an image of a whale smoking a cigar, and the new abstraction is a single "chunk" defined by the relation *smoking*, just as the *attack* and *defend* relations define a single structure in the chess example. The abstract relation is remembered, and the rest is reconstructed at recall to produce *cigar* from *whale*. This is similar to the explanation that Simon gives for the facilitation of imagery instructions in paired-associate learning.

Deep Structure as Image

This account differs from Simon's in that Simon suggests that the deep structure *is* the image. This conception, it seems to us, violates the principal observations that have been made about mental imagery. First, in Bower's experiments, the subjects do not construct a mental image on presentation of the pair of words and then continue to keep this image in mind through until recall. Rather, they use imagery to come to a unique relation between the stimulus and response terms, abstract this relation, and store away the abstraction. The abstraction would not contain all the detail of the original image, but it would be sufficient to enable the subjects to reconstruct *something like* their original mental image and hence to allow them to reconstruct the response term from the stimulus term. Second, an image is essentially a conscious construction, whenever it occurs, since we see the image being built up piece by piece: it does not emerge into consciousness in full complexity and detail. It thus seems that images are generated from a more abstract representation, and the generation is a piece by piece process (cf. Baylor, 1969). Third, if deep structure were the image, memory would be overburdened with too much surface detail—cognitive clutter, if you will. This detail is unnecessary since most of it can be constructed (or reconstructed) out of more general knowledge we have of objects and their internal relations. This is analogous to the construction of sentences: once we have decided in sufficient detail about what we want to say, there are only a few possible ways of expressing this content. In short, it seems useful to postulate two internal representations, one of which carries the meaning of the cognitive structure, while the other is a more detailed working image.

Mode-Specific Abstract Representations

This account also differs from Bower's (Chapter 2) in that Bower appears to postulate two modality-specific abstract representations (visual and verbal) and a grammar that interconnects the two. This conception has difficulties, in our view, because it does not contain a level of meaning that underlies the two. We think this separate level is needed, as we have said above, to account for the comparison process, memory for meaning, ambiguity of the surface structure of auditory and visual memories, and so on. Watt, in his analysis of Nevada cattle-brands, also shows that it is impossible to design a grammar of the kind Bower has suggested, at least for cattle brands. It is possible that Bower means for there to be an identifiable level—that we would call an abstract semantic representation—between the visual and the verbal code; it certainly would not be incompatible with what he seems to be saying. But we think it is important to make this level explicit. Once it is assumed that sentences and pictures both have the same kind of underlying representation, then it is possible to see the similarities and common principles operating in the use of both modalities.

A second difficulty with Bower's conception is that he suggests that both systems have a common generative grammar which underlies the generation of both verbal and visual images. It seems to us that the generative rules should be quite specific to the surface structures of the different modalities. The syntactic and phonological rules of language must be set up to handle linear strings, whereas the rules of sensory organization in the visual system must be set up to handle two- and three-dimensional structures. The problem in the visual system is really the time-honored problem of pattern and form perception. This is not to deny that the perception of speech and visual form share some common principles. But our point is that one must look at the highest level of abstraction, where the internal representations are stripped of their modal specificity so that they are neutral symbols, where the same cognitive principles apply. It is semantic rather than syntactic principles which are common to visual and verbal representations.

In summary, we have presented some data on how people judge whether or not a sentence is an accurate description of a picture. To account for these data, we have argued that it is necessary to assume that both sentences and pictures have abstract mental representations which are compared symbolically. These data cannot be accounted for by assuming that people compare modality-specific mental images—such as visual or auditory images—of the sentence and picture. From this, we have argued that visual and auditory images are modality-specific representations corresponding to more general modality-free representations, loosely called here *meaning*. There is evidence that meaning is the more basic representation for comparisons, durable memory, and the like, while images are working models for deriving new and different abstract representations. Images are therefore extremely useful, but the ultimate work-horse in most cognitive functions will probably turn out to be the more abstract meanings.

REFERENCES

Adams, J. A., & McIntyre, J. S. Natural language mediation and all-or-none learning. *Canadian Journal of Psychology*, 1967, **21**, 436-449.

Adams, J. A., & Montague, W. E. Retroactive inhibition and natural language mediation. *Journal of Verbal Learning and Verbal Behavior*, 1967, **6**, 528-535.

Alpern, G. D. The failure of nursery school enrichment program for culturally disadvantaged. *American Journal of Orthopsychiatry*, 1966, **36**, 244-245.

Anisfeld, M., & Knapp, M. Association, synonymity, and directionality in false recognition. *Journal of Experimental Psychology*, 1968, **77**, 171-179.

Asch, S. Reformulation of the problem of association. *American Psychologist*, 1969, **24**, 92-102.

Asch, S., Ceraso, J., & Heimer, W. Perceptual conditions of association. *Psychological Monographs*, 1960, **74**, No. 490.

Atkinson, R. C., Brelsford, J. W., & Shiffrin, R. M. Multiprocess models for memory with applications to a continuous presentation task. *Journal of Mathematical Psychology*, 1967, **4**, 277-300.

Averbach, E., & Coriell, A. S. Short-term memory in vision. *Bell System Technical Journal*, 1961, **40**, 309-328.

Averbach, E., & Sperling, G. Short-term storage of information in vision. In C. Cherry, (Ed.), *Information theory*. London: Butterworth, 1961.

Baddeley, A. D. Short-term memory for word sequences as a function of acoustic, semantic and formal similarity. *Quarterly Journal of Experimental Psychology*, 1966, **18**, 362-365. (a)

Baddeley, A. D. The influence of acoustic and semantic similarity on long-term memory for word sequences. *Quarterly Journal of Experimental Psychology*, 1966, **18**, 302-309. (b)

Baddeley, A. D. How does acoustic similarity influence short-term memory? *Quarterly Journal of Experimental Psychology*, 1968, **20**, 249-264.

Baddeley, A. D., & Dale, H. C. A. The effect of semantic similarity on retroactive interference in long- and short-term memory. *Journal of Verbal Learning and Verbal Behavior*, 1966, **5**, 417-420.

Barratt, P. E. Imagery and thinking. *Australian Journal of Psychology*, 1953, **5**, 154-164.

Bartlett, F. C. *Remembering: A study in experimental and social psychology*. Cambridge: Cambridge University Press, 1932.

Battig, W. F. Procedural problems in paired-associate learning research. *Psychonomic Monograph Supplement*, 1965, **1**, No. 1.

Baylor, G. W. *A treatise on the mind's eye: An empirical investigation of visual mental imagery*. Unpublished doctoral dissertation. Carnegie-Mellon University, 1971.

Baylor, G. W., & Simon, H. A. A chess mating combinations program. AFIPS Conference Proceedings, 1966 Spring Joint Computer Conference, Washington, D.C.: Spartan Books, 1966, **28**, 431-447.

Beals, R., Krantz, D. H., & Tversky, A. Foundations of multidimensional scaling. *Psychological Review*, 1968, **75**, 127-142.

Benton, A. L. *Right-left discrimination and finger localization*. New York: Harper, 1959.

Bereiter, C., & Engelmann, S. *Teaching disadvantaged children in the preschool*. Englewood Cliffs, N. J.: Prentice-Hall, 1966.

Berlyne, D. E. *Structure and direction in thinking*. New York: Wiley, 1965.

Blankenship, A. B., & Whitely, P. L. Proactive inhibition in the recall of advertising material. *Journal of Social Psychology*, 1941, **13**, 311-322.

Bobrow, S., & Bower, G.H. Comprehension and recall of sentences. *Journal of Experimental Psychology*, 1969, **80**, 455-461.

Bond, G. L. *The auditory and speech characteristics of poor readers*. Teachers College Contributions to Education, No. 657. New York: Columbia University, 1935.

Bond, G. L., & Dykstra, R. The cooperative research program in first-grade reading instruction. *Reading Research Quarterly*, 1967, **2** (complete).

Bower, G. H., & Bostrom, A. Absence of within-list PI and RI in short-term recognition memory. *Psychonomic Science*, 1968, **10**, 211-212.

Bower, G. H., & Clark, M. C. Narrative stories as mediators for serial learning. *Psychonomic Science*, 1969, **14**, 181-182.

Bowman, R. E., & Thurlow, W. R. Determinants of the effect of position in serial learning. *American Journal of Psychology*, 1963, **76**, 436-445.

Brelsford, J., Jr., Freund, R., & Rundus, D. Recency judgments in a short-term memory task. *Psychonomic Science*, 1967, **8**, 247-248.

Brelsford, J. W., Shiffrin, R. M., & Atkinson, R. C. Multiple reinforcement effects in short-term memory. *British Journal of Mathematical and Statistical Psychology*, 1968, **21**, 1-19.

Brooks, L. R. The suppression of visualization by reading. *Quarterly Journal of Experimental Psychology*, 1967, **19**, 289-299.

Brooks, L. R. Spatial and verbal components of the act of recall. *Canadian Journal of Psychology*, 1968, **22**, 349-368.

Brottman, M. A. Language remediation for the disadvantaged preschool child. *Monographs of Society for Research in Child Development*, 1968, **33**, (Whole No. 124).

Brown, J. Some tests of the decay theory of immediate memory. *Quarterly Journal of Experimental Psychology*, 1958, **10**, 12-21.

Brown, R., & Berko, J. Word association and the development of grammar. *Child Development*, 1960, **31**, 1-14.

Brown, R., & McNeill, D. The "tip of the tongue" phenomenon. *Journal of Verbal Learning and Verbal Behavior*, 1966, **5**, 325-337.

Bruce, D. J. The analysis of word sounds by young children. *British Journal of Educational Psychology*, 1964, **34**, 158-170.

Bruner, J. S., Olver, R. R., & Greenfield, P. M. (Eds.) *Studies in cognitive growth*. New York: Wiley, 1966.

Bugelski, B. R. Presentation time, total time, and mediation in paired-associate learning. *Journal of Experimental Psychology*, 1962, **63**, 409-412.

Bugelski, B. R. Images as mediators in one-trial paired-associate learning. II. Self-timing in successive lists. *Journal of Experimental Psychology*, 1968, **77**, 328-334.

Bugelski, B. R., & Cadwallader, T.C. A reappraisal of the transfer and retroaction surface. *Journal of Experimental Psychology*, 1956, **52**, 360-366.

Bugelski, B. R., Kidd, E., & Segmen, J. Image as a mediator in one-trial paired-associate learning. *Journal of Experimental Psychology*, 1968, **76**, 69-73.

Cattell, J. McK. Experiments on the association of ideas. *Mind*, 1887, **12**, 68-74.

Chall, J. *Learning to read: The great debate*. New York: McGraw-Hill, 1967.

Chase, W. G., & Calfee, R. C. Modality and similarity effects in short-term recognition memory. *Journal of Experimental Psychology*, 1969, **81**, 510-514.

Chase, W.G., & Clark, H. H. Semantics in the perception of verticality. *British Journal of Psychology*, 1971, **62**(3), 311-326.

Chase, W. G., & Posner, M. I. The effect of auditory and visual confusability on visual and memory search tasks. Paper presented at the meeting of the Midwestern Psychological Association, Chicago, May, 1965.

Chomsky, N. *Aspects of the theory of syntax*. Cambridge: MIT Press, 1965.

Clark, H. H. Linguistic processes in deductive reasoning. *Psychological Review*, 1969, **76**, 387-404.

Clark, H. H. Comprehending comparatives. In G. B. Flores d'Arcais & W. J. M. Levelt (Eds.), *Advances in psycholinguistics*. Amsterdam: North Holland, 1970.

Clark, H.H., & Card, S. K. Role of semantics in remembering comparative sentences. *Journal of Experimental Psychology*, 1969, **82**, 545-553.

Clark, H.H., & Chase, W.G. On the process of comparing sentences against pictures. *Cognitive Psychology*, 1972, in press.

Cohen, J. C., & Musgrave, B. S. Effects of formal similarity on cue selection in verbal paired-associate learning. *Journal of Experimental Psychology*, 1966, **71**, 829-838.

Cole, R. A., Haber, R. N., & Sales, B. D. Mechanisms of aural encoding: I. Distinctive features for consonants. *Perception and Psychophysics*, 1968, **3**, 281-284.

Coleman, J. S. *Introduction to mathematical sociology*. Glencoe, Ill.: The Free Press, 1964.

Collins, A. M., & Quillian, M. R. Retrieval time from semantic memory. *Journal of Verbal Learning and Verbal Behavior*, 1969, 8, 240-247.

Collins, A. M., & Quillian, M. R. Facilitating retrieval from semantic memory: The effect of repeating word concepts. In A.F. Sanders (Ed.), *Attention and Performance III, Acta Psychologica*, 1970a, 33, 304-314.

Collins, A.M., & Quillian, M.R. Does category size affect categorization time? *Journal of Verbal Learning and Verbal Behavior*, 1970b, 9, 432-438.

Conrad R. Errors of immediate memory. *British Journal of Psychology*, 1959, 50, 349-359.

Conrad, R. Serial order intrusions in immediate memory. *British Journal of Psychology*, 1960, 51, 45-48.

Conrad, R. Acoustic confusions and memory span for words. *Nature*, 1963, 197, 1029-1030.

Conrad, R. Acoustic confusions in immediate memory. *British Journal of Psychology*, 1964, 55, 75-83.

Conrad, R., Freeman, P. R., & Hull, A. J. Acoustic factors versus language factors in short-term memory. *Psychonomic Science*, 1965, 3, 57-58.

Conrad, R., & Hull, A. J. Information, acoustic confusion and memory span. *British Journal of Psychology*, 1964, 55, 429-432.

Corcoran, D. W. J., Carpenter, A., Webster, J. C., & Woodhead, M. M. An investigation of some techniques for training operators in skills of passive listening. Medical Research Council, Applied Psychology Research Unit, Cambridge, Rep. RNP/ 167/1096.

Corman, C. D., & Wickens, D. D. Retroactive inhibition in short-term memory. *Journal of Verbal Learning and Verbal Behavior*, 1968, 7, 16-19.

Cronbach, L. J. How can instruction be adapted to individual differences? In R. M. Gagne (Ed.), *Learning and individual differences*. Columbus, Ohio: Charles Merrill, 1967.

Dale, H. C. A. Semantic similarity and the A-B, C-D paradigm in STM. *Psychonomic Science*, 1967, 9, 79-80.

Dale, H. C. A., & Gregory, M. Evidence of semantic coding in short-term memory. *Psychonomic Science*, 1966, 5, 75-76.

Dallett, K. M. Implicit mediators in paired-associate learning. *Journal of Verbal Learning and Verbal Behavior*, 1964, 3, 209-214.

Dallett, K. M. Effects of within-list and between list acoustic similarity on the learning and retention of paired associates. *Journal of Experimental Psychology*, 1966 72, 667-677.

Davidson, H. A study of reversals in young children. *Journal of General Psychology*, 1934, 45, 452-465.

Davidson, R. E. Mediation and ability in paired-associate learning. *Journal of Educational Psychology*, 1964, 55, 352-356.

DeGroot, A. D. *Thought and choice in chess*. New York: Basic Books, 1965.

Dement, W., & Kleitman, N. The relation of eye movements during sleep to dream activity: An objective method for the study of dreaming. *Journal of Experimental Psychology*, 1957, 53, 339-346.

DeSoto, C., London, M., & Handel, S. Social reasoning and spatial paralogic. *Journal of Personality and Social Psychology*, 1965, **2**, 513-521.

Deutsch, C. P. Auditory discrimination and learning: social factors. In M. Deutsch (Ed.), *The disadvantaged child*. New York: Basic Books, 1967.

Donaldson, W., & Murdock, B. B., Jr. Criterion change in continuous recognition memory. *Journal of Experimental Psychology*, 1968, **76**, 325-330.

Dorfman, D. D., & Alf, E., Jr. Maximum likelihood estimation of parameters of signal detection theory—rating scale data. Mathematical Psychology Meetings, Stanford, California, 1968.

Dunn-Rankin, P. The similarity of lower-case letters of the English alphabet. *Journal of Verbal Learning and Verbal Behavior*, 1968, **7**, 990-995.

Ebenholtz, S. M. Serial learning: Position learning and sequential associations. *Journal of Experimental Psychology*, 1963, **66**, 353-362. (a)

Ebenholtz, S. M. Position mediated transfer between serial learning and a spatial discrimination task. *Journal of Experimental Psychology*, 1963, **65**, 603-608. (b)

Elkonin, D. B. The psychology of mastering the elements of reading. In B. Simon & J. Simon (Eds.), *Educational psychology in the U. S. S. R.* London: Routledge & Kegan Paul, 1963.

Entwisle, D. R. *Word associations of young children.* Baltimore, Md.: Johns Hopkins Press, 1966.

Entwisle, D. R., & Greenberger, E. Differences in the language of Negro and white grade-school children. Technical Report 19, Center for study of social organization of schools. Baltimore, Md.: Johns Hopkins University, 1968.

Epstein, W., Rock, I., & Zuckerman, C. B. Meaning and familiarity in associative learning. *Psychological Monographs*, 1960, **74**, No. 491.

Ervin, S. M. Change with age in the verbal determinants of word-association. *American Journal of Psychology*, 1961, **74**, 361-372.

Feifel, H., & Lorge, I. Qualitative differences in the vocabulary responses of children. *Journal of Educational Psychology*, 1950, **41**, 1-18.

Feigenbaum, E. A. An information processing theory of verbal learning. Rand Corp. Technical Report P 1817, 1959.

Feigenbaum, E. A. The simulation of verbal learning behavior. *Proceedings of the Western Joint Computer Conference*, 1961, **19**, 121-132.

Feigenbaum, E. A., & Simon, H. A. A theory of the serial position effect. *British Journal of Psychology*, 1962, **53**, 307-320.

Feldman, S. M., & Underwood, B. J. Stimulus recall following paired-associate learning. *Journal of Experimental Psychology*, 1957, **53**, 11-15.

Fellows, B. J. *The discriminative process and development.* New York: Pergamon, 1968.

Fillenbaum, S. Memory for gist: Some relevant variables. *Language and Speech*, 1966, **9**, 217-227.

Fillenbaum, S. Words as feature complexes: False recognition of antonyms and synonyms. *Journal of Experimental Psychology*, 1969, **82**, 400-402.

Flavell, J. H., & Hill, J. P. Developmental psychology. *Annual Review of Psychology*, 1969, **20**, 1-56.

Foss, D. J., Bever, T. G., & Silver, M. The comprehension and verification of ambiguous sentences. *Perception and Psychophysics*, 1968, **4**, 304-306.

Gagné, R. M. (Ed.) *Learning and individual differences*. Columbus, Ohio: Charles Merrill, 1967.

Galton, F. *Inquiries into human faculty*. London: Macmillan, 1883.

Gerstein, R. A. A suggested method for analyzing and extending the use of Bellevue-Wechsler vocabulary responses. *Journal of Consulting Psychology*, 1949, **13**, 366-370.

Gibson, E. J. A systematic application of the concepts of generalization and differentiation to verbal learning. *Psychological Review*, 1940, **47**, 196-229.

Gibson, E. J. Retroactive inhibition as a function of degree of generalization between tasks. *Journal of Experimental Psychology*, 1941, **28**, 93-115.

Gibson, E. J. Learning to read. *Science*, 1965, **148**, 1066-1072.

Gibson, E. J., Gibson, J. J., Pick, A. D., & Osser, H. A developmental study of the discrimination of letter-like forms. *Journal of Comparative and Physiological Psychology*, 1962, **55**, 897-906.

Gibson, E. J., & Yonas, A. A developmental study of visual search behavior. *Perception and Psychophysics*, 1966, **1**, 169-171.

Gibson, J. J. *The senses considered as perceptual systems*. New York: Houghton Mifflin Co., 1966.

Graham, K. R. Brightness contrast by hypnotic hallucination. *International Journal of Clinical and Experimental Hypnosis*, 1969, **XVII**, 62-73.

Green, B. F., Jr. Figure coherence in the kinetic depth effect. *Journal of Experimental Psychology*, 1961, **62**, 272-282.

Green, B. F., Jr. Descriptions and explanations: A comment on papers by Hoffman and Edwards. In B. Kleinmuntz (Ed.), *Formal representation of human judgment*. New York: Wiley, 1968, pp. 91-98.

Green, D. M., & Moses, F. L. On the equivalence of two recognition measures of short-term memory. *Psychological Bulletin*, 1966, **66**, 228-234.

Gregg, L. W., & Simon, H. A. An information-processing explanation of one-trial and incremental learning. *Journal of Verbal Learning and Verbal Behavior*, 1967, **6**, 780-787.

Gregg, L. W., & Simon, H. A. Process models and stochastic theories of simple concept formation. *Journal of Mathematical Psychology*, 1967, **4**, 246-276.

Haber, R. N. Perception and thought: An information-processing analysis. In J. F. Voss (Ed.), *Approaches to thought*. Columbus, Ohio: Charles Merrill, 1969.

Hanson, G. Dimensions in speech sound perception; an experimental study of vowel perception. *Ericsson Technics*, 1967, **23**, 3-175.

Harris. L. Discrimination of left-right directionality and development of the logic of relations. Paper presented to Society for Research in Child Development, Santa Monica, California, March, 1969.

Helleyer, S. Frequency of stimulus presentation and short-term decrement in recall. *Journal of Experimental Psychology*, 1962, 64, 650.

Henley, N. M., Noyes, H. L., & Deese, J. Semantic structure in short-term memory. *Journal of Experimental Psychology*, 1968, 77, 587-592.

Henrichs, J. V., & Buschke, H. Judgment of recency under steady-state conditions. *Journal of Experimental Psychology*, 1968, 78, 574-579.

Hildreth, G., Griffiths, N. J., & McGauvran, M. E. *Metropolitan readiness test*. New York: Harcourt, Brace and World, 1964.

Hill, M. B. A study of the process of word discrimination in individuals beginning to read. *Journal of Educational Research*, 1936, 29, 487-500.

Hintzman, D. Articulatory coding in short-term memory. *Journal of Verbal Learning and Verbal Behavior*, 1967, 6, 312-316.

Hintzman, D. Explorations with a discrimination net model of paired associates learning. *Journal of Mathematical Psychology*, 1968, 5, 123-162.

Hochberg, J. In the mind's eye. In R. N. Haber (Ed.), *Contemporary theory and research in visual perception*. New York: Holt, 1968.

Horowitz, L. M. Associative matching and intralist similarity. *Psychological Reports*, 1962, 10, 751-757.

Horowitz, L. M., Norman, S. A., & Day, R. S. Availability and associative symmetry. *Psychological Review,* 1966, 73, 1-15.

Houston, J. P. Mediation in serial learning. *Journal of Verbal Learning and Verbal Behavior*, 1964, 3, 369-370.

Houston, J. P. Unlearning of specific associations in the A-B, C-D paradigm. *Journal of Experimental Psychology*, 1967, 74, 254-258.

Howard, I. P., & Templeton, W. D. *Human spatial orientation*. New York: Wiley, 1966.

Hull, C. L. *Principles of behavior. An introduction to behavior theory*. New York: Appleton-Century-Crofts, 1943.

Humphrey, G. *Thinking: An introduction to its experimental psychology*. John Wiley & Sons, New York, 1951.

Hunt, E. B. *Concept learning: An information processing problem*. New York: John Wiley, 1962.

Huttenlocher, J. Children's ability to order and orient objects. *Child Development*, 1967, 38, 1169-1176. (a)

Huttenlocher, J. Discrimination of figure orientation: Effects of relative position. *Journal of Comparative and Physiological Psychology*, 1967, 63, 359-361. (b)

Huttenlocher, J. Constructing spatial images: A strategy in reasoning. *Psychological Review*, 1968, 75, 550-560.

Indow, T., & Kanazawa, K. Multidimensional mapping of Munsell colors varying in hue, chroma, and value. *Journal of Experimental Psychology*, 1960, 59, 330-336.

Irwin, O. C. Language and communication. In P. H. Mussen (Ed.), *Handbook of research methods in child development*. New York: Wiley, 1960.

Jacobson, E. Electrophysiology of mental activities. *American Journal of Psychology*, 1932, 44, 677-694.

James, W. *Principles of psychology, Vol. 2.* New York: Holt, 1890.

Jarrett, R. F., & Scheibe, K. E. Association chains and paired-associate learning. *Journal of Verbal Learning and Verbal Behavior*, 1962, 1, 264-268.

Jeffrey, W. E. Variables in early discrimination learning: I. Motor responses in the training of a left-right discrimination. *Child Development*, 1958, 29, 269-275.

Jeffrey, W. E., & Samuels, S. J. Effect of method of reading training on initial learning and transfer. *Journal of Verbal Learning and Verbal Behavior*, 1967, 6, 354-358.

Jenkins, J. R. Effects of incidental cues and encoding strategies on paired-associate learning. Unpublished doctoral dissertation. University of Minnesota, 1967.

Jensen, A. R., & Rohwer, W. D., Jr. The effect of verbal mediation on the learning and retention of paired-associates by retarded adults. *American Journal of Mental Deficiency,* 1963, 68, 80-84. (a)

Jensen, A. R., & Rohwer, W. D., Jr. Verbal mediation in paired-associate and serial learning. *Journal of Verbal Learning and Verbal Behavior*, 1963, 1, 346-352. (b)

Jensen, A. R., & Rohwer, W. D., Jr. What is learned in serial learning? *Journal of Verbal Learning and Verbal Behavior*, 1965, 4, 62-72.

Johnson, S. C. Hierarchical clustering schemes. *Psychometrika,* 1967, 32, 241-254.

Jost, A. Die Assoziationsfesfestigkeit in ihrer Abhangigkeit von der Verteilung der Wiederholungen. *Zeitschrift für Psychologie,* 1897, 14, 436-472.

Kamil, M. L., & Rudegeair, R. E. Assessment of phonological discrimination in children. Paper presented at Midwestern Psychological Association, Chicago, May, 1969.

Kamiya, J. EEG studies of voluntary control over our states of conseiousness. Colloquium talk at Stanford Psychology Department, Stanford, California, 1969.

Kaswan, J. Association of nonsense figures as a function of fittingness and intention to learn. *American Journal of Psychology*, 1957, 70, 447-450.

Katz, J. J., & Fodor, J. A. The structure of a semantic theory. *Language,* 1963, 39, 170-210.

Keppel, G. Retroactive inhibition of serial lists as a function of the presence or absence of positional cues. *Journal of Verbal Learning and Verbal Behavior*, 1964, 3, 511-517.

Kiess, H. O., & Montague, W. E. Natural language mediators in paired-associate learning. *Psychonomic Science*, 1965, 3, 549-550.

Kimble, G. A. Mediating associations. *Journal of Experimental Psychology*, 1968, 76, 263-266.

Kimura, D. Right temporal lobe damage. *Archives of Neurology*, 1963, 8, 264-271.

Kintsch, W. An experimental analysis of single stimulus tests and multiple-choice tests of recognition memory. *Journal of Experimental Psychology*, 1968, 76, 1-6.

Kleinmuntz, B. MMPI decision rules for the identification of college maladjustment: A digital computer approach. *Psychological Monograph*, 1963, 77, (14, Whole No. 577).

Kleinmuntz, B. The processing of clinical information by man and machine. In B. Kleinmuntz (Ed.), *Formal representation of human judgment.* New York: Wiley, 1968, pp. 149-186.

Kohler, W. *Gestalt psychology*. New York: Liveright, 1947.

Krauss, R. M., & Glucksberg, S. The development of communication: Competence as a function of age. *Child Development*, 1969, **40**, 255-266. (a)

Krauss, R. M., & Glucksberg, S. Some characteristics of children's messages. Paper presented at Society for Research in Child Development, Santa Monica, California, 1969. (b)

Kruskal, J. B. Multidimensional scaling by optimizing goodness of fit to a nonmetric hypothesis. *Psychometrika*, 1964, **29**, 1-27. (a)

Kruskal, J. B. Non-metric multidimensional scaling: A numerical method. *Psychometrika*, 1964, **29**, 115-129. (b)

Kurtz, K. H., & Hovland, C. I. The effect of verbalization during observation of stimulus-objects upon accuracy of recognition and recall. *Journal of Experimental Psychology*, 1953, **45**, 157-163.

Labov, W. Some sources of reading problems for Negro speakers of nonstandard English. In A. Frazier (Ed.), *New directions in elementary English*. Champaign, Ill.: National Council of Teachers of English, 1967.

Landauer, T. K., & Freedman, J. L. Information retrieval from long-term memory: Category size and recognition time. *Journal of Verbal Learning and Verbal Behavior*, 1968, **7**, 291-295.

Laughery, K. R. Computer simulation of short-term memory: A component decay model. In G. H. Bower & J. T. Spence, (Eds.), *The psychology of learning and motivation*, Vol. 3. New York: Academic Press, 1969, pp. 135-200.

Laughery, K. R., & Gregg, L. W. The simulation of human problem solving behavior. *Psychometrika*, 1962, **27**, 265-282.

Laughery, K. R., & Pinkus, A. L. Short-term memory: Effects of acoustic similarity presentation rate and presentation mode. *Psychonomic Science*, 1966, **6**, 285-286.

Leuba, C. Images as conditioned sensations. *Journal of Experimental Psychology*, 1940, **26**, 345-351.

Levelt, W. J. M. Psychological representation of syntactic structures. In T. G. Bever & W. Weksel (Eds.), *Studies in psycholinguistics, (In press)*.

Levelt, W. J.M. The scaling of syntactic relatedness: a new method in psycolinguistic research. *Psyconanic Science*, 1969, **17**, 351-352.

Levelt, W. J. M., Van De Geer, J. P., & Plomp, R. Triadic comparisons of musical intervals. *British Journal of Mathematical and Statistical Psychology*, 1966, **19**, 163-179.

Lockhart, R. S. Retrieval asymmetry in the recall of adjectives and nouns. *Journal of Experimental Psychology*, 1969, **79**, 12-17.

Lynch, K. *The image of the city*. Cambridge, Mass.: MIT Press, 1960.

Lyons, J. *Introduction to theoretical linguistics*. Cambridge: Cambridge University Press, 1968.

Martin, E. Stimulus meaningfulness and paired-association transfer: An encoding variability hypothesis. *Psychological Review*, 1968, **75**, 421-441.

McCarthy, D. Language development in children. In L. Carmichael (Ed.), *Manual of child psychology*. New York: Wiley, 1954.

McGeoch, J. A., & McDonald, W. T.   Meaningful relation and retroactive inhibition. *American Journal of Psychology*, 1931, **43**, 579-588.

McGeoch, J. A., & Irion, A. L.   *The psychology of human learning.* New York: Longmans, Green and Co., 1952.

McGovern, J. B.   Extinction of associations in four transfer paradigms. *Psychological Monographs,* 1964, Whole No. 593.

McKellar, P.   The investigation of mental images. In S. A. Barnett & A. McLaren, (Eds.), *Penguin Science Survey, 1965*: B. Harmondsworth, England: Penguin Books.

McLean, R. S., & Gregg, L. W.   Effects of induced chunking on temporal aspects of serial recitation. *Journal of Experimental Psychology,* 1967, **74**, 455-459.

McNeill, D.   A study of word association. *Journal of Verbal Learning and Verbal Behavior,* 1966, **5**, 548-557.

McNeill, J. D., & Stone, J.   Note on teaching children to hear separate sounds in spoken words. *Journal of Educational Psychology,* 1965, **56**, 13-15.

Melton, A. W.   Implications of short-term memory for a general theory of memory. *Journal of Verbal Learning and Verbal Behavior,* 1963, **2**, 1-21.

Melton, A. W., Sameroff, A., & Schubot, E. D.   Short-term recognition memory. Human Performance Center, The University of Michigan, Memorandum Report No. 2, May, 1963.

Melton, A. W., & VonLackum, W. J.   Retroactive and proactive inhibition in retention: Evidence for a two-factor theory of retroactive inhibition. *American Journal of Psychology,* 1941, **54**, 157-173.

Michon, J. A.   On the internal representation of associative networks. *Nederlands Tijdschrift voor de Psychologie,* 1968, **23**, 428-457.

Miller, G. A.   *Language and communication.* New York: McGraw Hill, 1951.

Miller, G. A.   The magical number seven, plus or minus two: Some limits on our capacity for processing information. *Psychological Review,* 1956, **63**, 81-97.

Miller, G. A.   Some psychological studies of grammar. *American Psychologist,* 1962, **17**, 748-762.

Miller, G. A., & Chomsky, N.   Finitary models of language users. In R. D. Luce, R. R. Bush, & E. Galanter (Eds.), *Handbook of mathematical psychology.* New York: Wiley, 1963, pp. 419-491.

Miller, W. F., & Shaw, A. C.   A picture calculus. Stanford Linear Accelerator Center, Public. 358, October 1967. Presented at conference on Emerging Concepts in Computer Graphics at University of Illinois, November 5-8, 1967.

Miller, W. F., & Shaw, A. C.   Linguistic methods in picture processing–A survey. Stanford Linear Accelerator Center, Public. 429, August 1968. Presented at 1968 Fall Joint Computer Conference, San Francisco, December 9-11, 1968.

Milner, B. Visual recognition and recall after right temporal-lobe excision in man. *Neuropsychologia,* 1968, **6**, 191-209.

Monroe, M.   *Children who cannot read.* Chicago: University of Chicago Press, 1932.

Montague, W. E., Adams, J. A., & Kiess, H. O.   Forgetting and natural language mediation. *Journal of Experimental Psychology,* 1966, **72**, 829-833.

Morris, D. *The naked ape: A zoologist's study of the human animal*. London: Cape, 1967.

Moyer, R. S., & Landauer, T. K. Time required for judgments of numerical inequality. *Nature*, 1967, **215**, 1519-1520.

Muehl, S., & Kremenak, S. Ability to match information within and between auditory and visual sense modalities and subsequent reading achievement. *Journal of Educational Psychology*, 1966, **57**, 230-239.

Murdock, B.B., Jr. The retention of individual items. *Journal of Experimental Psychology*, 1961, **62**, 618-625.

Murray, D. J. Articulation and acoustic confusability in short-term memory. *Journal of Experimental Psychology*, 1968, **78**, 679-684.

Natadze, R. Emergence of set on the basis of imaginal situations. *British Journal of Psychology*, 1960, **51**, 237-245.

Neisser, U. *Cognitive psychology*. New York: Appleton-Century Crofts, 1967.

Newell, A. On the analysis of human problem solving protocols. Paper presented to the International Symposium on Mathematical and Computational Methods in the Social Sciences, Rome, July 1966.

Norman, D. A. Acquisition and retention in short-term memory. *Journal of Experimental Psychology*, 1966, **72**, 369-381.

Norman, D. A. *Memory and attention*. New York: Wiley, 1969.

Norman, D. A., & Wickelgren, W. A. Strength theory of decision rules and latency in retrieval from short-term memory. *Journal of Mathematical Psychology*, 1969, **6**, 192-208.

Optical Society of America, Committee on Colorimetry. *The Science of color*. New York: Crowell, 1953.

Osgood, C. E. The similarity paradox in human learning. *Psychological Review*, 1949, **56**, 132-143.

Osgood, C. E. *Method and theory in experimental psychology*. New York: Oxford University Press, 1953.

Osgood, C. E., Suci, G. J., & Tannenbaum, P. H. *The measurement of meaning*. Urbana, Ill.: University Illinois Press, 1957.

Oswald, I. *Sleeping and waking*. New York: Elsevier, 1962.

Pailhous, J. Algorithme de deplacements chez le chauffeur de taxi. *Laboraratoire de Psychol. du Travail*, Paris, undated.

Paivio, A. Latency of verbal associations and imagery to noun stimuli as a function of abstractness and generality. *Canadian Journal of Psychology*, 1966, **20**, 378-387.

Paivio, A. A factor-analytic study of word attributes and verbal learning. *Journal of Verbal Learning and Verbal Behavior*, 1968, **7**, 41-49.

Paivio, A. Mental imagery in associative learning and memory. *Psychological Review*, 1969, **76**, 241-263.

Paivio, A., & Simpson, H. M. The effect of word abstractness and pleasantness on pupil size during an imagery task. *Psychonomic Science*, 1966, **5**, 55-56.

Paivio, A., Yuille, J. C., & Madigan, S. A.   Concreteness, imagery, and meaningfulness values for 925 nouns. *Journal of Experimental Psychology Monograph Supplement*, 1968, **76**, No. 1, 1-25.

Paivio, A., Yuille, J. C., & Smythe, P. C.   Stimulus and response abstractness, imagery and meaningfulness, and reported mediators in paired-associate learning. *Canadian Journal of Psychology*, 1966, **20**, 362-377.

Palermo, D. S., & Jenkins, J. J.   *Word Association norms.*   Minneapolis, Minn.: University of Minnesota Press, 1964.

Parks, T.   Post-retinal visual storage.   *American Journal of Psychology*, 1965, **78**, 145-147.

Peterson, L. R.   Search and judgment in memory. In B. Kleinmuntz (Ed.), *Concepts and the structure of memory*. New York: John Wiley and Sons, Inc., 1967, Chapter 7, pp. 153-180.

Peterson, L. R., & Peterson, M. J.   Short-term retention of individual verbal items. *Journal of Experimental Psychology*, 1959, **58**, 193-198.

Phillips, L. W.   Mediated verbal similarity as a determinant of the generalization of a conditioned GSR. *Journal of Experimental Psychology*, 1958, **55**, 56-62.

Piaget, J., & Inhelder, B.   *L'image mental chez l'enfant*. Paris: Presses Universitaires de France, 1966.

Pick, A. D.   Improvement of visual and tactual form discrimination. *Journal of Experimental Psychology*, 1965, **69**, 331-339.

Pols, L. C. W., Real-time recognition of spoken words, IEEE Transactions on Computers, 1971, **C-20**, 972-978.

Pols, L. C. W., Van der Kamp, L. J. H., & Plomp, R.   Perceptual and physical space of vowel sounds. Institute for Perception, Soesterberg, Technical Report IZF 1968, **25**.

Posner, M. I.   Abstraction and the process of recognition. In G.H. Bower & J.T. Spence (Eds.), *Advances in learning and motivation, Vol. III*. New York: Academic Press, 1969.

Posner, M. I., Boies, S. J., Eichelman, W. H., & Taylor, R. L.   Retention of visual and name codes of single letters. *Journal of Experimental Psychology Monographs,* 1969, **79**, No. 1, 1-16.

Posner, M. I., & Keele, S. W.   Decay of visual information from a single letter. *Science*, 1967, **158**, 137-139.

Posner, M. I., & Konick, A. F.   On the role of interference in short-term retention. *Journal of Experimental Psychology*, 1966, **72**, 221-231.

Posner, M. I., & Mitchell, R. F.   Chronometric analysis of classification. *Psychological Review*, 1967, **74**, 392-409.

Postman, L.   Short-term memory and incidental learning. In A. W. Melton (Ed.), *Categories of human learning*. New York: Academic Press, 1964, 146-202.

Postman, L.   Unlearning under conditions of successive interpolation. *Journal of Experimental Psychology*, 1965, **70**, 237-245.

Postman, L., & Stark, K.   Studies of learning to learn. *Journal of Verbal Learning and Verbal Behavior*, 1967, **3**, 339-353.

Prentice, W. C., & Asch, S. Paired associations with related and unrelated pairs of nonsense-figures. *American Journal of Psychology,* 1958, **71**, 247-254.

Pufall, P. B., & Furth, H. G. Recognition and learning of visual sequences in young children. *Child Development,* 1966, **37**, 827-836.

Quillian, M. R. Word concepts: A theory and simulation of some basic semantic capabilities. *Behavioral Science,* 1967, **12**, 410-430.

Quillian, M. R. Semantic memory. In M. Minsky (Ed.), Semantic information processing. Cambridge, Mass.: MIT Press, 1968.

Quillian, M. R. The teachable language comprehender: a simulation program and theory of language. *Communications Assn. Comp. Mach.,* 1969, **12**, 459-476.

Rapaport, A., & Fillenbaum, S. A structural anlaysis of the semantic space of color names. Multilithed Report No. 60, Psychometric Laboratory, University of North Carolina, May 1968.

Razran, G. H. S. Semantic, syntactic and phonetographic generalization of verbal conditioning. *Psychological Bulletin,* 1939, **36**, p. 578.

Reed, H. B. Associative aids: I. Their relation to learning, retention, and other associations. *Psychological Review,* 1918, **25**, 128-155.

Reitman, W. R. *Cognition and thought.* New York: John Wiley, 1965.

Richardson, A. Mental practice: a review and discussion. *Bulletin of the British Psychological Society,* 1963, **16**, No. 51.

Riess, B. F. Genetic changes in semantic conditioning. *Journal of Experimental Psychology,* 1946, **36**, 143-152.

Roberts, L. G. Machine perception of three-dimensional solids. In J. T. Tippitt (Ed.), *Optical and electro-optical information processing.* Cambridge, Mass.: MIT Press, 1965, Pp. 159-198.

Rohwer, W. D., Jr. Constraint, syntax and meaning in paired-associate learning. *Journal of Verbal Learning and Verbal Behavior,* 1966, **5**, 541-547.

Rohwer, W. D., Jr. Social class differences in the role of linguistic structures in paired-associate learning: Elaboration and learning proficiency. Final Report, Project No. 5-0605, University of California, Berkeley, 1967.

Romney, A. K., & d'Andrade, R. G. Cognitive aspects of English kinship terms. *American Anthropology,* 1964, **66**, 146-170.

Roskam, E. E. Ch. J. Metric analysis of ordinal data in psychology. Doctoral Dissertation, University of Leiden, The Netherlands, 1968.

Runquist, W. N. Intralist interference as a function of list length and interstimulus similarity. *Journal of Verbal Learning and Verbal Behavior,* 1966, **5**, 7-13.

Runquist, W. N., & Farley, F. H. The use of mediators in the learning of verbal paired-associates. *Journal of Verbal Learning and Verbal Behavior,* 1964, **3**, 280-285.

Russell, D. H., & Saadeh, I. Q. Qualitative levels in children's vocabularies. *Journal of Educational Psychology,* 1962, **4**, 170-174.

Ryle, G. *The concept of mind.* London: Hutchinson's University Library, 1949.

Sachs, J. S.   Recognition memory for syntactic and semantic aspects of connected discourse. *Perception and Psychophysics*, 1967, **2**, 437-442.

Sanday, P. R.   The problem of kinship terms and "psychological" reality: an information processing approach. Doctoral Thesis, University of Pittsburgh. (Abstract in Diss. Abstr. 1967, **27**, 3379-3380).

Saufley, W. H., Jr.   An analysis of cues in serial learning. *Journal of Experimental Psychology*, 1967, **74**, 414-419.

Schwartz, M.   Instructions to use verbal mediators in paired-associate learning. *Journal of Experimental Psychology*, 1969, **79**, 1-5.

Segal, S. J., & Fusella, V.   Imaging and perceiving in two sensory modalities. Paper presented at meetings of Eastern Psychological Association, Philadelphia, 1969.

Seymour, P. H. K.   Response latencies in judgments of spatial location. *British Journal of Psychology*, 1969, **60**, 31-39.

Shaw, A. C.   The formal description and parsing of pictures. Unpublished Doctoral dissertation, Stanford University, 1968, (SLAC Report No. 84, March, 1968).

Sheffield, F. D.   Theoretical considerations in the learning of complex sequential tasks from demonstration and practice. In A. A. Lumsdaine (Ed.), *Student response in programmed instruction*. Washington: National Academy of Sciences- National Research Council. Publication 943, 1961, 13-32.

Shepard, R. N.   The analysis of proximities: Multidimensional scaling with an unknown distance function I. *Psychometrika*, 1962, **27**, 125-140.

Shepard, R. N.   Attention and the metric structure of stimulus space. *Journal of Mathematical Psychology*, 1964, **1**, 54-87.

Shepard, R. N.   Recognition memory for words, sentences, and pictures. *Journal of Verbal Learning and Verbal Behavior*, 1967, **6**, 156-163.

Shepard, R. N., & Chang, J. J.   Forced-choice tests of recognition memory under steady-state conditions. *Journal of Verbal Learning and Verbal Behavior*, 1963, **2**, 93-101.

Shepard, R. N., & Metzler, J.   Mental rotation of three-dimensional objects. *Science*, 1971, **171**, 701-703.

Shepard, R. N., & Teghtsoonian, M.   Retention of information under conditions approaching a steady state. *Journal of Experimental Psychology*, 1961, **62**, 302-309.

Shuell, T. J., & Keppel, G.   A further test of the chain hypothesis of serial learning. *Journal of Verbal Learning and Verbal Behavior*, 1967, **3**, 439-445.

Siklossy, L.   Natural language learning by computer. Carnegie-Mellon University, unpublished doctoral dissertation, 1968.

Silberman, H. F.   Experimental analysis of a beginning reading skill. *Programmed Instruction*, 1964, **3**, 4-8.

Simon, H. A.   *Models of man, social and rational*. New York: Wiley, 1957.

Simon, H. A.   *The sciences of the artificial*. M.I.T. Press, Cambridge, Mass., 1969.

Simon, H. A.   The axiomatization of physical theories. *Philosophy of Science*, 1970, **37**, 16-26.

Simon, H. A., & Barenfeld, M. Information-processing analysis of perceptual processes in problem solving. *Psychological Review*, 1969, 76, 473-483.

Simon, H. A., & Feigenbaum, E. A. An information-processing theory of some effects of similarity, familiarization, and meaningfulness in verbal learning. *Journal of Verbal Learning and Verbal Behavior*, 1964, 3, 385-396.

Simon, H. A., & Kotovsky, K. Human acquisition of concepts for sequential patterns. *Psychological Review*, 1963, 70, 534-546.

Simpson, H. M., & Paivio, A. Effects on pupil size of manual and verbal indicators of cognitive task fulfillment. *Perception and Psychophysics*, 1968, 3, 185-190.

Singer, J. *Daydreaming: An introduction to the experimental study of inner experience.* New York: Random House, 1966.

Singer, J., & Antrobus, J. S. Eye movements during fantasies. *Archives of General Psychiatry*, 1965, 12, 71-76.

Skeel, M. H., Calfee, R. C., & Venezky, R. L. Perceptual confusions among fricatives in preschool children. Technical Report No. 73, Wisconsin Research and Development Center for Cognitive Learning, University of Wisconsin, February, 1969.

Skinner, B. F. *Science and human behavior.* New York: MacMillan Co., 1953.

Slamecka, N. J. Differentiation versus unlearning of verbal associations. *Journal of Experimental Psychology*, 1966, 71, 822-828.

Slamecka, N. J. Serial learning and order information. *Journal of Experimental Psychology*, 1967, 74, 62-66.

Smith, B. *Memory.* London: Geo. Allen & Unwin Ltd., 1966.

Sperling, G. The information available in brief visual presentations. *Psychological Monograph*, 1960, 74, (11, Whole No. 498).

Sperling, G. A model for visual memory tasks. *Journal of the Human Factors Society*, 1963, 5, 19-31.

Staats, A. W. *Learning, language, and cognition.* New York: Holt, Rinehart & Winston, 1968.

Start, K. B., & Richardson, A. Imagery and mental practice. *British Journal of Educational Psychology*, 1965, 34, 280-284.

Stern, C. Evaluation language curricula for preschool children. In M. A. Brottman (Ed.), *Language remediation for the disadvantaged preschool child. Monographs of Society for Research in Child Development*, 1968, 33, (Whole No. 124).

Sternberg, S. The discovery of processing stages: Extensions of Donders' method. In W. G. Koster (Ed.), *Attention and performance II. Acta Psychologica*, 1969, 30, 276-315. (a)

Sternberg, S. Memory scanning: Mental processes revealed by reaction time experiments. *American Scientist*, 1969, 57, 421-457. (b)

Strang, H. R. The effects of letter directionality cueing and response mode upon the acquisition of letter reversal discriminations in four-year-old children. Unpublished doctoral dissertation, University of Kansas, 1967.

Sutherland, I. E. Sketchpad: A man-machine graphical communication system. Lincoln Lab. Technical Report No. 296; MIT, Lexington, Mass., 1963.

Sutherland, N. S., & Bowman, R.   Discrimination of circles and squares with and without knobs by goldfish. *Quarterly Journal of Experimental Psychology*, 1969, **21**, 330-338.

Tanner, W. P., Jr., & Swets, J. A.   A decision making theory of visual detection. *Psychological Review*, 1954, **61**, 401-409.

Templin, M. C.   *Certain language skills in children.*   Minneapolis: University of Minnesota Press, 1957.

Thorndike, E. L., & Lorge, I.   *The teacher's word book of 30,000 words.*   New York: Columbia University Press, 1944.

Thurstone, L. L.   A law of comparative judgment. *Psychological Review*, 1927, **34**, 273-286.

Tinker, M. A.   Recent studies of eye movements in reading. *Psychological Bulletin*, 1958, **55**, 215-231.

Torgerson, W. S.   A theoretical and empirical investigation of multidimensional scaling. Thesis, Princeton. Quoted in: *Theory and methods of scaling.*   New York: Wiley, 1958. Pp. 280-290.

Tulving, E., & Osler, S.   Effectiveness of retrieval cues in memory for words. *Journal of Experimental Psychology*, 1968, **77**, 593-601.

Tulving, E., & Pearlstone, Z.   Availability versus accessibility of information in memory for words. *Journal of Verbal Learning & Verbal Behavior*, 1966, **5**, 381-391.

Turvey, M. T.   Evidence of a connotative dimension in short-term memory as a function of retention interval. *Psychonomic Science*, 1967, **9**, 547-548.

Tversky, B.   Pictorial and verbal encoding in short-term memory. Technical Report No. 10, Human Performance Center, Department of Psychology, University of Michigan, October, 1968.

Uhr, L. (Ed.)   *Pattern recognition.*   New York: Wiley, 1966.

Underwood, B. J.   Studies of distributed practice: VIII. Learning and retention of paired nonsense syllables as a function of intralist similarity. *Journal of Experimental Psychology*, 1953, **45**, 133-142.

Underwood, B. J.   Stimulus selection in verbal learning. In C. N. Cofer & B. S. Musgrave (Eds.), *Verbal behavior and learning.*   New York: McGraw-Hill, 1963. Pp. 33-70.

Underwood, B. J.   False recognition produced by implicit verbal responses. *Journal of Experimental Psychology*, 1965, **70**, 122-129.

Underwood, B. J., & Freund, J. S.   Errors in recognition learning and retention. *Journal of Experimental Psychology*, 1968, **78**, 55-63.

Underwood, B. J., & Goad, D.   Studies of distributed practice: I. The influence of intra-list similarity in serial learning. *Journal of Experimental Psychology*, 1951, **42**, 125-134.

Underwood, B. J., & Schultz, R. W.   *Meaningfulness and verbal learning.*   Chicago: Lippincott, 1960.

Van de Geer, J. P.   Matching K sets of configurations. Dept. Data Theory Social Sciences, University of Leiden, Technical Report RN 005-68, 1968.

Van de Geer, J. P., & Jaspars, J. M. F.   Cognitive functions. *Annual Review of Psychology*, 1966, **17**, 145-176.

Venezky, R. L., Calfee, R. C., & Chapman, R. Skills required for learning to read: a preliminary analysis. *Education*, 1969, 89, 298-302.

Vernon, M. D. *Backwardness in reading: A study of its nature and origin.* Cambridge, England: University Press, 1960.

Wagenaar, W. A., & Padmos, P. The significance of a stress percentage obtained with Kruskal's multi-dimensional scaling technique. Institute for Perception, Soesterberg, Technical Report IZF 1968-22.

Wallace, W. H., Turner, S. H., & Perkins, C. C. Preliminary studies of human information storage. Signal Corps. Project No. 132C, Institute for Cooperative Research, University of Pennsylvania, December, 1957.

Wallach, H., & Averbach, E. Memory modalities. *American Journal of Psychology*, 1955, 68, 249-257.

Watt, W. C. *Morphology of the Nevada Cattlebrands and their Blazons, Part One.* National Bureau of Standards Report 9050, Washington, D. C., 1966.

Watt, W. C. *Morphology of the Nevada Cattlebrands and their Blazons, Part Two.* Department of Computer Science, Carnegie-Mellon University, 1967, (a)

Watt, W. C. Structural properties of the Nevada Cattlebrands. *Computer Science Research Review,* Carnegie-Mellon University, 1967, 20-27. (b)

Waugh, N. C., & Norman, D. A. Primary memory. *Psychological Review*, 1965, 72, 89-104.

Wickelgren, W. A. Size of rehearsal group and short-term memory. *Journal of Experimental Psychology*, 1964, 68, 413-419.

Wickelgren, W. A. Acoustic similarity and retroactive interference in short-term memory. *Journal of Verbal Learning and Verbal Behavior*, 1965, 4, 53-61. (a)

Wickelgren, W. A. Acoustic similarity and intrusion errors in short-term memory. *Journal of Experimental Psychology*, 1965, 70, 102-108. (b)

Wickelgren, W. A. Similarity and intrusions in short-term memory for consonant-vowel digrams. *Quarterly Journal of Experimental Psychology*, 1965, 17, 241-246. (c)

Wickelgren, W. A. Distinctive features and errors in short-term memory for English vowels. *Journal of the Acoustical Society of America*, 1965, 38, 583-588. (d)

Wickelgren, W. A. Short-term memory for phonemically similar lists. *American Journal of Psychology*, 1965, 78, 567-574. (e)

Wickelgren, W. A. Short-term memory for repeated and non-repeated items. *Quarterly Journal of Experimental Psychology*, 1965, 17, 14-25. (f)

Wickelgren, W. A. Distinctive features and errors in short-term memory for English consonants. *Journal of the Acoustical Society of America*, 1966, 39, 388-398. (a)

Wickelgren, W. A. Phonemic similarity and interference in short-term memory for single letters. *Journal of Experimental Psychology*, 1966, 71, 396-404. (b)

Wickelgren, W. A. Associative intrusions in short-term recall. *Journal of Experimental Psychology*, 1966, 72, 853-858. (c)

Wickelgren, W. A. Rehearsal grouping and hierarchical organization of serial position cues in short-term memory. *Quarterly Journal of Experimental Psychology*, 1967, 19, 97-102. (a)

Wickelgren, W. A. Exponential decay and independence from irrelevant associations in short-term recognition memory for serial order. *Journal of Experimental Psychology*, 1967, 73, 165-171. (b)

Wickelgren, W. A. Unidimensional strength theory and component analysis of noise in absolute comparative judgments. *Journal of Mathematical Psychology*, 1968, 5, 102-122. (a)

Wickelgren, W. A. Associative strength theory of recognition memory for pitch. *Journal of Mathematical Psychology*, 1969, 6, 13-61. (a)

Wickelgren, W. A. Auditory or articulatory coding in verbal short-term memory. *Psychological Review*, 1969, 76, 232-235. (b)

Wickelgren, W. A. Context-sensitive coding, associative memory, and serial order in (speech) behavior. *Psychological Review*, 1969, 76, 1-15. (c)

Wickelgren, W. A. Learned specification of concept neurons. *Bulletin of Mathematical Biophysics*, 1969, 31, 123-142. (d)

Wickelgren, W. A. Context-sensitive coding in speech recognition, articulation, and development. In K. N. Leibovic (Ed.), *Information processing in the nervous system*. New York: Springer-Verlag, 1969, 85-95. (e)

Wickelgren, W. A. Multitrace strength theory. In D. A. Norman (Ed.), *Models of memory*, New York: Academic Press, 1970, Pp. 65-102. (a)

Wickelgren, W. A. Time, interference, and rate of presentation in short-term recognition memory for items. *Journal of Mathematical Psychology*, 1970, 7, 219-235. (b)

Wickelgren, W. A., & Whitman, P. T. Visual very-short-term memory is nonassociative. *Journal of Experimental Psychology*, 1970, 84, 277-281.

Wickelgren, W. A., & Norman, D. A. Strength models and serial position in short-term recognition memory. *Journal of Mathematical Psychology*, 1966, 3, 316-347.

Wickens, D. D., & Eckler, G. R. Semantic as opposed to acoustic encoding in STM. *Psychonomic Science*, 1968, 12, 63.

Wickens, D. D., & Simpson, H. K. Semantic versus phonetic encoding in short-term memory. Paper presented at Midwestern Psychological Association, 1968.

Williams, L. G. The effect of target specification on objects fixated during visual search. *Perception and Psychophysics*, 1966, 1, 315-318.

Williams, T. Some studies in game playing with a digital computer. Carnegie-Institute of Technology, unpublished doctoral dissertation, 1965.

Winnick, W. A., & Dornbush, R. L. Role of positional cues in serial rote learning. *American Journal of Psychology*, 1963, 66, 419-421.

Wittengenstein, L. *Tractatus Logico-Philosophicus*. London: Routledge, Kogan Paul, 1922.

Wood, G., & Bolt, M. Mediation and mediation time in paired-associate learning. *Journal of Experimental Psychology*, 1968, 78, 15-20.

Yarbus, A. L. *Eye movements and vision*. New York: Plenum, 1967.

Yntema, D. B., & Trask, F. P.   Recall as a search process. *Journal of Verbal Learning and Verbal Behavior*, 1963, **2**, 65-74.

Young, R. K.   A comparison of two methods of learning serial associations. *American Journal of Psychology*, 1959, **72**, 554-559.

Young, R. K.   The stimulus in serial verbal learning. *American Journal of Psychology*, 1961, **74**, 517-528.

Young, R. K.   Tests of three hypotheses about the effective stimulus in serial learning. *Journal of Experimental Psychology*, 1962, **63**, 307-313.

Young, R. K.   Serial Learning. In T. R. Dixon & D. L. Horton (Eds.), *Verbal behavior and general behavior theory*. Englewood Cliffs, N. J.: Prentice Hall, 1968. Pp. 122-148.

Young, R. K., & Casey, M.   Transfer from serial to paired-associate learning. *Journal of Experimental Psychology*, 1964, **67**, 594-595.

Young, R. K., & Clark, J.   Compound-stimulus hypothesis in serial learning. *Journal of Experimental Psychology*, 1964, **67**, 301-302.

Young, R. M., & Chase, W. G.   Additive stages in the comparison of sentences and pictures. Presented at the Midwestern Psychological Association Conference, Chicago, May, 1971.

Yuille, J. C.   Concreteness without imagery in PA learning. *Psychonomic Science*, 1968, **11**, 55-56.

Yuille, J. C., & Paivio, A.   Latency of imaginal and verbal mediators as a function of stimulus and response concreteness-imagery. *Journal of Experimental Psychology*, 1967, **75**, 540-544

Yuille, J. C., & Paivio, A.   Imagery and verbal mediation instructions in paired-associate learning. *Journal of Experimental Psychology*, 1968, **78**, 436-441.

AUTHOR INDEX

253

SUBJECT INDEX

Additivity, 206
Algebra word problem, 195–196
Alpha activity, 60
Ambiguity, 66, 132
Ammons Picture Vocabulary Test, 174
Animal hierarchies (in children's learning),
    102–105
Anomalous sentences, 126–128
Anticipation method, 8
Aphasia, 194
Appearance, 52–55
Association learning, 3–4, 119
    all-or-none, 2
    mental imagery and, 51–88, 183–204
Attention, 7–10
    noticing processes, 202–203, 226–229

Behavioral oscillation, 40
Behaviorism, 51, 89, 183–186
Brain localization, 64, 190
Brook's experiments, 61–62, 224

Chess, 226–229
Chronometric analysis, 206
Chunking, 16, 70, 230
    induced, 5–7, 203
    STM capacity, 187–188
Coding, 5, 19, 20–22, 29–36
    allophonic, 34
    axioms of, 26–27
    dual-code theory, 83–86
    models of, 207–219
    verbal versus pictorial, 63, 197–200
Cognition, 36–37

cognitive skills, 141–149
cognitive theory, 89–91
    imagist theory of, 55–56
    see also Information processing, theory of;
        Multitrace theory
Cognitive processes, see Association learning;
    Attention; Chunking; Coding; Decision
    processes; Familiarization; Imagery;
    Rehearsal; and Retrieval
Cognitive tasks, algebra word problem, 195–
    196
    animal hierarchies, 102–105
    Brooks' experiments, 61–62, 224
    Chess, 226–229
    sentence-picture task, 205–206
    word matrix experiment, 100–102
    see also Geometry routines
Color, 53
Comprehension, 57, 82, 117–137, 224
Computer programs, 1–4. See also EPAM;
    Perceiver program; and Teachable
    Language Comprehender
Computer simulation, 1–4, 8–9, 115, 134
Confusion matrix, 110–111
    in semantic networks, 128
Confusions, 153, 194
    sorting, 172
Concept, 21, 27, 56, 83–84, 124, 158
Content-addressability, 30
Cue distinctiveness, 78–79; see also Stimulus
    distinctiveness

Data base, 14–15, 90–91
Data space, data structures, 89–91

259